CW00688465

ADVANCES IN COGNITIVE LOAD THEORY

Cognitive load theory uses our knowledge of how people learn, think and solve problems to design instruction. In turn, instructional design is the central activity of classroom teachers, of curriculum designers, and of publishers of textbooks and educational materials, including digital information. Characteristically, the theory is used to generate hypotheses that are tested using randomised controlled trials. Cognitive load theory rests on a base of hundreds of randomised controlled trials testing many thousands of primary and secondary school children as well as adults.

That research has been conducted by many research groups from around the world and has resulted in a wide range of novel instructional procedures that have been tested for effectiveness. *Advances in Cognitive Load Theory*, in describing current research, continues in this tradition. Exploring a wide range of instructional issues dealt with by the theory, it covers all general curriculum areas critical to educational and training institutions and outlines recent extensions to other psycho-educational constructs including motivation and engagement.

With contributions from the leading figures from around the world, this book provides a one-stop-shop for the latest in cognitive load theory research and guidelines for how the findings can be applied in practice.

Sharon Tindall-Ford is an Associate Professor of Educational Psychology at the University of Wollongong. Her research interests in the area of cognition and instruction have focused on a number of cognitive load effects including the modality effect, worked example effect, imagination effect and self management of cognitive load. She is particularly interested in how these effects are implemented within primary and secondary classrooms.

Shirley Agostinho is an Associate Professor of Educational Technology at the University of Wollongong. Her research focuses on how teachers design and how learners support their own learning using digital technologies. Her interest in cognitive load theory is concerned with how learners can apply cognitive load theory principles to support their learning.

John Sweller is an Emeritus Professor of Educational Psychology at the University of New South Wales. His research is associated with cognitive load theory. The theory is a contributor to research on issues associated with human cognition, its links to evolution by natural selection, and the consequences for instructional design.

LOCAL/GLOBAL ISSUES IN EDUCATION

Greg Thompson Murdoch University, Australia
Peter Renshaw University of Queensland, Australia

This series investigates the interplay between the local and the global in contemporary education policy and practice. While globalisation is transforming local education systems, the local cannot be conceived as homogeneous or passive. Local policy advocates, educators and researchers mediate globalisation by adapting, resisting and amplifying its effects and influences. In this book series, the local perspective taken is from Australia, whose geographical and cultural positioning provides a unique analytical lens through which processes of globalisation in education can be explored and understood. Published in association with the Australian Association for Research in Education, this series includes high-quality empirical, theoretical and conceptual work that uses a range of qualitative and quantitative methods to address contemporary challenges in education.

ADVANCES IN COGNITIVE LOAD THEORY

Rethinking Teaching

Edited by Sharon Tindall-Ford, Shirley Agostinho and John Sweller

Routledge
Taylor & Francis Group

LONDON AND NEW YORK

First published 2020
by Routledge
2 Park Square, Milton Park, Abingdon, Oxon OX14 4RN

and by Routledge
52 Vanderbilt Avenue, New York, NY 10017

Routledge is an imprint of the Taylor & Francis Group, an informa business

© 2020 selection and editorial matter, Sharon Tindall-Ford, Shirley Agostinho and John Sweller; individual chapters, the contributors

The right of Sharon Tindall-Ford, Shirley Agostinho and John Sweller to be identified as the author[/s] of the editorial material, and of the authors for their individual chapters, has been asserted in accordance with sections 77 and 78 of the Copyright, Designs and Patents Act 1988.

All rights reserved. No part of this book may be reprinted or reproduced or utilised in any form or by any electronic, mechanical, or other means, now known or hereafter invented, including photocopying and recording, or in any information storage or retrieval system, without permission in writing from the publishers.

Trademark notice: Product or corporate names may be trademarks or registered trademarks, and are used only for identification and explanation without intent to infringe.

British Library Cataloguing in Publication Data
A catalogue record for this book is available from the British Library

Library of Congress Cataloging-in-Publication Data
Names: Tindall-Ford, Sharon.
Title: Advances in cognitive load theory : rethinking teaching / edited by Sharon Tindall-Ford, Shirley Agostinho and John Sweller.
Description: Milton Park, Abingdon, Oxon ; New York, NY : Routledge, 2019.
Identifiers: LCCN 2019004035| ISBN 9780367246884 (hardback) | ISBN 9780367246907 (pbk.) | ISBN 9780429283895 (ebook)
Subjects: LCSH: Learning, Psychology of. | Cognitive learning. | Educational psychology.
Classification: LCC LB1060 .A29 2019 | DDC 370.15/23–dc23
LC record available at https://lccn.loc.gov/2019004035

ISBN: 978-0-367-24688-4 (hbk)
ISBN: 978-0-367-24690-7 (pbk)
ISBN: 978-0-429-28389-5 (ebk)

Typeset in Bembo
by Taylor & Francis Books

MIX
Paper from
responsible sources
FSC
www.fsc.org   FSC™ C013985

Printed in the United Kingdom
by Henry Ling Limited

CONTENTS

PART 4
New effects and new conditions required for old effects 155

ILLUSTRATIONS

Figures

Tables

CONTRIBUTORS

Shirley Agostinho is an Associate Professor of Educational Technology at the University of Wollongong. Her research focuses on how teachers design and how learners support their own learning using digital technologies. Her interest in cognitive load theory is concerned with how learners can apply cognitive load theory principles to support their learning.

Paul Ayres is an Emeritus Professor of Educational Psychology at the University of New South Wales, Sydney, Australia. He has a long association with cognitive load theory and was a member of the original group who pioneered the theory. His research has been conducted on many of the key areas of cognitive load theory, such as split-attention, isolating elements, the goal-free effect, the expertise reversal effect, and the transient information effect of instructional animations and videos.

Lisa Bender has a Master's Degree in psychology from the University of Ulm, Germany. In 2018, she started working at the Institute of Psychology, University of Freiburg (Germany), Educational and Developmental Psychology (Prof. Renkl). She works on a project, funded by the German Research Foundation (Eitel & Renkl), on the boundary conditions of the seductive-details effect. Lisa works also as a therapist for children with specific developmental and attention deficits. Her main research interests refer to learning from multiple representations and learning difficulties.

Roland Brünken is Full Professor in Education at Saarland University. He received his doctoral degree in psychology from Erfurt University in 1998 and was Associate Professor in Educational Psychology from 2003 to 2006 at Göttingen University. Since 2006 he has worked at Saarland University. His research areas include learning and instruction, computer-based learning, expertise development and traffic psychology. He has published over 100 peer reviewed journal articles and several books, including an edited book on cognitive load theory and a German textbook on educational psychology. Roland Brünken has received more than €1 Million in external funding from several research institutions for his work.

Juan C. Castro–Alonso is a researcher in the STEM Group at the Center for Advanced Research in Education (CIAE), Universidad de Chile, Santiago, Chile. He is a Biochemist, Master in Communication and Education, and holds a PhD in Education. His interests are cognitive load theory, educational psychology, visuospatial processing and spatial ability, STEM and biology education, sex effects, and multimedia learning. He is currently investigating how learners' characteristics can affect their performance on a battery of adaptable computer tests measuring visuospatial processing.

Paul Chandler is Pro Vice-Chancellor (Inclusion & Outreach) at UOW. He has been a former Australian Research Council Fellow (UNSW) and Dean of Education (UOW). He has accumulated substantial research project funding into cognition and instruction. He is Foundation Chair of the $44 million Early Start Project at UOW. Prof. Chandler has received many research and teaching awards, including the ARC/Thomson Direct Award, as one of 10 most valuable Australian scientists. Prof. Chandler has recently been appointed to four new boards, including the position of Executive Director of the NSW Educational Standards Authority.

Theresa Dicke is a post-doc research fellow at the Institute for Positive Psychology and Education at the Australian Catholic University. Her research interests lie in the realm of Organizational, Health, and Educational Psychology. Applying complex quantitative methods, she has extensively studied the role of (occupational) wellbeing and achievement in school; thus, focusing on students', teachers', and principals' perspectives alike.

Alexander Eitel finished his diploma degree in psychology in 2009 (University of Tübingen). From 2009 to 2015, he worked at the Knowledge Media Research Center Tübingen (lab of Prof. Scheiter), where he received his PhD in 2013. After one semester of teaching as deputy professor at the Freiburg University of Education in 2015, he started working in the department of Educational and Developmental Psychology at the University of Freiburg (lab of Prof. Renkl). To date, Alexander has (co-) authored 22 publications in peer-reviewed journals, nine of them in *Learning and Instruction*. He is an elected coordinator of the EARLI Special Interest Group 2 ("Comprehension of Text and Graphics") until 2021. His main research interests refer to learning from multiple representations, and retrieval-based learning.

Paul Evans is Senior Lecturer in the School of Education, University of New South Wales, Australia. His expertise is in educational psychology, particularly in relation to motivation, engagement, learning and teaching, and cognitive load. His research covers a wide range of domains and settings, including schools, music studios, and workplaces, and spanning childhood, adolescence, and adulthood.

Paul Ginns is Associate Professor in Educational Psychology at the Sydney School of Education and Social Work, University of Sydney. His research has two broad foci. The first applies theories from cognitive science and embodied cognition to instructional design. This program of research draws on models of human cognitive architecture to maximise the effectiveness and efficiency of learning, through appropriate management of cognitive load. In this program of research, he has published both original research, and meta-analytic reviews of specific instructional design effects. The second research program seeks to understand the systemic relations between students' approaches to and engagement in learning, their perceptions of the teaching and learning environment, and subsequent learning outcomes

Chih-Yi Hsu is a physics teacher at the National Tou-Liu Senior High School in Taiwan. He received his PhD in education from the University of New South Wales in Sydney, Australia. His research interests include cognitive load theory, multimedia learning, science education, and metacognitive learning.

Slava Kalyuga is Professor of Educational Psychology at the School of Education, the University of New South Wales, Sydney. His research interests are in cognitive processes in learning, cognitive load theory, and evidence-based instructional design principles. Prof Kalyuga is the author of four books and more than 130 refereed papers and book chapters. He has been an associate editor of *Learning and Instruction*.

Yves Karlen is a professor for learning and instruction in secondary school education at the School of Education at University of Applied Sciences and Arts Northwestern Switzerland FHNW. One of his main research interest lies in the field of self-regulated learning, thus, focusing on students' metacognitive and motivational processes and teachers' beliefs, knowledge and competencies to promote self-regulated learning in classrooms.

Femke Kirschner is a researcher and educational consultant and trainer for Educational Consultancy & Professional Development at the Faculty of Social and Behavioural Sciences, Utrecht University. Her fascination for looking at collaborative learning from a cognitive perspective did not end with her dissertation (2009) called "United Brains for Complex Learning". Since then she has held post doc positions at both the Erasmus University Rotterdam and Utrecht University. Currently, next to doing research, she is an educational consultant and trainer which gives her the opportunity to use her knowledge in optimising education.

Paul A. Kirschner is a Distinguished University Professor at the Open University of the Netherlands as well as Visiting Professor of Education with a special emphasis on Learning and Interaction in Teacher Education at the University of Oulu, Finland. He is a Research Fellow of the American Educational Research Association, the International Society of the Learning Sciences, and the Netherlands Institute for Advanced Study in the Humanities and Social Science. He is a former member of the Dutch Educational Council, advisor to the Minister of Education and is presently a member of the Scientific Technical Council of the Foundation for University Computing Facilities (SURF WTR).

Andreas Korbach is a postdoc at Saarland University working for the research group of Prof. Dr. Roland Brünken. He received his doctoral degree in educational science from Saarland University in 2017 as research assistant of Prof. Dr. Babette Park. His research areas are the development of instruments for cognitive load measurement, eye-movement analysis for multimedia learning contexts and the promotion of media literacy. He has published several peer reviewed journal articles and numerous conference contributions.

Yu-Chen Kuo is a research assistant at the Department of Educational Psychology and Counselling in National Taiwan Normal University.

Amy Kydd is a secondary mathematics teacher at Pymble Ladies' College, where she has taught since finishing university. The data reported in this study were collected as part of Amy's Honours thesis for a Bachelor of Education (Secondary Education: Humanities and Social Sciences), from The University of Sydney.

Wayne Leahy is a Senior Lecturer and researcher at Macquarie University. His subject area is cognitive processes and instruction within the framework of cognitive load theory. Wayne is currently researching the boundary conditions of study and practice procedures as well as the impact of transient verbal information and the relationship to dual modality presentations. He has a special interest in instructional design and its applicability to elementary aged students.

Jimmie Leppink is currently Senior Lecturer in Medical Education at Hull York Medical School, University of York. His research, consultancy, and teaching activities focus on learning analytics, assessment, instructional design, methodology, and statistics.

Detlev Leutner is a professor for instructional psychology at Duisburg-Essen University, Germany. His research interests are cognitive load, learning with multimedia, self-regulated learning and metacognition, problem solving competencies, large-scale assessment, teacher training, and higher education.

Yi-Chun Lin is a postdoctoral research fellow at the Department of Educational Psychology and Counselling in National Taiwan Normal University.

Tzu-Chien Liu is a professor at the Department of Educational Psychology and Counseling & Institute for Research Excellence in Learning Sciences in National Taiwan Normal University. He has contributed to both theoretical and empirical work associated with cognitive load theory and its applications to education for many years. Dr Liu is now the associate editor of the *Journal of Research in Education Sciences* which is a top journal in the education field of Taiwan (Scopus).

Nadine Marcus is an Associate Professor in Human Computer Interaction at University of New South Wales, Australia. Her research focuses on the design of multimedia educational technology to improve learning, and involves the collection of empirical data to inform multimedia theories of instructional design, as well as the creation of an eLearning software platform, known as the Adaptive eLearning Platform (AeLP). Within the field of Cognitive Load Theory she has been influential in the discovery of animation, element interactivity and transient information effects. She has published extensively in peer reviewed journals and conferences within the domains of Educational Technology, Online Learning and Interface Design.

Andrew J. Martin is Scientia Professor and Professor of Educational Psychology in the School of Education, University of New South Wales, Australia. His research interests include motivation, engagement, learning, achievement, and quantitative research methods.

Myrto Mavilidi is a Post Doc Research Associate in the department of Education, at the University of Newcastle. She has been involved in several research projects in educational psychology about cognitive load theory, embodied cognition and learning, and cognitive development, as well as strategies to reduce test anxiety and improve learning performance. Her current research interests are looking at the effects of performing movements on cognition and learning.

Faisal Mirza completed his PhD at the University of Wollongong in 2018 investigating the self-management of redundant information.

Anthony (Tony) Okely is Senior Professor and Director of Research at Early Start, University of Wollongong, Australia. He has been awarded over \$11 Million in competitive funding, and published more than 200 journal articles that have been cited more than 10,000 times. Tony's research focuses on physical activity, sedentary behaviour, and motor development in children. Tony led the research team that developed and updated the Australian Physical Activity Recommendations for Children 0–5 years. He is also part of the Guideline Development Group for the WHO guidelines on physical activity, sedentary and sleep behaviours in children under five years of age.

Kim Ouwehand is a dual Post Doc Research Associate in the Department of Psychology, Education and Child Studies at the Erasmus University Rotterdam, the Netherlands. In her first project she focuses on the improvement of instructional design from a CLT-perspective. A main focus within this project is on the effects of observing and producing gestures on learning and memory. Additional research interests are in the effects of the physical learning environment on learning and cognitive functioning more generally. In her second project she focuses on learning opportunities and work conditions of teachers in the Netherlands and internationally.

Fred Paas is a Professor of Educational Psychology at Erasmus University Rotterdam, Rotterdam, The Netherlands, and Professorial Fellow at the University of Wollongong in Australia. His main research interest is in instructional control of cognitive load in lifelong learning of complex tasks. Prof. Paas has been identified as the world's most productive researcher in the five top journals in the field of Educational Psychology, from 2009–2014. He is the editor-in-chief of the journal *Educational Psychology Review*, editorial board member of the *Journal of Educational Psychology*, and a fellow of the American Educational Research Association.

Babette Park is Associate Professor in Education at Saarland University and Visiting Professor in Educational Psychology at Justus-Liebig University Giessen. She finished her German PhD in Psychology in 2010. Since 2012, she has held a chair in Education funded by the German Federal Ministry of Education and Research. Her research group runs basic-oriented research to develop instruments for measuring cognitive load, instructional-psychological research investigating cognitive and affective processes in multimedia learning, and application-oriented research by focusing on conditions and determinants of successful teaching in higher education. Babette Park has published numerous international peer-reviewed journal articles and book chapters and is a member of the Cognitive-Load-Theory Advisory Committee for the annual International Cognitive Load Theory Conference.

Sébastien Puma is a lecturer in cognitive psychology at the School of Education of Cergy-Pontoise. He was awarded his PhD (2016) from the University of Toulouse, France. His research questions focused on the involvement of working memory and attention during learning sessions, and ways to measure it. He is now part of a national research program investigating the use of Digital Games-Based Learning environments to foster arithmetic learning.

Alexander Renkl finished his diploma degree in psychology in 1987 (RWTH Aachen). From 1988 to 1990, he worked at the Max-Planck Institute of Psychological Research, Munich (Germany) and received his doctoral degree from the University of Heidelberg in 1991. He spent several years (1991 to 1997) at the University of Munich before he became a Professor of Educational Psychology at the University of Education in Schwäbisch Gmünd (Germany). Since 1999, he has been Professor of Educational and Developmental Psychology at the University of Freiburg. He has (co-) authored over 300 publications. These publications have substantial impact (Google Scholar: h = 70; retrieved 03/17/2018). His main research interests refer to example-based learning, self-explanations, learning from multiple representations, learning strategies, learning by journal writing, and teachers' pedagogical and psychological knowledge.

Corinna Schuster is a PhD student at the Department of Research on Learning and Instruction at Ruhr-University Bochum, Germany. Her main areas of interest are self-regulated learning and transfer processes. In her doctoral thesis, she develops and evaluates concepts to implement metacognitive strategies into regular school classes in order to foster learning performance.

Stoo Sepp is a PhD Candidate at the University of Wollongong, Australia, exploring the effects of the production and observation of pointing and tracing gestures in the use of gesture-based learning technologies. His interests in the area of ICT-based gesture research focus on informing the sound integration of innovative technologies to support learning in an array of educational contexts.

Ferdinand Stebner is a post-doc researcher at the Department of Research on Learning and Instruction at Ruhr-University Bochum, Germany. His main areas of research are self-regulated learning, multimedia learning, medical education, Cognitive Load Theory, and research on implementation and transfer processes in daily school life.

John Sweller is an Emeritus Professor of Educational Psychology at the University of New South Wales. His research is associated with cognitive load theory. The theory is a contributor to research on issues associated with human cognition, its links to evolution by natural selection, and the consequences for instructional design.

Sharon Tindall-Ford is an Associate Professor of Educational Psychology at the University of Wollongong. Her research interests in the area of cognition and instruction have focused on a number of cognitive load effects including the modality effect, worked example effect, imagination effect and self management of cognitive load. She is particularly interested in how these effects are implemented within primary and secondary classrooms.

André Tricot is a professor of psychology at the School of Education, University of Toulouse. He was awarded his PhD in Cognitive Psychology (1995) from Aix-Marseille University, France. In 2014–2015, he was the head of the group that designed grades 1, 2 and 3 of new curricula for primary schools in France. André's main research topics concern the relationships between natural memory and processing (human cognitive system) and artificial memory (documents). The main question of this research is: How does designing artificial memory help natural memory instead of overloading it? Applications are in instructional design, human–computer interaction, ergonomics and transport safety.

Tamara van Gog is Full Professor of Educational Sciences at the Department of Education of Utrecht University. Her research focuses on instructional design to foster: example-based learning; self-monitoring and self-regulated learning; teachers' monitoring and regulation of students' learning; (embodied cognition in) multimedia learning; and critical thinking (in professional domains).

Jeroen J. G. van Merriënboer is Full Professor of Learning and Instruction, and Research Director of the School of Health Professions Education (SHE) at Maastricht University. His research focuses on instructional design and the use of new technologies in the health professions and is largely based on four-component instructional design (4C/ID) and cognitive load theory.

Joachim Wirth is a professor for research on learning and instruction at Ruhr-University Bochum, Germany. His research covers both, the assessment and support of self-regulated learning and problem solving, multimedia learning and cognitive load, and higher education. He is especially interested in transfer of insight from experimental studies into school practice.

Mona Wong obtained her PhD (Educational Psychology) from the University of New South Wales, Sydney, Australia, in 2016 and her bachelor's degree (Cognitive Science) from The University of Hong Kong, in 2008. Her doctorate thesis examined the effectiveness of instructional animations based on cognitive load theory. With an interest in exploring learning as a cognitive function, her research area mainly lies in cognitive load theory, the science of learning, instructional animation design (and its possible gender effects), embodied cognition, and evolutionary psychology.

Jimmy Zambrano R. is an Ecuadorian who got interested in educational research working as a primary school teacher. He has had formal instruction in educational sciences, distance education, and human resource management. He is currently a member of the International Society of the Learning Sciences and is finishing a PhD at the Open University of the Netherlands with a focus on cognitive load factors in collaborative learning.

1

COGNITIVE LOAD THEORY

John Sweller

In this introductory chapter I discuss how human cognitive architecture allows us to learn, think and solve problems and how that architecture can be used to design instruction. Cognitive load theory (Sweller, 2015, 2016; Sweller, Ayres, & Kalyuga, 2011) is underpinned by our understanding of human cognitive architecture to generate hypotheses of potentially novel instructional procedures. The effectiveness of those procedures is tested using randomised, controlled trials with current instructional procedures providing control conditions. Characteristically, to avoid altering multiple variables simultaneously, multiple controlled trials are required and carried out. The result, over more than 30 years, is a theory that has continually evolved as new data and new concepts become available, delivering a large corpus of cognitive load effects that provide efficacious instructional procedures. The chapters of this volume reflect a continuation of this tradition.

In its current formulation, the cognitive architecture used by cognitive load theory is heavily influenced by evolutionary psychology, used both to indicate that category of knowledge that is amenable to instruction and to provide the structures and functions of human cognition that deal with instructable knowledge. Together, knowledge categories along with the structures and functions of human cognitive architecture based on evolutionary psychology provide an important part of the theoretical base for cognitive load theory. In this introduction, both will be considered separately.

Categories of knowledge

Knowledge can be categorised in many different ways but very few categories have instructional implications. One categorisation scheme that has important instructional implications is based on evolutionary educational psychology (Geary, 2008, 2012; Geary & Berch, 2016; Paas & Sweller, 2012).

Geary divides knowledge into biologically (or evolutionary) primary and secondary categories. We have specifically evolved to acquire biologically primary knowledge. Examples are learning to listen to and speak a native language, learning general problem-solving strategies such as generalising from one problem solution to another, or learning to recognise faces. There are several important characteristics of biologically primary knowledge. It is modular with only limited overlap between one category of primary knowledge and another. The modularity of primary skills is due to the differing epochs during which each skill evolved. For example, our ability to learn to listen to and speak a native language and our ability to learn to generalise problem solutions to other similar problems are likely to have evolved independently at different times.

Another important characteristic of biologically primary knowledge is that much of it is generic-cognitive. A generic-cognitive skill is a basic, mental skill that applies to a variety of domains. Learning to use a general problem-solving strategy provides an example of a generic-cognitive skill. As a more specific example, a means-ends strategy (Newell & Simon, 1972), in which we attempt to reduce the differences between where we are in a problem and the goal of a problem, is used by most animals attempting to reach a food source. We, along with many animals, have evolved to acquire that skill and many other generic-cognitive skills.

Because we have evolved to automatically acquire biologically primary skills such as generic-cognitive skills, they can be learned by most people but cannot be taught (Tricot & Sweller, 2014). Due to the vital importance of most generic-cognitive skills, it is easy to assume that they should be the subject of instruction. For example, there is frequent advocacy for teaching general problem-solving skills that apply to a variety of unrelated problems. An example is the means-ends strategy described in the previous paragraph. Despite the importance of generic-cognitive skills and the advocacy in favour of teaching them, there is very limited evidence that teaching them improves general performance over a range of tasks (Sala & Gobet, 2017). Of course, if we have evolved to acquire generic-cognitive skills without tuition, attempts to teach such skills are likely to be futile (Sweller, 2015; Tricot & Sweller, 2014).

Biologically secondary knowledge differs from primary knowledge in several instructionally relevant areas, beginning with the fact that unlike primary knowledge, it is instructable. Indeed, the clearest examples of biologically secondary knowledge can be found in educationally relevant areas. Almost everything taught in educational contexts consists of biologically secondary knowledge. Schools and other educational institutions were invented because of the need to teach biologically secondary areas.

Unlike primary knowledge, secondary knowledge is not modular and so we have not specifically evolved to acquire various categories of secondary knowledge. Instead, similar procedures and the same cognitive architecture are used to acquire all types of secondary knowledge. There are two other major differences between biologically primary and secondary knowledge. While, as indicated above, much biologically primary knowledge is generic-cognitive, secondary knowledge is largely domain-specific. We may have evolved to solve a large variety of problems using a generic-cognitive problem-solving strategy such as means-ends analysis but we are most unlikely to have evolved to solve an algebra problem such as $(a + b)/c = d$, solve for a, by multiplying out the denominator on the left-hand side as the first move. That strategy is specific to a particular class of algebra problem and of no use when solving any other category of problems. Unlike generic-cognitive skills, it needs to be taught and deliberately learned because we have not specifically evolved to acquire this strategy.

In addition, biologically secondary, domain-specific skills need to be explicitly taught and deliberately learned (Kirschner, Sweller, & Clark, 2006; Sweller, Kirschner, & Clark, 2007). Because we have not specifically evolved to acquire them, they will not be automatically learned like biologically primary, generic-cognitive skills. As a consequence, explicit instruction is vital in most areas. The frequent failure of our field to distinguish between biologically primary, generic-cognitive knowledge and biologically secondary, domain-specific knowledge has had the unfortunate consequence that many instructional designers and many instructional theories assume that because we are able to learn easily and automatically without explicit instruction outside of educational contexts, that the same limited guidance procedures are educationally superior to explicit instruction.

There are differences between how we learn within an education context as opposed to learning in environments external to formal education, but those differences are due to the different categories of knowledge being dealt with. An example of the problems that can arise by ignoring the distinction between biologically primary, generic-cognitive and biologically secondary, domain-specific skills, can be found by considering the examples above of learning to use a general problem-solving strategy such as means-ends analysis externally to an education context as opposed to learning to solve an algebraic equation. The generic means-ends strategy is never explicitly taught because it does not need to be taught. Because of its importance, it is acquired automatically as a biologically primary skill and so it would be futile to attempt to teach it. In contrast, learning that we need to multiply out the denominator when solving a particular algebra problem is a domain-specific, biologically secondary skill that we will not learn unless it is taught. Assuming that the two skills belong to the same category and are acquired in the same way and so should be taught in the same way is likely to result in instructionally flawed procedures.

Human cognitive architecture

Cognitive load theory is mainly concerned with biologically secondary information because most educationally relevant areas deal with such information. Biologically secondary information is processed, stored and used according to a specific cognitive architecture. That architecture is used by cognitive load theory and can be outlined by five basic structures and functions. It should be noted that the same processes govern the functioning of evolution by natural selection (Sweller &

Sweller, 2006). Both human cognition and evolution by natural selection are examples of natural information processing systems and as a consequence, the two systems are closely analogous.

Long-term memory structure and function. Knowledge is the driver of intellectual performance, and knowledge is stored in schematic form in long-term memory. Our ability to store knowledge is a biologically primary skill. Curiously, until relatively recently, intellectual performance tended to be associated more with terms such as "thinking", "problem-solving" or "creativity" rather than "knowledge". Even more curiously, we have known of the centrality of knowledge to problem-solving skill for a very long time. De Groot (1965), in a book first published in 1946, demonstrated that the only obvious difference between more able and less able chess players was their knowledge of large numbers of chess board configurations. A good chess player has learned to recognise chess board configurations and the best moves associated with them. Chess is a game of problem solving but problem-solving skill can be entirely explained by biologically secondary, domain-specific knowledge held in long-term memory. No other explanation has been required for over the last 70 years. The same base of biologically secondary, domain-specific skill can be assumed to apply to every acquired, knowledge-based area including areas taught in educational institutions. Skilled performers in all such areas have acquired enormous stores of schematic knowledge held in long-term memory. Accordingly, instructional procedures need to place their emphasis on knowledge acquisition.

Borrowing and reorganising function. How is knowledge best acquired? Humans have evolved to acquire knowledge, including biologically secondary knowledge, from others. It is a biologically primary skill. We are one of the few species to have evolved to both present information to and acquire information from other members of the species. Instruction should facilitate that process by an appropriate organisation of written, spoken and diagrammatic material. Cognitive load theory was devised to assist in the realisation of this goal of effective and efficient knowledge transfer between people.

Randomness as genesis function. While the most effective method of obtaining information is from other people either directly or via media, sometimes that information is unavailable either because it cannot be accessed or because it has not yet been invented. Under those circumstances, problem solving can provide an alternative route. All problem-solving strategies consist of an amalgam of knowledge and random generation and test. We will use knowledge as far as possible to solve problems but if knowledge cannot be used to generate a problem-solving move, we have no choice but to randomly generate a move and test it for effectiveness. We do not need to be taught this procedure because it is biologically primary. Random generation and test can work but it is slow and inefficient compared to obtaining relevant information from another person. In instructional contexts, it should not be used as a substitute for providing learners with information.

Working memory structure and function when processing novel information. After it is perceived, novel information obtained from the external environment is first processed by working memory. Information can be obtained either from others via the borrowing and reorganising function or during problem solving via the randomness as genesis function. Once processed, if potentially useful subsequently, it can be stored in long-term memory. When dealing with novel information, this structure is characterised by its very limited capacity (Cowan, 2001; Miller, 1956) and duration (Peterson & Peterson, 1959). No more than 3–4 items of information can be processed in working memory at a time and cannot be held without rehearsal for more than about 20 seconds. This structure is central to cognitive load theory. By definition, learners deal with novel information. Instructional procedures that ignore this structure are likely to be random in their effectiveness.

Working memory structure and function when processing familiar information. Working memory not only processes novel information obtained via the senses, it also processes familiar information that has been stored in long-term memory using the previously described structures and functions. Unlike working memory when dealing with novel information, there are no known limits when working memory deals with organised, familiar information transferred from long-term memory. When activated by appropriate environmental signals, working memory can transfer large amounts of automated information from long-term memory, keep that information active in working memory for indefinite periods, and so allow the generation of action appropriate to that environment. This function of working memory when processing familiar information stored in long-term memory provides the ultimate justification of the cognitive system and explains the importance of education. Our ability to effortlessly and appropriately access and process huge amounts of automated, biologically secondary information explains the transformational consequences of education.

Instructional consequences of human cognitive architecture

The above cognitive architecture provides the base for the instructional design procedures used by cognitive load theory. Assuming that architecture, the major function of instruction is to alter the contents of long-term memory. Once altered, that information can be transferred to working memory transforming the ability of learners to function in a particular environment. They can derive meaning from print where others only see apparently random squiggles; they can immediately and effortlessly solve mathematical problems that others find impossibly complex. In general, what is otherwise meaningless and unintelligible can become obvious, routine and automatic. Of course, before reaching this state, novel, biologically secondary information must be transferred to long-term memory from the environment via a severely restricted working memory. Facilitating this process is the primary function of cognitive load theory. In order to do so, further categorisation of information using the concept of element interactivity is required.

Element interactivity

Element interactivity is a central concept of cognitive load theory (Sweller, 2010). Some information consists of individual, largely unrelated elements of information. Where elements of information are unrelated, they can be processed with minimal or no reference to each other. For example, if you need to learn some of the nouns of a foreign language or the symbols of the chemical periodic table, each element can be learned without reference to any other element. Element interactivity is low. In contrast, at the other extreme, some information can be very high in element interactivity because each element interacts with a multitude of other elements. For example, if a student must learn how to balance a chemical equation or solve an algebra problem, no element can vary without affecting many of the other elements. Any change to a pro-numeral in an algebra equation has consequences for the entire equation.

These differences in element interactivity have working memory consequences. Learning the nouns of a foreign language is likely to be a very difficult, time-consuming task but it does not impose a heavy working memory load because element interactivity is low. In contrast, learning to solve an algebra problem such as $(a + b)/c = d$, solve for a, involves far fewer elements but for a novice algebra student, also can be difficult, although for a different reason. Any step to solve the algebra problem has consequences for the other elements that constitute the problem because the elements interact. Interaction between elements means all of the elements must be processed in working memory simultaneously. The task is difficult, not just because there are many elements but because there are many elements that must be processed simultaneously in working memory. Instruction that is difficult because it imposes a heavy working memory load has very different instructional design implications from instruction that is difficult because it requires the assimilation of many elements that do not interact and so do not impose a heavy working memory load. For this reason, differences in element interactivity are central to cognitive load theory.

Categories of cognitive load. There are two basic sources of element interactivity: intrinsic and extraneous leading to intrinsic and extraneous cognitive load. Intrinsic cognitive load, as the name implies, is intrinsic to the information being dealt with. The two areas discussed above provide examples. Learning the nouns of a foreign language provides an example of a low intrinsic cognitive load while learning how to solve algebra problems provides an example of a high intrinsic cognitive load. Unsurprisingly, cognitive load theory is primarily concerned with information that has a high intrinsic cognitive load.

Intrinsic cognitive load is fixed for a given instructional area and given levels of expertise (Chen, Kalyuga, & Sweller, 2017; Sweller, 1994). It can be altered by altering what is taught. More importantly, expertise alters element interactivity by altering the composition of elements. For example, an expert in solving the above algebra problem may immediately recognise the problem and its solution using the environmental organising and linking principle to retrieve the information from long-term memory. The entire problem and its solution may constitute a single element. In this manner, expertise reduces element interactivity and intrinsic cognitive load.

Element interactivity is not only central to intrinsic cognitive load but also determines extraneous cognitive load. This category of cognitive load is determined by instructional procedures rather than the intrinsic nature of the information. Some instructional procedures require learners to process many multiple elements simultaneously while other procedures have the same learning goals but reduce the number of elements that need to be simultaneously processed. The ultimate success or otherwise of cognitive load theory is determined by its ability to generate instructional procedures that reduce element interactivity and so reduce working memory load thus increasing the transfer of information to be stored in long-term memory.

Advances in cognitive load theory discussed in this volume

As cognitive load theory developed, it has been used to generate a large number of instructional effects by reducing element interactivity, primarily associated with extraneous cognitive load (Sweller et al., 2011). As discussed at the beginning of this chapter, each effect is based on randomised, controlled trials comparing an instructional design derived from the theory with a conventional or standard procedure as the control. The new work discussed in this volume provides a summary of theoretical developments over recent years and the empirical consequences of that development. That work is summarised next.

General theoretical advances

This book provides a number of interesting theoretical advances within cognitive load theory research. In Chapter 2, Martin and Evans combine the heavy working memory load experienced by novice learners with the expertise reversal effect to promulgate their Load Reduction Instruction thesis. They advocate that initial learning should be associated with a heavy emphasis on explicit instruction followed by a gradual reduction in guidance with increasing knowledge. In some ways, Load Reduction Instruction is a generalisation of Renkl's more specific guidance fading effect according to which the use of worked examples should be faded to be replaced by problem solving with increases in expertise. Martin and Evans' argument of appropriately managing cognitive load to support learner motivation and engagement, resulting in enhanced learning, is very convincing.

Zambrano, R. Kirschner and F. Kirschner in Chapter 3 correctly point out that cognitive load theory has been primarily concerned with individual learning rather than collaborative learning. They also point out that the field of collaborative learning currently does not have a unifying theory and that cognitive load theory is ideally placed to fulfil that role. They provide a compelling case by using the theory to explain when collaborative learning should and should not be effective.

The structure and capacity of working memory is central to cognitive load theory. In Chapter 4, Puma and Tricot provide a novel history of the use by cognitive load theory of various working memory models. They advocate consideration of the Time Based Resource Sharing Model, indicating that it may better fit the range of data generated by cognitive load theory. This relatively recently developed model has not been used by most cognitive load theorists and the argument that it should be considered, is persuasive.

Specific research advances and research procedures

Cognitive load theory scholars and researchers are continuously developing and refining new research procedures and advances in cognitive load theory. This section records some of that recent work. In Chapter 5 Liu, Lin, and Kuo discuss some of the difficulties associated with conducting randomised, controlled trials in regular classrooms. They pointed out that using electronic slideshows in virtual classrooms may eliminate many of the issues associated with real classrooms but still retain appropriate levels of internal and ecological validity. By successfully demonstrating the split-attention effect using an arrow-line cueing procedure, they demonstrated the efficacy of using a virtual classroom to test cognitive load theory instructional design principles.

In Chapter 6, Leppink, Paas, van Gog, and van Merriënboer provide us with an innovative measure that may be used within cognitive load theory research to support learner self-assessment and task selection. The researchers discuss a measure that is intended to indicate the extent to which learners are able to determine and choose an appropriate level of difficulty of tasks that facilitate further learning. In effect, the measure determines the extent to which learners can select tasks with appropriate levels of cognitive load.

Wong, Castro-Alonso, Ayres, and Paas in Chapter 7, introduce a new, exceptionally interesting theoretical point. They indicate that the transient information effect increases extraneous cognitive load when using animations but, of course, using information that is high in element interactivity also will increase element interactivity. Accordingly, the effectiveness of animations can be hypothesised to depend on an interaction between transience and element interactivity. They indicate that there are some data in support of this hypothesis but, of course, it requires explicit, experimental testing.

Castro-Alonso, Ayres, Wong, and Paas in Chapter 8, point out that various spatial ability tests correlate with ability to learn from multi-media learning materials. In some cases the relation between the test and the learning materials is clear but in other cases there seems little relation between the two. Nevertheless, the authors indicate that the correlation seems to stand up even when the spatial ability test and the learning materials ostensibly have very little relation. While research is needed to determine the exact relation between spatial ability and multimedia learning, it is clear that especially for learners with poor spatial ability, it is very important that cognitive load be reduced as much as possible.

Human movement, pointing, tracing and gesturing

An innovative area of research emerging within cognitive load theory, is the use of gestures and human movement to enhance learning. Chapter 9 by Mavilidi, Ouwehand, Okely, Chandler, and Paas summarises several papers that investigated the effects of learner movement on learning. In results using movement as a biologically primary activity to leverage learning biologically secondary information, they consistently found that appropriate body movements facilitated learning everything from mathematics to second language vocabulary. In the process, there is every likelihood that they have initiated a new, very important area of cognitive load theory.

Chapter 10, by Ginns and Kydd is concerned with the effect of asking learners to point and trace while learning. Students learning about the human circulatory system were asked to point and trace while learning and compared to learners who were instructed not to use their hands. The hypothesis was that pointing and tracing is biologically primary and so may leverage learning the biologically secondary information that constitutes knowledge of the circulatory system. In other words, pointing and tracing may reduce cognitive load. Evidence for improved performance when pointing and tracing associated with a reduction in cognitive load was obtained.

Sepp, Agostinho, Tindall-Ford and Paas in Chapter 11, contend that touch-based ICT tools provide unique opportunities to investigate and capture learners' gestures when learning and interacting with ICT tools. Chapter 11 synthesises research investigating gesturing within ICT. The synthesis is followed by a recent study investigating learners making multiple gestures when using an ipad to learn geometry concepts. This chapter makes an important contribution to the understanding of how educators can effectively use gesture-based learning materials and apps in their classrooms.

In Chapter 12, Park, Korbach, Ginns, and Brünken provide a theoretical account of the factors that may be relevant to explaining the benefits associated with pointing and tracing when learning. Haptic processes such as the pointing and tracing effect are becoming increasingly important in cognitive load theory and the theoretical integration of experimental results based on these haptic processes is urgent. This chapter initiates this process by outlining several possible directions that need to be considered.

New effects and new conditions required for old effects

Cognitive load theory is continually evolving resulting in new effects and additional understanding of old effects. Chapter 13 by Mirza, Agostinho, Tindall-Ford, Paas and Chandler discusses a relatively new cognitive load theory effect: self-management of cognitive load. The researchers argue that learners do not always have the benefit of learning from cognitive compliant instructional materials and as such learners should be taught to apply the principles of cognitive load theory and self-manage cognitive load. The chapter summarises a series of experiments that have investigated self-management of cognitive load when learning from split-attention materials. New research investigating self-management of redundant information is presented, with a discussion on the various forms of redundancy and how this may affect the effectiveness of self-management.

An extension of the self-management effect is discussed by Eitel and Renkl in Chapter 14. The researchers point out that often, the extraneous load associated with cognitive load effects such as the redundancy and split-attention effects can be avoided not only by restructuring the information as discussed in Chapter 13, but by informing learners how to appropriately use the information. This "informed use" effect, extends the original idea of self-management. The research provides a potential new pathway to reducing extraneous cognitive load – and a new research area.

Cognitive load theorists have investigated the efficacy of animations in supporting learning. In Chapter 15, Ayres, Castro-Alonso, Wong, Marcus, and Paas survey the copious research that has been carried out on instructional use of animations. It is frequently assumed that the use of animations is invariably beneficial. In fact, the most common result is no difference between animations and static graphics with frequent findings of animations having negative learning outcomes. The authors analyse the conditions which contribute to the effectiveness or otherwise of instructional animations.

In Chapter 16, Stebner, Schuster, Dicke, Karlen, Wirth, and Leutner apply cognitive load theory to self-regulated learning. Since self-regulated learning is a generic-cognitive skill that is likely to be largely biologically primary, according to the current version of the theory it is unlikely to be teachable in the same way as the domain-specific, biologically secondary skills that are the subject of most cognitive load theory research. Stebner et al. validly point out that teaching any generic-cognitive skill needs to be associated with far transfer since that is the aim of such skills and at this point, teaching self-regulated learning has not been shown to generate far transfer improvements.

Kalyuga and Hsu's Chapter 17 provides new data bearing on the controversy generated by the suggestion that students should be presented problems to solve prior to explicit instruction, even if they cannot solve those problems. The researchers compared problem solving only, problem solving with guidance about the relevant principles, problem solving with principle guidance and reflection on the solution attempts, and fully guided worked examples, all followed by explicit instruction. They found that problem solving with principle guidance and reflection was superior to problem solving alone or problem solving with guidance, with no other significant effects. A problem solving only procedure resulted in the least learning.

Leahy and Sweller discuss the centrality of element interactivity to cognitive load theory. In Chapter 18 the researchers discuss the application of the concept to resolve contradictions in the empirical work associated with the generation, worked example and testing effects.

In conclusion, the history of cognitive load theory is a history of constant theoretical and empirical development. My co-editors and I hope readers see the current volume as a continuation of that progress.

References

Chen, O., Kalyuga, S., & Sweller, J. (2017). The expertise reversal effect is a variant of the more general element interactivity effect. *Educational Psychology Review, 29*, 393–405. doi:10.1007/s10648-016-9359-1.

Cowan, N. (2001). The magical number 4 in short-term memory: A reconsideration of mental storage capacity. *Behavioral and Brain Sciences*, 24, 87–114.

De Groot, A. (1965). *Thought and choice in chess*. The Hague, Netherlands: Mouton. (Original work published 1946).

Geary, D. (2008). An evolutionarily informed education science. *Educational Psychologist*, 43, 179–195.

Geary, D. (2012). Evolutionary Educational Psychology. In K. Harris, S. Graham, & T. Urdan (Eds.), *APA Educational Psychology Handbook* (Vol. 1, pp. 597–621). Washington, D.C.: American Psychological Association.

Geary, D., & Berch, D. (2016). Evolution and children's cognitive and academic development. In D. Geary, & D. Berch (Eds.), *Evolutionary perspectives on child development and education* (pp. 217–249). Switzerland: Springer.

Kirschner, P., Sweller, J., & Clark, R. (2006). Why minimal guidance during instruction does not work: An analysis of the failure of constructivist, discovery, problem-based, experiential and inquiry-based teaching. *Educational Psychologist*, 41, 75–86.

Miller, G. A. (1956). The magical number seven, plus or minus two: Some limits on our capacity for processing information. *Psychological Review*, 63, 81–97.

Newell, A., & Simon, H. A. (1972). *Human problem solving*. Englewood Cliffs, NJ: Prentice Hall.

Paas, F., & Sweller, J. (2012). An evolutionary upgrade of cognitive load theory: Using the human motor system and collaboration to support the learning of complex cognitive tasks. *Educational Psychology Review, 24*, 27–45. doi:10.1007/s10648-011-9179-2.

Peterson, L., & Peterson, M. J. (1959). Short-term retention of individual verbal items. *Journal of Experimental Psychology*, 58, 193–198.

Sala, G., & Gobet, F. (2017). Does far transfer exist? Negative evidence from chess, music and working memory training. *Current Directions in Psychological Science, 26*, 515–520. doi:10.1177/0963721417712760.

Sweller, J. (2010). Element interactivity and intrinsic, extraneous and germane cognitive load. *Educational Psychology Review*, 22, 123–138.

Sweller, J. (2015). In academe, what is learned and how is it learned? *Current Directions in Psychological Science*, 24, 190–194.

Sweller, J. (2016). Working memory, long-term memory and instructional design. *Journal of Applied Research in Memory and Cognition*, 5, 360–367.

Sweller, J., Ayres, P., & Kalyuga, S. (2011). *Cognitive load theory*. New York: Springer.

Sweller, J., Kirschner, P., & Clark, R. E. (2007). Why minimally guided teaching techniques do not work: A reply to commentaries. *Educational Psychologist*, 42, 115–121.

Sweller, J., & Sweller, S. (2006). Natural information processing systems. *Evolutionary Psychology*, 4, 434–458.

Tricot, A., & Sweller, J. (2014). Domain-specific knowledge and why teaching generic skills does not work. *Educational Psychology Review, 26*, 265–283. doi:10.1007/s10648-013-9243-1.

PART 1

General theoretical advances

2

LOAD REDUCTION INSTRUCTION (LRI)

Sequencing explicit instruction and guided discovery to enhance students' motivation, engagement, learning, and achievement

Andrew J. Martin and Paul Evans

UNIVERSITY OF NEW SOUTH WALES, AUSTRALIA

There are significant academic demands at school and these demands tend to escalate as students move from elementary school to middle school to high school. Over this time, there is an increase in frequency and difficulty of homework, assignments, tests, and subject difficulty (Anderman, 2013; Anderman & Mueller, 2010; Graham & Hill, 2003; Hanewald, 2013; Kvalsund, 2000; Martin, 2015, 2016; Martin, Way, Bobis & Anderson, 2015; Zeedyk, Gallacher, Henderson, Hope, Husband, & Lindsay, 2003). This escalation in academic challenge imposes increasing cognitive demands on students. As students transition through school, there are also accompanying declines in motivation and engagement (Eccles & Roesser, 2009; Martin, 2007, 2009; Wang & Eccles, 2012; see also Booth & Gerard, 2014; Gillen-O'Neel & Fuligni, 2013). These challenges suggest the need to approach instruction in ways that help manage the cognitive burden on learners. Cognitive psychology has identified instructional principles and strategies that are aimed at easing the cognitive burden on students as they learn and achieve. This chapter outlines a recently developed instructional framework that accommodates the cognitive demands of learning and the cognitive boundary conditions of learners. This approach is referred to as "load reduction instruction" (LRI; Martin, 2016; Martin & Evans, 2018). As described more fully below (see also Figure 2.1), LRI encompasses five key principles: (1) reducing the difficulty of instruction during initial learning, (2) instructional support and scaffolding, (3) ample structured practice, (4) appropriate provision of instructional feedback-feedforward (combination of corrective information and specific improvement-oriented guidance), and (5) independent application.

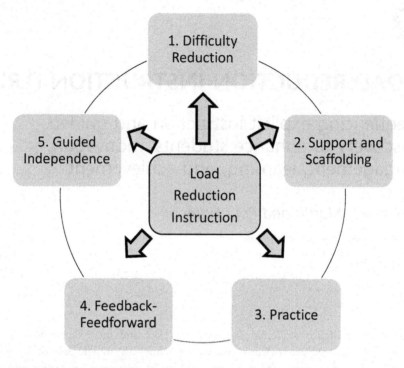

FIGURE 2.1 Load reduction instruction (LRI) framework
Source: adapted from Martin (2016).

Load reduction instruction

An underlying tenet of LRI is that learners are initially novices in academic skill and subject matter. Thus, a structured approach to instruction is important in the early phases of learning. According to cognitive load theory (CLT), teachers can impose two kinds of cognitive load on their students. Intrinsic cognitive load relates to the inherent difficulty of the instructional material. Teachers manage intrinsic cognitive load by presenting instructional material that is appropriate to students' level of knowledge—for example, when students know enough about algebra and solving basic equations, learning how to solve simultaneous equations is within their grasp. The degree to which solving simultaneous equations is difficult for the students is reflective of the intrinsic cognitive load of solving simultaneous equations. Extraneous cognitive load relates to the way the material is structured and presented. Instructional material can be presented clearly and explicitly to students, in a way that guides them through the learning, or it can be structured in a way that requires students themselves to work out the structure of the information, search and explore among a range of potential solutions, or pull information together from a range of sources in which they have relatively little knowledge. Extraneous cognitive load does not contribute to learning (hence the name) and is thus seen as an unnecessary burden on students (Sweller, Ayres, & Kalyuga, 2011).

Following from key elements of CLT, then, load reduction instruction refers mainly to a range of strategies intended to reduce extraneous cognitive load, and to a lesser extent, intrinsic cognitive load (Martin, 2016). When learners are novices (as they often are by virtue of them being learners, especially in the beginning of a unit of work or at the commencement of studying a particular subject), a structured and systematic approach is necessary to reduce extraneous cognitive load (and to some extent, intrinsic cognitive load). As learners develop the requisite skill and subject matter in a domain, there is an appropriate time for guided discovery and exploratory approaches (Liem & Martin, 2013; see also Kalyuga, Ayres, Chandler, & Sweller, 2003). That is, as they move beyond novice status and have automated core skills and knowledge, they can engage in guided discovery and exploratory learning that can make the most of this skill and knowledge. LRI thus posits that explicit and constructivist learning (and teaching) are interconnected— the effectiveness of one is dependent on the effectiveness of the other (Martin, 2016). In contrast, when discovery and exploration are carried out without the requisite skill and subject matter, extraneous cognitive load inhibits the quality of learning and has negative effects on motivation and engagement.

In presenting the LRI framework in this chapter, we emphasise that there are other frameworks that have recognised the roles of both explicit and discovery approaches (e.g., "balanced instruction", "gradual release of responsibility", "enhanced discovery learning" etc.; e.g., Alfieri, Brooks, Aldrich, & Tenenbaum, 2011; Fisher & Frey, 2008; Marzano, 2011; Maynes, Julien-Schultz, & Dunn, 2010; Pearson & Gallagher, 1983; Pressley & Allington, 2014), and so we position LRI on this landscape. In doing so, we make the point that these other instructional approaches are not necessarily designed to reduce and/or manage the cognitive burden on learners (even though they may well do this). In contrast, LRI is fundamentally motivated, by design, to reduce extraneous cognitive load (and to a lesser extent, intrinsic cognitive load).

Working and long-term memory

The human mind is composed of working and long-term memory and these are primary mechanisms for how people learn (Kirschner, Sweller, & Clark, 2006; Sweller, 2012; Winne & Nesbit, 2010). Working memory is responsible for receiving and processing information—solving problems, performing tasks, etc.— including new and unfamiliar information. Learning occurs when information is effectively "moved" from working memory and encoded in long-term memory in a way that can be later retrieved as required (Kirschner et al., 2006; Sweller, 2012; Winne & Nesbit, 2010). Working memory is therefore central for processing and encoding memory.

A major challenge for educators and learners is that working memory is very limited. This is a particular headwind for educators when they need to teach new material or present novel subject matter (Sweller, Ayres, & Kalyuga, 2011; Winne & Nesbit, 2010). Although figures vary, it has been suggested that unless rehearsed, working memory is limited to approximately seven (or less) elements and lost within up to 30 seconds (Atkinson & Shiffrin, 1971; Baddeley, 1994; Miller, 1956). A great deal of instruction comprises information exceeding these limits and this further underscores the need for instructional approaches that manage the cognitive burden on learners. According to Kirschner and colleagues: "Any instructional theory that ignores the limits of working memory when dealing with novel information or ignores the disappearance of those limits when dealing with familiar information is unlikely to be effective" (2006, p. 77).

Overly burdening working memory is therefore easy to do, and it can be a major barrier to learning. If overly burdened, there is risk that content will not be understood, information will not be encoded effectively in long-term memory, and/or information will be confused or misinterpreted (Rosenshine, 2009; Tobias, 1982). It is thus important for educators to deliver instruction, present content, and organise tasks and activities in ways that do not excessively tax working memory.

At the same time, long-term memory is not so limited—it has vast capacity. Therefore, if learners can effectively store information in long-term memory and if their working memory can successfully access this stored information, then effective learning can occur. This is particularly useful because information that has been encoded in long-term memory consumes fewer working memory resources when it is recalled, compared with when it is presented as novel. Given this, learners are greatly assisted in their learning if educators can develop and deliver instruction that can help the learner process information between working memory and long-term memory, and present instructional material that frees working memory from unnecessary burden (Martin, 2015, 2016; Paas, Renkl, & Sweller, 2003; Sweller, 2003, 2004; Winne & Nesbit, 2010).

Fluency, automaticity, independent learning, and LRI principles #1–5

Fluency and automaticity in skill and knowledge mean that when skill and knowledge are recalled into working memory, fewer working memory resources are consumed. This frees up working memory and the reduced burden allows the learner to process novel information into long-term memory (Rosenshine, 2009). Over time, the learner develops a vast volume of long-term memory and in so doing, develops expertise in areas in which long-term memory has sufficiently developed.

From a practice perspective, Martin (2016; see also Martin & Evans, 2018) has described how fluency and automaticity can be developed through LRI's first four principles, as follows: (#1) reducing the difficulty of instruction in the initial stages of learning (see also Mayer & Moreno, 2010); (#2) providing appropriate support and scaffolding to learn the relevant skill and knowledge (see also Renkl, 2014; Renkl & Atkinson, 2010); (#3) allowing sufficient opportunity for practice (see also Nandagopal & Ericsson, 2012; Purdie & Ellis, 2005; Rosenshine, 2009); and (#4) providing appropriate feedback-feedforward (combination of corrective information and specific improvement-oriented guidance) as needed (see also Hattie, 2009; Mayer & Moreno, 2010; Schute, 2008). Beginning learners will require ample time dedicated to each of these four LRI principles and due care would be exercised by the educator before moving from one LRI element to the next. More developed learners, or high ability learners, may require relatively less time in the early stages of LRI principles #1 to #4 (Martin, 2016).

As fluency and automaticity free up the learner's working memory, he/she is then well placed to apply their automated and fluent skill and knowledge to novel tasks, to higher-order reasoning and thinking, or to guided discovery learning (Martin, 2016). In other words, as expertise develops, learners are able to manipulate and use knowledge in novel and creative ways, with relatively less reliance on the involvement of an instructor. Without the requisite expertise, such tasks tend not to result in learning, and instead overburden learners' working memory by engaging in tasks (such as problem-solving and means-ends analysis) that do not contribute to learning. This represents principle #5: guided independent learning. Thus, LRI harnesses the benefits of both explicit and constructivist approaches and emphasises that each approach is implicated in the other. In so doing, however, it also emphasises that the order in which this process occurs is critical. Inadequate attention to the LRI principles #1–4 or privileging LRI principle #5 too early in the learning process may pose too great a cognitive burden on the learner. However, if there is insufficient attention to LRI principle #5 after the learner has become fluent in skill and/or knowledge, the learner may also be burdened.

In some support for this latter notion, CLT researchers have shown that once learners become expert (i.e., develop sufficient fluency and/or automaticity), they actually benefit more from problem-solving approaches, and their learning may be impeded by overly explicit and structured approaches—the so-called expertise reversal effect (e.g., Kalyuga, 2007; Kalyuga, Ayres, Chandler, & Sweller, 2003; Kalyuga, Chandler, Tuovinen, & Sweller, 2001). Following from appropriate explicit input, instructional support, guided practice, and feedback-feedforward from the instructor (e.g., LRI principles #1–4), students now have the required prior knowledge, they have developed adequate fluency and/or automaticity, and their working memory is not so taxed in a way typical of novices. Therefore, more demanding subject matter can now be presented to the learner (Kalyuga et al., 2003). Taken together, with adequate foregrounding (i.e., LRI principles #1–4), there is a point in the learning process when more independence (i.e., LRI principle #5) is important (Liem & Martin, 2013; Martin, 2015, 2016; Martin & Evans, 2018; Mayer, 2004).

Importantly, however, LRI principle #5 (independent learning) is not without its qualifications. For example, Liem and Martin (2013; see also Pressley et al., 2003) outlined a range of independent learning options available to the educator and learner, traversing pure independent learning (predominantly unguided independent application) through to guided independent learning (predominantly scaffolded and assisted independent learning). They observed that guidance in the independent learning phase of LRI is still important because it helps manage the cognitive burden on learners' working memory. As noted earlier, when working memory is overly burdened, there is a risk that the intended learning will not occur (Martin, 2016). Thus, LRI advocates for guided independent learning rather than pure independent learning. Indeed, naïve or misplaced emphasis on pure independent learning has generated frustration among researchers:

> Like some zombie that keeps returning from its grave, pure discovery continues to have its advocates. However, anyone who takes an evidence-based approach to educational practice must ask the same question: Where is the evidence that it works? In spite of calls for free discovery in every decade, the supporting evidence is hard to find.
>
> *(Mayer, 2004, p. 17)*

The process of explicit instruction through to guided discovery learning

As discussed above, there is a time in the learning process when more novelty, complexity, and independence are important for further learning (Mayer, 2004). Indeed, CLT has recognised the need to distinguish between optimal learning approaches for novices and optimal learning approaches appropriate for more advanced learners. For this reason, CLT researchers have explored approaches aimed

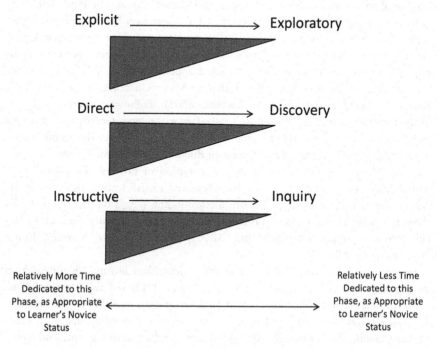

FIGURE 2.2 LRI process: from explicit to exploratory, direct to discovery, and instructive to inquiry

at smoothing the often rigid dichotomisation of explicit and discovery-oriented approaches (e.g., see Kalyuga & Singh, 2015).

Given this, Martin (2016) proposed a sequence of teaching and learning that draws on explicit through to guided discovery-oriented learning. Martin (2016) emphasised that the effectiveness of each part of this process relies on the recognition that learners can range in their relative novice and expert status. Depending on which stage they are at in the learning process, learners differ in the volume of working memory consumed by the present instruction, the schematic knowledge that can be recalled from long-term memory, and the fluency and automaticity with which knowledge can be recalled. Figure 2.2 demonstrates this.

Figure 2.2 is a general model of the LRI process in that it is relevant to most learners. These learners require sufficient time and attention in the explicit instructional stage. This helps provide a foundation for a guided discovery phase. For high ability students, relatively less time and attention are directed at the explicit instructional stage as these learners progress more rapidly to a guided exploratory and discovery phase—however, some time engaged in this phase is nonetheless necessary—otherwise they run the risk of being a relatively unskilled discoverer or uninformed inquirer.

Load reduction instruction and academic outcomes

Across a range of empirical studies, meta-analyses and reviews, principles under-pinning and informing LRI are associated with motivation, engagement, learning, and achievement outcomes (Cromley & Byrnes, 2012; Lee & Anderson, 2013; Liem & Martin, 2013; Mayer, 2004). For example, in early work, Adams and Engelmann (1996) demonstrated that explicit instruction evinced positive effects on basic skills (e.g., spelling, word recognition, numeracy) and cognitive skills (e.g., math problem solving, reading comprehension). Adams and Engelmann (1996) also found positive effects for motivation (e.g., self-concept, attributions). A meta-analysis conducted by Haas (2005) concluded that explicit instruction appeared to be the most effective method of teaching algebra. As relevant to key principles under LRI, its success was attributed to pacing and scaffolding as well as some level of guided and independent practice. Hattie's (2009) meta-analysis of educational factors associated with achievement had explicit instruction ranked 26th (of 138 effects) in terms of its link to achievement. A meta-analysis by Alfieri and colleagues (2011) demonstrated that principles emphasised under LRI were significantly implicated in achievement. For example, they found that worked examples demonstrated the strongest effects; this was followed by the effects of feedback, direct teaching, and explanations. In their review of meta-analyses conducted into explicit and dis-covery instructional approaches, Liem and Martin (2013) concluded that more explicit approaches help alleviate cognitive burden and assist the processing of instructional material between working memory and long-term memory (also see Alfieri et al., 2011; Kirschner et al., 2006). Notably, they also concluded that there are positive academic outcomes when independent learning took place after an appropriate amount and level of explicit input.

Alongside learning and achievement yields, Martin (2016) drew numerous connections between LRI and academic motivation and engagement. Instructors' own reasons for choosing relatively unguided discovery approaches often point to motivational benefits—that is, they may be concerned that teaching that is too prescriptive and directed is less enjoyable for students. In other words, it may be seen that there is a payoff between the amount of guidance and instruction, and the amount of motivation and engagement. However, LRI poses that this is not the case, and that indeed, LRI promotes motivation and engagement. This is because LRI factors (e.g., sufficient practice and feedback-feedforward) underpin learning competence (Archer & Hughes, 2011) and this is likely to be positively linked to motivation factors such as self-efficacy and persistence (Martin, 2016). Recently, research on structure—the extent to which teachers provide clear directions, explicit plans for the lesson, guidance, and feedback—showed that it resulted in students being more engaged in class and learning more effectively (Jang, Reeve, & Deci, 2010; Sierens, Vansteenkiste, Goossens, Soenens, & Dochy, 2009; Vansteenkiste et al., 2012). Martin and Evans (2018) proposed also that LRI factors (e.g., reducing task difficulty during initial learning) may reduce problematic motivation factors such as anxiety and disengagement (Ashcraft & Kirk, 2001; Martin, 2016). Martin and Evans (2018) also described how LRI seeks to reduce difficulty and burden on learners and that this should also have positive effects on their capacity to deal with academic adversity (e.g., academic buoyancy, academic resilience; Martin & Marsh, 2008). Thus, alongside academic achievement, LRI also promotes motivation, interest, competence, and engagement.

Assessing load reduction instruction—the Load Reduction Instruction Scale (LRIS) and early findings

Building on the conceptual work into the LRI framework, Martin and Evans (2018) developed an instrument to assess the five LRI principles and that could be used in correlational (and experimental) research to enable data collection in various individual and group contexts. This tool—the Load Reduction Instruction Scale (LRIS)—comprised five factors that represented the five principles of LRI. Each of these five factors was represented by five items—thus, a 25-item instrument (see Table 2.1). Martin and Evans (2018) administered the LRIS to 393 year 9 (25%), year 10 (36%), and year 11 (39%) high school students. These students were drawn from 40 mathematics classrooms located in two independent schools (one single-sex girls, $n = 142$; one co-educational girls and boys, $n = 251$) in Sydney, Australia. The average age of participants was 15.55 ($SD = .97$) years and just over half (57%) the sample comprised girls. As well as the LRIS, students were assessed on various academic outcomes, including their positive motivation (valuing, self-efficacy, mastery orientation), positive engagement (planning and

TABLE 2.1 Load Reduction Instruction Scale (LRIS)

Difficulty reduction

When we learn something new in this class, the teacher starts with the easy parts

When we learn something new in this class, the teacher makes sure it's not too hard at first

When we start a new topic in this class, the teacher starts with the basics

When we learn new things in this class, the teacher makes it easy at first

When we start learning a new concept in this class, the teacher makes it easy to understand

Support and scaffolding

As we work on tasks or activities in this class, the teacher gives good assistance

As we do our schoolwork in this class, we get the help we need from the teacher

In this class the teacher is available for help when we need it

In this class we can always ask for help from the teacher if we are having trouble

In this class the teacher provides support while we are learning

Practice

In this class the teacher makes sure we practice things we learn

In this class the teacher makes sure we go over the main ideas

In this class the teacher makes sure we get enough practice before moving on to new tasks or activities

In this class the teacher makes sure we practice important things we learn many times over

We are always able to practice what we have learned in this class

Feedback-feedforward

In this class the teacher gives us lots of feedback on our work

In this class the teacher often tells us how to improve our work

In this class the teacher gives us good ideas to help us do our schoolwork

In this class the teacher provides constructive feedback that helps us learn

In this class the teacher's feedback is useful

Guided independence

Once we know what we're doing in this class, the teacher lets us work on our own

Once we know what we're doing in this class, the teacher gives us questions to answer on our own

Once we know what we're doing in this class, the teacher gives us schoolwork to figure out by ourselves

Once we know what we're doing in this class, the teacher gives us a chance to work independently

Once we know what we're doing in this class, the teacher provides time to practice on our own

Martin & Evans, 2018, with permission.

Rated: 1=Strongly disagree, 2=Disagree, 3=Somewhat disagree, 4=Neither disagree nor agree, 5=Somewhat agree, 6=Agree, 7=Strongly agree.

monitoring, persistence, task management), negative motivation (failure avoidance, anxiety, uncertain control), negative engagement (self-handicapping, disengagement), academic buoyancy (capacity to successfully deal with academic adversity and setback), and mathematics achievement. As a validity check, students were also administered items that assessed intrinsic cognitive load and extraneous cognitive load (two "classic" factors under CLT) in the mathematics class.

In terms of psychometric properties, each of the five LRIS factors was reliable (coefficient omega ranged from .92 to .94) and factor analysis supported a five-factor model (mean factor loadings ranged from .84 to .93). There was also support for the feasibility of an overarching LRI factor (based on higher-order factor analysis). When testing for differences between classrooms, Martin and Evans (2018) found significant variation in LRI factors from class-to-class, suggesting that teachers varied in the extent to which they implement LRI. Martin and Evans (2018) also found LRI was negatively associated with both intrinsic cognitive load and extraneous cognitive load, but significantly more so for extraneous load (as our earlier argument would support).

There were significant correlations between the LRIS and various academic outcomes. For example, LRI was significantly and positively associated with positive motivation and positive engagement, and significantly inversely associated with negative engagement. In line with claims that LRI is aimed at easing the load on learners moving from novice to expert (Martin, 2016), it was found that LRI was significantly and positively associated with academic buoyancy. Finally, consistent with research into each element of LRI (see Martin, 2016 for a review), Martin and Evans (2018) found achievement was significantly and positively correlated with difficulty reduction (factor 1; e.g., Mayer & Moreno, 2010), support and scaffolding (factor 2; e.g., Renkl, 2014), practice (factor 3; e.g., Purdie & Ellis, 2005), feedback-feedforward (factor 4; e.g., Hattie, 2009), and guided independence (factor 5; e.g., Liem & Martin, 2013).

Implications for assessment and practice

This chapter has outlined a recently developed instructional framework that seeks to account for the realities of students' working and long-term memory as they progress from novice to relative expert status. Following from this, we suggest numerous implications for assessment and practice.

Implications for assessment

In regard to assessment implications, the LRIS is suggested to be psychometrically sound and associated with major educational outcomes such as motivation, engagement, and achievement. It thus appears to be a viable instrument for research seeking to further explore aspects of LRI and its role in learning. As well as this, Martin and Evans (2018) have suggested numerous ways that the LRIS can be used in practice. They estimated that the whole instrument can be completed in about 10–15 minutes, depending on the literacy levels and age of respondents. Also, given the nature of the wording, the LRIS can be administered in different school subjects (the Martin & Evans study was in mathematics). They also identified the possibility of schools administering specific scales that may be of key interest. For example, feedback-feedforward (principle #4) is central to effective instruction (Hattie, 2009) and the LRIS feedback-feedforward items might be administered to respondents in such cases. The LRIS might also be used as an observation checklist for classroom/teacher practice, with findings then being used to assist micro-teaching opportunities (Hattie, 2009). Alternatively, teachers could use the LRIS as a tool for self-reflection (e.g., reflecting on how students in the classroom might rate the teacher on each LRIS factor). Depending on what this reveals, teachers might then adjust instruction to better ease the cognitive burden on their students.

Implications for practice

Following from each of the five principles of LRI (and the five LRIS factors), there are implications for pedagogy. Martin (2016) has outlined many pedagogical strategies for each part of the LRI framework and we refer the reader to that work for a more comprehensive range of pedagogical strategy. Here, we briefly identify an indicative few for illustrative purposes. With regard to reducing difficulty in the initial stages of learning (principle #1), pre-training and segmenting (or, "chunking") have been suggested (e.g., Martin, 2010; Mayer & Moreno, 2010). For provision of support and scaffolding (principle #2) and in line with CLT (Sweller, 2012), the use of worked examples, prompting, and structured templates have been identified (e.g., Renkl, 2014; Renkl & Atkinson, 2010). For provision of ample practice (principle #3), deliberate and mental rehearsal have been recommended (e.g., Ginns, 2005; Nandagopal & Ericsson, 2012; Purdie & Ellis, 2005; Sweller, 2012). For feedback-feedforward (principle #4), corrective and improvement-oriented information have been identified (e.g., Basso & Belardinelli, 2006; Hattie, 2009). Finally, for guided independence (principle #5), supported discovery learning has been suggested (e.g., Mayer, 2004). The bulk of this advice has been administered in relation to general or "mainstream" student populations. However, given the recognised yield of explicit instructional techniques for at-risk learners (e.g., McMullen & Madelaine, 2014; Rupley, Blair & Nichols, 2009; Swanson & Sachse-Lee, 2000), research among these learners might also incorporate LRI considerations. Taken together, there is a strong empirical foundation for various instructional practices to foster and promote effective learning under the LRI framework.

Conclusion

Load reduction instruction (LRI) is an instructional approach that aims to appropriately manage cognitive load in order to assist students' learning. Following from research and conceptualising under CLT, students are typically novices at first in terms of academic skill and subject matter and so a structured and somewhat directive approach to instructional practice is helpful as it reduces cognitive load in the early stages of learning. As learners develop fluency and automaticity in skill and subject matter, LRI emphasises the importance of moving learners to guided independent learning. Given this, LRI encompasses five key principles: (1) reducing the difficulty of instruction during initial learning, (2) instructional support and scaffolding, (3) ample structured practice, (4) appropriate provision of instructional feedback-feedforward, and (5) independent application. There is promising research (using the Load Reduction Instruction Scale; LRIS) suggesting that the factors under the LRI framework are significantly associated with important educational outcomes. It is thus evident that clear, structured, and well guided instruction has significant implications for students' learning and achievement.

References

Adams, G., & Engelmann, S. (1996). *Research on Direct Instruction: 25 years beyond DISTAR*. Seattle, WA: Educational Achievement Systems.

Alfieri, L., Brooks, P. J., Aldrich, N. J., & Tenenbaum, H. R. (2011). Does discovery-based instruction enhance learning? *Journal of Educational Psychology*, 103, 1–18. doi:10.1037/a0021017.

Anderman, E. M. (2013). Middle school transitions. In J. Hattie, & E. M. Anderman (Eds.). *International guide to student achievement*. Routledge: New York.

Anderman, E. M., & Mueller, C. E. (2010). Middle school transitions and adolescent development. In J. L. Meece & J. S. Eccles (Eds.). *Handbook of research on schools, schooling, and human development*. Routledge: New York.

Archer, A. L., & Hughes, C. A. (2011). *Explicit instruction: Effective and efficient teaching*. Guilford Press.

Ashcraft, M. H., & Kirk, E. P. (2001). The relationships among working memory, math anxiety, and performance. *Journal of Experimental Psychology: General*, 130, 224–237. doi:10.1037/0096-3445.130.2.224.

Atkinson, R. C., & Shiffrin, R. M. (1971). The control of short-term memory. *Scientific American*, 225, 82–91.

Baddeley, A. (1994). The magical number seven: Still magic after all these years? *Psychological Review*, 101, 353–356. doi:10.1037/0033-295X.101.2.353.

Basso, D., & Belardinelli, M. O. (2006). The role of the feedforward paradigm in cognitive psychology. *Cognitive Processing*, 7, 73–88. doi:10.1007/s10339-006-0034-1.

Booth, M. Z., & Gerard, J. M. (2014). Adolescents' stage-environment fit in middle and high school: The relationship between students' perceptions of their schools and themselves. *Youth and Society*, 46, 735–755.

Cromley, J. G., & Byrnes, J. P. (2012). Instruction and cognition. *Wiley Interdisciplinary Reviews: Cognitive Science*, 3, 545–553. doi:10.1002/wcs.1192.

Eccles, J. S., & Roesser, R. W. (2009). Schools, academic motivation, and stage-environment fit (pp. 404–434). In R. M. Lerner, & L. Steinber (Eds.) *Handbook of adolescent psychology* (3rd ed.). Hoboken, N.J.: John Wiley & Sons.

Fisher, D., & Frey, N. (2008). *Better learning through structured teaching: A framework for the gradual release of responsibility*. Alexandria, VA: Association for Supervision and Curriculum Development.

Gillen-O'Neel, C., & Fuligni, A. (2013). A longitudinal study of school belonging and academic motivation across high school. *Child Development*, 84, 678–692.

Ginns, P. (2005). Meta-analysis of the modality effect. *Learning and Instruction*, 15, 313–331. doi:10.1016/j.learninstruc.2005.07.001.

Graham, C., & Hill, M. (2003). *Negotiating the transition to secondary school*. Scottish Council for Research in Education. Edinburgh: Scotland.

Haas, M. (2005). Teaching methods for secondary algebra: A meta-analysis of findings. *NASSP Bulletin*, 89, 24–46. doi:10.1177/019263650508964204.

Hanewald, R. (2013). Transition between primary and secondary school: Why it is important and how it can be supported. *Australian Journal of Teacher Education*, 38, 62–74. doi:10.14221/ajte.2013v38n1.7.

Hattie, J. (2009). *Visible learning: A synthesis of over 800 meta-analyses relating to achievement*. London and New York: Routledge.

Jang, H., Reeve, J., & Deci, E. L. (2010). Engaging students in learning activities: It is not autonomy support or structure, but autonomy support and structure. *Journal of Educational Psychology*, 102, 588–600. doi:10.1037/a0019682.

Kalyuga, S. (2007). Expertise reversal effect and its implications for learner-tailored instruction. *Educational Psychology Review*, 19, 509–539. doi:10.1007/s10648-007-9054-3.

Kalyuga, S., Ayres, P., Chandler, P., & Sweller, J. (2003). The expertise reversal effect. *Educational Psychologist*, 38, 23–31. doi:10.1207/S15326985EP3801_4.

Kalyuga, S., Chandler, P., Tuovinen, J., & Sweller, J. (2001). When problem solving is superior to studying worked examples. *Journal of Educational Psychology*, 93, 579–588. doi:10.1037/0022-0663.93.3.579.

Kalyuga, S., & Singh, A-M. (2015). Rethinking the boundaries of cognitive load theory in complex learning. *Educational Psychology Review*. doi:10.1007/s10648-015-9352-0.

Kirschner, P. A., Sweller, J., & Clark, R. E. (2006). Why minimal guidance during instruction does not work: An analysis of the failure of constructivist, discovery, problem-based, experiential, and inquiry-based teaching. *Educational Psychologist*, 41, 75–86. doi:10.1207/s15326985ep4102_1.

Kvalsund, R. (2000). The transition from primary to secondary level in smaller and larger rural schools in Norway: Comparing differences in context and social meaning. *International Journal of Educational Research*, 33, 401–424. doi:10.1016/S0883-0355(00)00025-00022.

Lee, H. S., & Anderson, J. R. (2013). Student learning: What has instruction got to do with it? *Annual Review of Psychology*, 64, 445–469. doi:10.1146/annurev-psych-113011-143833.

Liem, G.A.D., & Martin, A.J. (2013). Direct instruction and academic achievement. In J. Hattie & E. Anderman (Eds.). *International guide to student achievement*. Oxford: Routledge.

Martin, A. J. (2007). Examining a multidimensional model of student motivation and engagement using a construct validation approach. *British Journal of Educational Psychology*, 77, 413–440. doi:10.1348/000709906X118036.

Martin, A. J. (2009). Motivation and engagement across the academic lifespan: A developmental construct validity study of elementary school, high school, and university/college students. *Educational and Psychological Measurement*, 69, 794–824. doi:10.1177/0013164409 332214.

Martin, A. J. (2010). *Building classroom success: Eliminating academic fear and failure*. New York: Continuum.

Martin, A. J. (2015). Teaching academically at-risk students in middle school: The roles of explicit instruction and guided discovery learning. In S. Groundwater-Smith, & N.

Mockler (Eds.). *Big fish, little fish: Teaching and learning in the middle years*. Cambridge: Cambridge University Press.

Martin, A. J. (2016). *Using Load Reduction Instruction (LRI) to boost motivation and engagement*. Leicester, UK: British Psychological Society.

Martin, A. J., & Evans, P. (2018). Load Reduction Instruction: Exploring a framework that assesses explicit instruction through to independent learning. *Teaching and Teacher Education*, 73, 203–214. doi:10.1016/j.tate.2018.03.018.

Martin, A. J., & Marsh, H. W. (2008). Academic buoyancy: Towards an understanding of students' everyday academic resilience. *Journal of School Psychology*, 46, 53–83.

Martin, A. J., Way, J., Bobis, J., & Anderson, J. (2015). Exploring the ups and downs of mathematics engagement in the middle years of school. *Journal of Early Adolescence*, 35, 199–244. doi:10.1177/0272431614529365.

Marzano, R. J. (2011). Art and science of teaching/The perils and promises of discovery learning. *Educational Leadership*, 69, 86–87.

Mayer, R. E. (2004). Should there be a three-strikes rule against pure discovery learning? The case for guided methods of instruction. *American Psychologist*, 59, 14–19. doi:10.1037/0003-066X.59.1.14.

Mayer, R.E., & Moreno, R. (2010). Techniques that reduce extraneous cognitive load and manage intrinsic cognitive load during multimedia learning (pp. 131–152). In J. L. Plass., R. Moreno, & R. Brunken (Eds.). *Cognitive load theory*. Cambridge: Cambridge University Press.

Maynes, N., Julien-Schultz, L., & Dunn, C. (2010). Modeling and the Gradual Release of Responsibility: What Does It Look Like in the Classroom? *Brock Education Journal*, 19, 65–77.

McMullen, F., & Madelaine, A. (2014) Why is there so much resistance to Direct Instruction? *Australian Journal of Learning Difficulties*, 19, 137–151 doi:10.1080/19404158.2014.962065.

Miller, G. A. (1956). The magical number seven, plus or minus two: Some limits on our capacity for processing information. *Psychological Review*, 63, 81–97.

Nandagopal, K., & Ericsson, K. A. (2012). Enhancing students' performance in traditional education: Implications from the expert performance approach and deliberate practice (pp. 257–293). In K. R. Harris., S. Graham., & T. Urdan (Eds). *APA educational psychology handbook*. Washington: American Psychological Association. doi:10.1037/13273-010.

Paas, F., Renkl, A., & Sweller, J. (2003). Cognitive load theory and instructional design: Recent developments. *Educational Psychologist*, 38, 1–4. doi:10.1207/S15326985EP3801_1.

Pearson, P. D., & Gallagher, M. (1983). The instruction of reading comprehension. *Contemporary Educational Psychology*, 8, 317–344. doi:10.1016/0361-476X(83)90019-X.

Pressley, M., & Allington, R. L. (2014). *Reading instruction that works: The case for balanced teaching*. New York, NY: Guilford Publications.

Pressley, M., Roehrig, A. D., Raphael, L., Dolezal, S., Bohn, C., Mohan, L., Wharton-McDonald, R., Bogner, K., & Hogan, K. (2003). Teaching processes in elementary and secondary education. In W. M. Reynolds, & G. E. Miller (Eds.). *Handbook of educational psychology*. New Jersey: John Wiley & Sons. doi:10.1002/0471264385.wei0708.

Purdie, N., & Ellis, L. (2005). *A review of the empirical evidence identifying effective interventions and teaching practices for students with learning difficulties in Years 4, 5, and 6*. Melbourne: Australian Council for Educational Research.

Renkl, A. (2014). Toward an instructionally oriented theory of example-based learning. *Cognitive Science*, 38, 1–37. doi:10.1111/cogs.12086.

Renkl, A., & Atkinson, R. K. (2010). Learning from worked-out examples and problem solving (pp. 91–108). In J. L. Plass., R. Moreno., & R. Brunken (Eds.). *Cognitive load theory*. Cambridge: Cambridge University Press.

Rosenshine, B. V. (2009). The empirical support for direct instruction. In S. Tobias, & T. M. Duffy (Eds.). *Constructivist instruction: Success or failure?* New York: Routledge.

Rupley, W. H., Blair, T. R., & Nichols, W. D. (2009). Effective reading instruction for struggling readers: The role of direct/explicit teaching. *Reading and Writing Quarterly*, 25, 125–138. doi:10.1080/10573560802683523.

Schute, V. J. (2008). Focus on formative feedback. *Review of Educational Research*, 78, 153–189. doi:10.3102/0034654307313795.

Sierens, E., Vansteenkiste, M., Goossens, L., Soenens, B., & Dochy, F. (2009). The synergistic relationship of perceived autonomy support and structure in the prediction of self-regulated learning. *British Journal of Educational Psychology*, 79, 57–68. doi:10.1348/000709908X304398.

Swanson, H. L., & Sachse-Lee, C. (2000). A meta-analysis of single-subject-design intervention research for students with LD. *Journal of Learning Disabilities*, 33, 114–136. doi:10.1177/002221940003300201.

Sweller, J. (2003). Evolution of human cognitive architecture (pp. 215–266). In B. Ross (Ed.), *The psychology of learning and motivation*, Vol. 43. Academic Press, San Diego. doi:10.1016/s0079-7421(03)01015–01016.

Sweller, J. (2004). Instructional design consequences of an analogy between evolution by natural selection and human cognitive architecture. *Instructional Science*, 32, 9–31. doi:10.1023/B:TRUC.0000021808.72598.4d.

Sweller, J. (2012). Human cognitive architecture: Why some instructional procedures work and others do not (pp. 295–325). In K. R. Harris., S. Graham., & T. Urdan (Eds.). *APA educational psychology handbook*. Washington: American Psychological Association. doi:10.1037/13273-011.

Sweller, J., Ayres, P., & Kalyuga, S. (2011). *Cognitive load theory*. New York: Springer. doi:10.1007/978-1-4419-8126-4.

Tobias, S. (1982). When do instructional methods make a difference? *Educational Researcher*, 11, 4–10. doi:10.2307/1174134.

Vansteenkiste, M., Sierens, E., Goossens, L., Soenens, B., Dochy, F., Mouratidis, A., … Beyers, W. (2012). Identifying configurations of perceived teacher autonomy support and structure: Associations with self-regulated learning, motivation and problem behavior. *Learning and Instruction*, 22, 431–439. doi:10.1016/j.learninstruc.2012.04.002.

Wang, M. T., & Eccles, J. S. (2012). Adolescent behavioral, emotional, and cognitive engagement trajectories in school and their differential relations to educational success. *Journal of Research on Adolescence*, 22, 31–39.

Winne, P. H., & Nesbit, J. C. (2010). The psychology of academic achievement. *Annual Review of Psychology*, 61, 653–678. doi:10.1146/annurev.psych.093008.100348.

Zeedyk, M. S., Gallacher, J., Henderson, M., Hope, G., Husband, B., & Lindsay, K. (2003). Negotiating the transition from primary to secondary school perceptions of pupils, parents and teachers. *School Psychology International*, 24, 67–79. doi:10.1177/014303430302400101.

3

HOW COGNITIVE LOAD THEORY CAN BE APPLIED TO COLLABORATIVE LEARNING

Collaborative cognitive load theory

Jimmy Zambrano R.

OPEN UNIVERSITEIT, THE NETHERLANDS

Paul A. Kirschner

OPEN UNIVERSITEIT, THE NETHERLANDS; UNIVERSITY OF OULU, FINLAND

Femke Kirschner

UTRECHT UNIVERSITY, THE NETHERLANDS

Cognitive load theory (CLT) lies at the base of the design and implementation of effective and efficient individual instruction (Sweller, Ayres, & Kalyuga, 2011). In essence, CLT holds that our cognitive architecture and how we process information is limited by the capacity and duration of our working memory (WM) activities, directly affecting learning. Learning tasks cause learners to expend WM resources (i.e., cognitive load associated with cognitive processes) due to a learning task's inherent complexity (i.e., interacting information elements related to the task and the additional elements related to the instructional approach), and long-term memory (LTM) schemes.

Modern learning is increasingly moving from individual learning to teams (i.e., collaborative learning) for acquiring lifelong learning and working skills (Hmelo-Silver & Chinn, 2015). The problem is that, in contrast to individual learning, there is limited well-researched, evidence-informed theory to guide designing, developing, and implementing collaborative learning. One consequence of this void is poor implementation and, thus, ineffective, inefficient and unsatisfying use of collaborative learning both for the teacher and for the learner. Another consequence is that, due to this poor implementation, teachers and learners waste precious resources (i.e., time, effort, money) on ineffective and inefficient learning and teaching inside and outside of the classroom (i.e., computer-supported collaborative learning; CSCL). Finally, this represents a severely missed chance for learners to acquire necessary work-life skills.

State of the art: cognitive load theory

Knowledge can be categorised in many different ways (e.g., a priori, a posteriori, explicit, implicit/tacit, declarative, procedural, propositional etc.). In the context of this chapter, a choice has been made to use a categorisation that has a more or less direct effect on learning and instruction. CLT sees Geary's (2012) distinction between biologically primary and secondary knowledge, which include skills and the knowledge produced by them, as a useful categorisation scheme for educational purposes that can lead to different instructional procedures. We have, as a species, evolved to acquire *biologically primary* knowledge almost effortlessly and without explicit instruction due to group support of the members of a community. Generally, because they are more or less effortlessly acquired, biologically primary knowledge does not need to be formally taught. Examples of such primary skills are hearing, listening, and joint attention (Callaghan et al., 2011; Tomasello & Rakoczy, 2003), and their respective derived primary knowledge is planning, generalising, speaking in one's native language (Sweller, 2015; Tricot & Sweller, 2014). Collaboration is also a biologically primary skill that we have evolved to acquire (Paas & Sweller, 2012). We have, however, not evolved to acquire *biologically secondary* knowledge without intentionally designed effective learning environments. To acquire this knowledge, substantial effort and therefore proper support and guidance is required (i.e., instruction; Kirschner, Sweller, & Clark, 2006; Sweller, Kirschner, & Clark, 2007). Without explicit instruction and appropriate biologically primary skills, acquiring domain-specific tasks is severely compromised. Some examples of secondary skills and domains are: reading and writing one or more non-native languages, computer programming, solving engineering and science problems, analysing philosophical theories, or other learning tasks for which guided instruction is required and we, therefore, learn in an instructional context.

All our knowledge and learning is shaped and limited by our cognitive system and how it functions. The way in which biologically secondary knowledge is constructed by the human cognitive system is analogous to the way in which evolution by natural selection processes information (Sweller & Sweller, 2006). This architecture is described in five principles which are summarised in Table 3.1.

When presented with novel information, there are two additive sources of cognitive load imposed on WM (Sweller, 2010) which combined should not exceed its limits. *Intrinsic load* deals with the inherent complexity of the information in a learning task that needs to be learned. It is defined in terms of the amount of novel interacting information elements in a task; the higher the number of novel interacting elements, the more complex the task especially when time is an issue. Time is almost always an issue, since learning to successfully solve a problem demands the rapid processing of many interconnected elements (Ricker & Cowan, 2018). For example, learning to solve the equation $5(3 - 4x)$ seems to be similar to solving $-7(-4 + 2x)$. However, the second problem is more complex (thus causing more cognitive load) because it requires considering the negative sign before 7

TABLE 3.1 Natural information processing system principles

Principle	Function
Information store	Primary and secondary knowledge and skills are stored in LTM.
Borrowing and reorganising	The knowledge store is mostly borrowed from other's knowledge and is reorganised in a particular way.
Randomness as genesis	In the absence of relevant knowledge, required new/novel knowledge is created by random generate-and-test processes.
Narrow limits of change	Limited capacity and duration of WM processing prevent rapid random changes of the store.
Environmental organising and linking	Interacting with the environment requires signals that allow transferring organised information from LTM to WM to perform appropriate actions.

which generates more connections between elements and potentially more errors of multiplication (Ayres, 2006).

In addition, there may be interacting elements unrelated to the intrinsic complexity of the task that imposes *extraneous load*[1] on working memory. This load can be controlled by instructors and be varied by using different instructional procedures. Some procedures (e.g., discovery or inquiry learning) impose more unproductive load on WM than others (e.g., worked examples, process worksheets) (Atkinson, Derry, Renkl, & Wortham, 2000) and demand more time on the task.

Both types of cognitive load interact with each other as well as with the learner's level of expertise (Chen, Kalyuga, & Sweller, 2016). If the task has a high level of intrinsic interacting elements, a learner who has relevant knowledge in LTM (i.e., an advanced learner) will experience a lower cognitive load and achieve better learning than a novice with little relevant knowledge in LTM. If extraneous interacting elements are added (e.g., if the learner must apply a discovery strategy), the task will overwhelm the learner and impede her/his learning. Learning will also be impeded when an advanced learner (i.e., a learner with considerable prior knowledge or experience in the subject area) receives instruction that combines new with redundant information (e.g., diagrams with integrated text) (Kalyuga, Chandler, & Sweller, 1998). The embedded texts interfere with the information already available in LTM, increase the cognitive load, and, thus, reduce the performance (i.e., expertise reversal effect; Chen et al., 2016). Research in and application of CLT has led to the development of a broad range of instructional procedures to reduce extraneous load and increase productive load to facilitate learning (see Sweller et al., 2011).

Beyond the state of the art: Collaborative Cognitive Load Theory

CLT allows for the design of effective and efficient individual learning and informs good instructional design for individuals (e.g., Paas, Renkl, & Sweller, 2003; Van Merriënboer & Kirschner, 2018) as well as for the design of multimedia learning

(Mayer, 2014). What has not yet been attempted, and what the field sorely needs, is a cognitive theory for collaborative learning; Collaborative Cognitive Load Theory (CCLT). Learning collaboratively involves two or more learners who actively contribute to attaining a mutual learning goal and who share the effort needed to reach this goal (Teasley & Roschelle, 1993). As an instructional method, collaborative learning uniquely affects extraneous cognitive load as learners must interact with their teammates to communicate with each other over and coordinate their actions on a task. The collaborative cognitive load represents both an extra and inevitable cost. However, considering the principle of mutual cognitive inter-dependence, the cognitive load associated with collaboration may benefit learning especially when learning environments are highly complex (F. Kirschner, Paas, & Kirschner, 2011).

Cognitive architecture and evolutionary categories of knowledge

Considering the advances of the developmental comparative psychology, namely evolutionary dynamics (Rand & Nowak, 2013; Tomasello & Gonzalez-Cabrera, 2017), we propose considering a crucial, new principle for the human cognition specific to the *processes* of collaborative learning, namely the *mutual cognitive inter-dependence principle* (P. A. Kirschner, Sweller, Kirschner, & Zambrano R., 2018). We suggest that collaboration is the decisive organising principle for the develop-ment and functioning of the human cognitive architecture. When determining the cognitive principles in collaborative conditions, it is crucially important to include the effects of interaction between natural information processing systems. Envir-onmental variations are a crucial factor for genetic evolution, and mutations must be stored in a reservoir of information for being transmitted through reproduction. Something similar happens in human cognition with respect to cultural knowl-edge. Changes in the information store are produced and reproduced through learning and instruction processes. However, for natural and cultural selection to work, mutual collaboration between individuals and groups is required (Geary & Huffman, 2002; Sterelny, 2012; Tomasello & Rakoczy, 2003). Genetic and cog-nitive evolution depends on the mutual interdependence of group members, where the fittest collaborate by modelling and transmitting relevant information (e.g., skills, knowledge, artifacts and so forth) to the group (Sterelny, 2012).

From a cognitive load perspective, collaboration around specific domain tasks is beneficial but has cognitive costs due to intrinsic transactional activities (Geary, 2012; Geary & Huffman, 2002; Hinsz, Tindale, & Vollrath, 1997; P. A. Kirschner et al., 2018). In cultural reproduction, experts for example invest cognitive costs in novice learners collaborating with them providing tailored instructional environments to their previous schemes (Collins, Brown, & Newman, 1987; Zhang, Kalyuga, Lee, & Lei, 2016). In groups of learners with heterogeneous knowledge, advanced learners invest transactional resources that benefit novices, and novices in turn pay the cog-nitive cost of learning from/with experts, other learners, or well-designed (i.e., by instructors) learning materials. Domain-specific experts and advanced learners borrow or collaborate giving their knowledge and skills to others, and novices reorganise their previous schemes. In other words, the interaction between collaboration, learning environments, and expertise can explain better the principles and evolution of human cognitive architecture (Coolidge, Wynn, & Overmann, 2013). This suggests that the key to genetic and cultural evolution is not only individual cognitive fitness but the mutual cognitive interdependence (Allen & Nowak, 2016).

Humans have evolved to work together in mutualistic contexts (Rand & Nowak, 2013). Interacting and collaborating in environments requiring this behaviour provides a major purpose for the evolutionary development of communication (Tomasello, 2008). If we have evolved to acquire joint knowledge, then collaboration may be biologically primary or *general knowledge* and places little strain on WM (Paas & Sweller, 2012). However, as collaboration depends on the cognitive environment in which it is carried out (i.e., the subject area/domain, context), it does not follow that we are able to collaborate appropriately while acquiring biologically secondary *task-specific knowledge* (i.e., where there is a greater strain on WM). Collaboratively acquiring task-specific knowledge requires learners obtaining appropriate support and guidance to work together (Zambrano, Kirschner, & Kirschner, 2018b) for particular domains (e.g., solving a math problem vs. writing a prose text). Effective and efficient collaboration depends on the quality of the communication and coordination *related* to the specific characteristics of the learning task (P. A. Kirschner et al., 2018). Since learning in school-domains requires primary knowledge (e.g., communicating with each other, sharing attention), it can be argued that humans have evolved also to acquire biologically secondary knowledge through collaboration (Zambrano et al., 2018b; Zhang et al., 2016; Zhang, Kalyuga, Lee, Lei, & Jiao, 2015). Consequently, team mates can and should develop *generalised domain skills* (Kalyuga, 2015) at the group level.

Transaction costs and prior knowledge

Collaborative cognitive load is productive when the inter-individual activities facilitate better and efficient knowledge than individual learning. There are theoretical grounds to hypothesise that group learning can reduce element interactivity while increasing productive load at the individual level. Good collaborative learning induces *collective working memory* (F. Kirschner et al., 2011) that otherwise does not exist. In collaborative tasks, the various interacting elements of the task can be distributed among multiple WMs (i.e., the group members) reducing the cognitive load on a single WM. Under individual learning, a single WM must process all interacting elements. Those multiple WMs constitute a collective memory larger than a single one. Collaboration as an instructional procedure thereby changes the total cognitive load at the individual level. Also, having generalised domain group skills means that during collaborative learning information can come from collaborators based on the borrowing and reorganising principle and, thereby, is likely to become available exactly when needed, resulting in decreased load and increased learning (Gupta & Hollingshead, 2010).

Communication and coordination during collaborative learning bring transaction costs (F. Kirschner, Paas, & Kirschner, 2009; Yamane, 1996) in terms of cognitive load. These are the costs "of setting up, enforcing, and maintaining the reciprocal obligations, or contracts that keep the members of a team together [and] ... represent the 'overhead' of the team ... to allow a work team to produce more than the sum of its parts" (Ciborra & Olson, 1988, p. 95). In collaborative learning, the communication and coordination costs are the extra cognitive load that have to be taken into account caused by the acts learners must carry out when studying, communicating with each other and coordinating both their own learning and that of others (Janssen, Kirschner, Erkens, Kirschner, & Paas, 2010; F. Kirschner et al., 2009).

As transactive activities impose additional costs in terms of cognitive load, these activities can either impede or improve learning. Collective WM is effective when a group takes advantage of its larger collective capacity (e.g., when the task is extremely complex) and also exchanges productive transactive activities (F. Kirschner et al., 2011; Wegner, 1995). To obtain maximum benefit from the collective WM effect, the effects of the distribution of the task elements among multiple WMs must be examined. Assuming stable motivation and prior knowledge, the way information items and the processes to carry out a learning task are distributed can generate different transactional activities. For example, the collaboration between three students to solve quadratic equations may vary depending on how the constants and variables have been distributed, what the position of the values is in relation to the equal sign (e.g., to perform calculations the values $-2x^2 + 5x =$ must be moved to the right side of the equation), and which mathematical operations must be carried out (e.g., does it include fractions, or is it necessary to use a formula or factoring). Depending on the distribution of the elements, a member would have to perform some operations individually (i.e., homogeneous distribution), with another member, or between all (i.e., heterogeneous distribution) to solve each step of the problem. Additionally, transactional activities can vary substantially, affecting learning when the same task elements are distributed among four or five group members. It can be expected that the collaborative cognitive load will be lower if the distribution is homogeneous and if groups have an appropriate number of members. Distribution and size of the team are determined based on the types and number of transactional activities required to solve a complex problem.

Transactive activities also can be enhanced by providing different group schemes. These schemes can be understood as a continuum between the familiarity between the members of a group (e.g., classroom norms; Janssen, Erkens, Kirschner, & Kanselaar, 2009) and sharing knowledge about how to collaborate for specific tasks (Fransen, Weinberger, & Kirschner, 2013). From this spectrum of alternatives (see Table 3.2), knowledge specialisation may reduce the extraneous cognitive load among group members by avoiding the overlap in individual knowledge and providing the group with access to a larger reservoir of information across domains (Gupta & Hollingshead, 2010; Tindale & Sheffey, 2002). At the moment, we know that learners with a low

TABLE 3.2 Collaborative cognitive load effects and their hypotheses

Effects	Description
Information distribution	The more heterogeneously the information is distributed among team members working on a learning task, the higher the extraneous load caused by transactive activities (communication and coordination).
Team size	The more members in a team working on a learning task, the higher the extraneous load caused by transactive activities (communication and coordination).
Familiarity	The more team members know each other well (i.e., are familiar with each other), but have not had experience working with each other on a learning task, the lower extraneous load caused by communication.
Experience	The more experience team members have working with each other on unrelated learning tasks, the lower the extraneous load caused by transactive activities (communication and coordination).
Task-group experience	The more experience team members have coordinating their actions on specific tasks relatively related to the learning task at hand (i.e., they know what to expect from each other in terms of task execution), the lower extraneous load caused by coordination.
Task expertise	The greater the expertise of team members in the task domain, the lower the extraneous load caused by transactive activities (communication and coordination).

level of previous knowledge benefit from collaborative learning when they form heterogeneous groups instead of homogeneous groups (Zhang et al., 2015; Zhang et al., 2016). In line with this, we can expect that when one or more group members have relevant knowledge needed to carry out the task, collaborative learning becomes more effective and efficient especially under high cognitive load (i.e., via a temporal restriction) conditions (Prichard & Ashleigh, 2007).

Generalised domain knowledge (Kalyuga, 2013) at the group level may also reduce the unproductive cognitive load when group members have acquired appropriate schemes of collaborative work. All learners have general knowledge (i.e., general schemes) about how to collaborate with others. For example, whom to work with, general rules of collaboration, general rules of courtesy, interpersonal expectations, and so on. However, these previous acquired schemes can interfere with the specific demands of the collaborative learning task at hand (e.g., when a task requires shared calculation or involves argumentative writing). When members of a group do not have appropriate prior knowledge to collaborate with each other, they may expend WM resources on communication or interactions unrelated to the learning tasks instead of, for instance organising and coordinating work-processes among each other (i.e., socially shared regulatory activities; Järvelä & Hadwin, 2013; Zambrano, Kirschner, & Kirschner, 2018a). This extraneous load could have been reduced when group members have had experience working together on analog or transferable tasks (Kalyuga, 2013; Peterson & Wissman, 2018). Group learners must receive instructional guidance and support (e.g., task-based scripts or training) until they appropriate a socially-shared domain scheme. These group schemes allow learners to reduce their cognitive load and focus their WM resources on transactional activities that enable the acquisition of better/more appropriate specific knowledge schemes (Zambrano et al., 2018a).

The advantage of having a greater WM capacity and either shared generalised or specific domain knowledge has important implications for collaborative learning. Bringing together learners in a group is no guarantee that they will work and learn properly both as group and as individuals within the group. They must develop a shared mental model or collective scheme of cognitive interdependence on how to effectively communicate and coordinate their transactional activities. Groups must form adequate processes of and procedures for working together (Fransen et al., 2013; Prichard & Ashleigh, 2007) that allow them to experience and further develop the expertise that they have, share group knowledge, appropriately distribute available task information amongst themselves, and exploit the quality of participation of each group member in carrying out the task at hand. Consequently, one could state that for complex tasks/problems, collaboration becomes a scaffold (just like worked examples) for the individuals' knowledge acquisition processes. Collaboration will be effective if it becomes a scaffold in this sense. If it does not, or if it in itself adds too much extraneous load, it will be harmful (P. A. Kirschner et al., 2018).

Conclusion: educational implications of research

The execution of a collaborative learning task is an interaction between the characteristics of the task, the individual learners, and the team. Thus, the general framework used by CLT is directly applicable to collaborative learning but needs specific additions to account for collaboration. The major additions required when dealing with collaborative learning are a) the *mutual cognitive interdependence principle* for the human cognitive architecture, and b) the concepts of the collective WM (i.e., multiple individual working memories) and generalised domain group knowledge along with the effects, due to the transactional activities. These additions provide novel hypotheses associated with the effects of differential domain-specific knowledge on collaborative effectiveness. This leads to a number of hypotheses (i.e., implications) as to the effects mentioned above for future research, summarised in Table 3.2.

Using CCLT to conduct research on collaborative learning means that we can go beyond determining whether the effects found in individual learning conditions and measurement methods work in collaborative conditions, and test new hypotheses and measurements that explain the specific complex interactions between students and multiple information resources. Furthermore, the specialised focus on collaborative learning provides teachers with clear and to-the-point instructional guidelines (i.e., the CCLT effects) for designing effective collaborative learning environments. The instructional guidelines support teachers to think about the cognitive properties of their students and the effect that a specific task and a specific group composition will have on the cognitive process that will take place. Using CCLT, the choice for collaborative learning as an instructional tool, will always be an informed one.

Note

1 According to Kalyuga (2011, p. 1), "[I]n its traditional treatment, germane load is essentially indistinguishable from intrinsic load, and therefore this concept may be redundant ... the dual intrinsic/extraneous framework is sufficient and non-redundant and makes boundaries of the theory transparent. As such, germane load is not treated as an additive source of load here."

References

Allen, B., & Nowak, M. A. (2016). There is no inclusive fitness at the level of the individual. *Current Opinion in Behavioral Sciences, 12,* 122–128. doi:10.1016/j.cobeha.2016.10.002.

Atkinson, R. K., Derry, S. J., Renkl, A., & Wortham, D. (2000). Learning from examples: Instructional principles from the worked examples research. *Review of Educational Research, 70*(2), 181–214. doi:10.3102/00346543070002181.

Ayres, P. (2006). Using subjective measures to detect variations of intrinsic cognitive load within problems. *Learning and Instruction, 16*(5), 389–400. doi:10.1016/j.learninstruc.2006.09.001.

Callaghan, T. C., Moll, H., Rakoczy, H., Warneken, F., Liszkowski, U., Behne, T., & Tomasello, M. (2011). *Early social cognition in three cultural contexts.* Boston: Wiley-Blackwell.

Chen, O., Kalyuga, S., & Sweller, J. (2016). The expertise reversal effect is a variant of the more general element interactivity effect. *Educational Psychology Review,* 1–13. doi:10.1007/s10648-016-9359-1.

Ciborra, C. C., & Olson, M. H. (1988). Encountering electronic work groups: A transaction costs perspective. *Office Technology and People, 4*(4), 285–298. doi:10.1108/eb022667.

Collins, A., Brown, J. S., & Newman, S. E. (1987) *Cognitive apprenticeship: Teaching the craft of reading, writing, and mathematics. Technical Report No. 403.* Retrieved from Cambridge, MA. https://files.eric.ed.gov/fulltext/ED284181.pdf.

Coolidge, F. L., Wynn, T., & Overmann, K. A. (2013). The evolution of working memory. In T. P. Alloway & R. G. Alloway (Eds.), *Working memory: The connected intelligence* (pp. 37–60). New York, NY: Psychology Press.

Fransen, J., Weinberger, A., & Kirschner, P. A. (2013). Team effectiveness and team development in CSCL. *Educational Psychologist, 48*(1), 9–24. doi:10.1080/00461520.2012.747947.

Geary, D. C. (2012). Evolutionary educational psychology. In K. R. Harris, S. Graham, T. Urdan, C. B. McCormick, G. M. Sinatra, & J. Sweller (Eds.), *APA educational psychology handbook, Vol 1: Theories, constructs, and critical issues* (pp. 597–621). Washington, DC: American Psychological Association.

Geary, D. C., & Huffman, K. J. (2002). Brain and cognitive evolution: Forms of modularity and functions of mind. *Psychological Bulletin, 128*(5), 667–698. doi:10.1037/0033-2909.128.5.667.

Gupta, N., & Hollingshead, A. B. (2010). Differentiated versus integrated transactive memory effectiveness: It depends on the task. *Group Dynamics: Theory, Research, and Practice, 14*(4), 384–398. doi:10.1037/a0019992.

Hinsz, V. B., Tindale, R. S., & Vollrath, D. A. (1997). The emerging conceptualization of groups as information processors. *Psychological Bulletin, 121*(1), 43–64. doi:10.1037/0033-2909.121. 1. 43.

Hmelo-Silver, C., & Chinn, C. A. (2015). Collaborative learning. In L. Corno & E. M. Anderman (Eds.), *Handbook of educational psychology* (3rd ed.). New York, NY: Routledge.

Janssen, J., Erkens, G., Kirschner, P. A., & Kanselaar, G. (2009). Influence of group member familiarity on online collaborative learning. *Computers in Human Behavior, 25*(1), 161–170. doi:10.1016/j.chb.2008.08.010.

Janssen, J., Kirschner, F., Erkens, G., Kirschner, P. A., & Paas, F. (2010). Making the black box of collaborative learning transparent: Combining process-oriented and cognitive load approaches. *Educational Psychology Review, 22*(2), 139–154. doi:10.1007/s10648-010-9131-x.

Järvelä, S., & Hadwin, A. F. (2013). New frontiers: Regulating learning in CSCL. *Educational Psychologist, 48*(1), 25–39. doi:10.1080/00461520.2012.748006.

Kalyuga, S. (2011). Cognitive load theory: How many types of load does it really need? *Educational Psychology Review, 23*(1), 1–19. doi:10.1007/s10648-010-9150-7.

Kalyuga, S. (2013). Enhancing transfer by learning generalized domain knowledge structures. *European Journal of Psychology of Education, 28*(4), 1477–1493. doi:10.1007/s10212-013-0176-3.

Kalyuga, S. (2015). *Instructional guidance: A cognitive load perspective*. Charlotte, NC: Information Age Publishing, Inc.

Kalyuga, S., Chandler, P., & Sweller, J. (1998). Levels of expertise and instructional design. *Human Factors: The Journal of the Human Factors and Ergonomics Society, 40*(1), 1–17. doi:10.1518/001872098779480587.

Kirschner, F., Paas, F., & Kirschner, P. A. (2009). Individual and group-based learning from complex cognitive tasks: Effects on retention and transfer efficiency. *Computers in Human Behavior, 25*(2), 306–314. doi:10.1016/j.chb.2008.12.008.

Kirschner, F., Paas, F., & Kirschner, P. A. (2011). Task complexity as a driver for collaborative learning efficiency: The collective working-memory effect. *Applied Cognitive Psychology, 25*(4), 615–624. doi:10.1002/acp.1730.

Kirschner, P. A., Sweller, J., & Clark, R. (2006). Why minimal guidance during instruction does not work: An analysis of the failure of constructivist, discovery, problem-based, experiential and inquiry-based teaching. *Educational Psychologist, 41*, 75–86 doi:10.1207/s15326985ep4102_1.

Kirschner, P. A., Sweller, J., Kirschner, F., & Zambrano, R. J. (2018). From cognitive load theory to collaborative cognitive load theory. *International Journal of Computer-Supported Collaborative Learning, 13*(2), 213–233. doi:10.1007/s11412-018-9277-y.

Mayer, R. E. (Ed.) (2014). *The Cambridge handbook of multimedia learning* (2nd. ed.). New York: Cambridge University Press.

Paas, F., Renkl, A., & Sweller, J. (2003). Cognitive load theory and instructional design: Recent developments. *Educational Psychologist, 38*(1), 1–4. doi:10.1207/s15326985ep3801_1.

Paas, F., & Sweller, J. (2012). An evolutionary upgrade of cognitive load theory: Using the human motor system and collaboration to support the learning of complex cognitive tasks. *Educational Psychology Review, 24*(1), 27–45. doi:10.1007/s10648-011-9179-2.

Peterson, D. J., & Wissman, K. T. (2018). The testing effect and analogical problem-solving. *Memory*, 1–7. doi:10.1080/09658211.2018.1491603.

Prichard, J. S., & Ashleigh, M. J. (2007). The effects of team-skills training on transactive memory and performance. *Small Group Research, 38*(6), 696–726. doi:10.1177/1046496407304923.

Rand, D. G., & Nowak, M. A. (2013). Human cooperation. *Trends in Cognitive Sciences, 17*(8), 413–425. doi:10.1016/j.tics.2013.06.003.

Ricker, T. J., & Cowan, N. (2018). Cognitive load as a measure of capture of the focus of attention. In R. Zheng (Ed.), *Cognitive load measurement and application: A theoretical framework for meaningful research and practice* (pp. 129–146). New York, NY: Routledge.

Sterelny, K. (2012). *The evolved apprentice: How evolution made humans unique*. Cambridge, MA: The MIT Press.

Sweller, J. (2010). Element interactivity and intrinsic, extraneous and germane cognitive load. *Educational Psychology Review*, 22, 123–138.

Sweller, J. (2015). In academe, what is learned and how is it learned? *Current Directions in Psychological Science*, 24, 190–194 doi:10.1177/0963721415569570.

Sweller, J. (2017). Without an understanding of human cognitive architecture, instruction is blind. *The ACE conference*. Retrieved from https://youtu.be/gOLPfi9Ls-w.

Sweller, J., Ayres, P., & Kalyuga, S. (2011). *Cognitive load theory*. New York, NY: Springer.

Sweller, J., Kirschner, P. A., & Clark, R. E. (2007). Why minimally guided teaching techniques do not work: A reply to commentaries. *Educational Psychologist*, 42, 115–121 doi:10.1080/00461520701263426.

Sweller, J., & Sweller, S. (2006). Natural information processing systems. *Evolutionary Psychology*, 4(1), 434–458. doi:10.1177/147470490600400135.

Teasley, S. D., & Roschelle, J. (1993). Constructing a joint problem space: The computer as a tool for sharing knowledge. In S. P. Lajoie (Ed.), *Computers as cognitive tools: Technology in education* (pp. 229–258). Hillsdale, NJ; England: Lawrence Erlbaum Associates, Inc.

Tindale, R. S., & Sheffey, S. (2002). Shared Information, cognitive load, and group memory. *Group Processes & Intergroup Relations*, 5(1), 5–18.

Tomasello, M. (2008). *Origins of human communication*. Cambridge, Mass.: MIT Press.

Tomasello, M., & Gonzalez-Cabrera, I. (2017). The role of ontogeny in the evolution of human cooperation. *Human Nature*, 28(3), 275–288. doi:10.1007/s12110-017-9291-1.

Tomasello, M., & Rakoczy, H. (2003). What makes human cognition unique? From individual to shared to collective intentionality. *Mind & Language*, 18(2), 121–147. doi:10.1111/1468-0017.00217.

Tricot, A., & Sweller, J. (2014). Domain-specific knowledge and why teaching generic skills does not work. *Educational Psychology Review*, 26, 265–283. doi:10.1007/s10648-013-9243-1.

Van Merriënboer, J. J. G., & Kirschner, P. A. (2018). *Ten steps to complex learning: A systematic approach to four-component instructional design* (3th ed.). New York, NY: Routledge.

Wegner, D. M. (1995). A computer network model of human transactive memory. *Social Cognition*, 13(3), 319–339. doi:10.1521/soco.1995.13.3.319.

Yamane, D. (1996) Collaboration and its discontents: Steps toward overcoming barriers to successful group projects. *Teaching Sociology*, 24(4), 378–383. doi:10.2307/1318875.

Zambrano, R. J., Kirschner, F., & Kirschner, P. A. (2018a). *The benefits of task-based prior group experience on collaborative learning: A mixed-methods study*. Manuscript accepted for publication.

Zambrano, R. J., Kirschner, F., & Kirschner, P. A. (2018b). The effect of the prior collaborative experience on the effectiveness and efficiency of collaborative learning. In J. Kay & R. Luckin (Eds.), *Rethinking learning in the digital age: Making the learning sciences count*, 13th International Conference of the Learning Sciences (ICLS) (Vol. 1, pp. 112–114). London: International Society of the Learning Sciences.

Zhang, L., Kalyuga, S., Lee, C., & Lei, C. (2016). Effectiveness of collaborative learning of computer programming under different learning group formations according to students' prior knowledge: A cognitive load perspective. *Journal of Interactive Learning Research*, 27 (2), 171–192. Retrieved from http://www.learntechlib.org/p/111825.

Zhang, L., Kalyuga, S., Lee, C. H., Lei, C., & Jiao, J. (2015). *Effectiveness of collaborative learning with complex tasks under different learning group formations: A cognitive load perspective*. Paper presented at the Hybrid Learning: Innovation in Educational Practices: 8th International Conference, ICHL 2015, Wuhan, China, July 27–29, 2015, Proceedings.

4

COGNITIVE LOAD THEORY AND WORKING MEMORY MODELS

Comings and goings

Sébastien Puma

UNIVERSITY OF CERGY-PONTOISE AND PARAGRAPHE LABORATORY (EA 349)

André Tricot

UNIVERSITY OF TOULOUSE 2 JEAN JAURES AND CLLE-LTC LABORATORY (CNRS UMR 5263)

Cognitive load theory aims at improving academic learning by providing guidance for effective instructional design. According to this theory, when engaging in academic learning, students have to invest their resources in three types of cognitive load: intrinsic, devoted to information processing imposed by the learning task; extraneous, devoted to additional information processing imposed by the learning material presentation; and germane, devoted to learning itself, i.e. changing knowledge in long-term memory. Sometimes it is not possible to distinguish intrinsic and germane load. For example, when the learning task is to understand a text, the learning goal is also to understand this text.

Cognitive load theory uses working memory and attentional models to describe cognitive resources involved in these learning activities. It relies on existing working memory models to interpret empirical findings. Yet, some of the empirical effects unravelled by cognitive load theory challenged the model used to the point where it became necessary to adopt another working memory model. The history of cognitive load theory is thus a cycle between empirical findings and working memory models. The aim of this chapter is to describe this cycle before presenting emerging questions and discussing how a new working memory model could address them.

In their book on working memory models, Shah and Miyake (1999) proposed a series of criteria any working memory model should clearly address. Some of these criteria will be used to present the respective contributions of the models to the field of cognitive load theory. These criteria are: "the basic mechanisms and representations in working memory", "the unitary versus non-unitary nature of working memory", "the nature of working memory limits", "the relationship of working memory to long-term memory and knowledge", and "the relationship of working memory to attention and consciousness". Three models, namely, Baddeley's (1986) multiple component model, Ericsson and Kintsch's (1995) long-term working memory model and Barrouillet and Camos' (2015) Time Based Resource Sharing model will be presented in this chapter, in a chronological order, as a means to deal with the way cognitive load theory brings new challenges and questions to working memory research and how, in turn, working memory research brings answers and theoretical perspectives to cognitive load theory. The challenges yet to be addressed and the limits of these relations will also be discussed.

Cognitive load theory before explicit references to working memory models

Cognitive load theory dealt with matters of limited cognitive resources (Sweller, 1988; Sweller & Levine, 1982) before using references to working memory models. It focused on how to describe the limited cognitive resources invested during learning and proposed the worked example effect and goal free effect to address the idea that students had limited cognitive resources available (e.g., Broadbent, 1958; Atkinson & Shiffrin, 1968). At this early stage of cognitive load theory, working memory models and cognitive architecture were not explicitly mentioned in publications.

The worked example effect

One of the first findings of cognitive load theory, the worked example effect was based upon the idea that cognitive resources are available for learning in limited amounts (Sweller, Ayres, & Kalyuga, 2011). Based on this idea, the worked example effect showed that novice students learned better from working on understanding the solution of a solved problem, than trying to solve the same problem on their own. Thus, freeing some of the resources that were initially dedicated to find the correct answer by providing the solution actually improved problem solving and learning outcomes. According to cognitive load theory, this result was explained by a reduction of extraneous load, with a constant intrinsic load, resulting in more resources devoted to germane load. This was assumed to result in more resources dedicated to transfer information to long-term memory, in other words, in learning. At that point, there was no necessity for cognitive load theory to consider working memory models, since the idea of a limited amount of cognitive resources was sufficient.

The goal free effect

Another of the early cognitive load theory findings, the goal free effect, is based on the same idea as the worked example effect: freeing cognitive resources involved in problem solving helps learning (Sweller, Ayres, & Kalyuga, 2011). When novice learners try to solve a problem, they mainly use novice strategies, e.g. means-end analysis (Newell & Simon, 1972). This strategy, though largely transferable from one topic to another, is highly demanding. It requires learners to elaborate a problem state representation, to actively maintain the goal of the problem in working memory, and all steps between the current problem state representation and the goal state, to complete the problem solution. Cognitive load theory showed that removing the goal prevented students from adopting this costly strategy, freeing cognitive resources, and thus improved learning outcomes (Sweller, 1988).

Initially, cognitive load theory dealt with learning materials where the learning task was a problem to solve. The theory obtained improvements in learning by modifying the extraneous load: the problem solving task itself was changed, with the goal free effect and the worked example effect. Gradually, the learning materials became more complex, involving texts, graphs, sounds, animations and pictures. Cognitive load theory dealt with multimedia learning and, at the same time, multimedia learning researchers discovered cognitive load theory. But when using multimedia materials, simple "limited short term memory resources" as described by Miller (1956) or Atkinson and Shiffrin (1968) are not sufficient. It became necessary to use working memory models to explain why cognitive load changes. Baddeley's (1986) multicomponent model became very useful to generate new hypotheses and to explain new results.

Cognitive load theory and the multicomponent model

An early working memory model used in the cognitive load theory framework (Sweller, Van Merrienboer & Paas, 1998), Baddeley's multi-component model (e.g., Baddeley & Hitch, 1974; Baddeley, 1986) assumed that short-term memory was also the cognitive place where information was manipulated. Changing the name, from short-term memory to working memory (Miller, Galanter, & Pribram 1960), was a change of paradigm, from a passive storage place to an active manipulation place. A major contribution of the multicomponent model of working memory was to unify what were several models of short-term storage of information passing through different modality channels into a single model. This model included two slave systems, the phonological loop and the visuo-spatial sketchpad, and a central executive responsible for attention allocation. It accounted for independence between verbal and visual information retention (e.g. Baddeley, 1966) but also for interference in the processing of cross modal information. In this non-unitary model, units of information in the form of chunks (Miller, 1956) were maintained in two components (verbal and visual) depending on their nature. From these components, they could be used for further processing by the central executive, conceived as an attentional module, or at least responsible for the allocation of attentional resources.

In this conception, as in the conception of cognitive load theory, working memory was described as the gatekeeper of long-term memory. Thus, any element to be placed in long-term memory (i.e. to be learned) had to pass through working memory. This description of working memory as distinct from long-term memory reflected a two way communication system, with long-term memory required when storing chunks of information. Increased long-term memory content (i.e. superior expertise) helped creating larger chunks. The number of chunks that could be held in working memory was limited to seven plus or minus two (Miller, 1956) but the mechanisms responsible for this limitation and forgetting in working memory were not described. Two hypotheses competed to explain this limitation and fast forgetting in working memory: interference and decay. With respect to the interference hypothesis, elements or chunks held in working memory could stay there for any duration, provided no other element entered working memory. If any other information was placed in working memory, then it would take a place and, if no place was available, would replace previous information. On the other hand, the decay hypothesis assumed that elements placed in working memory have an activation level that will decrease over time, that is, that an element's trace decays as time passes. This hypothesis assumes elements in working memory need to be refreshed to counter this time related decay and thus forgetting. The multi-component model is consistent with both hypotheses though the time related decay hypothesis might be favoured (Baddeley, 2012).

Modality effect

The major contribution of this model to cognitive load theory is probably the modality effect. The modality effect "arises when audio information replacing written text information, referring to a map, graph, diagram or tabular information results in enhanced processing and learning" (Leahy & Sweller 2016, p. 108). The multicomponent model, assuming two slave systems for maintenance and manipulation of information depending on their modalities is well suited to describe this effect. Information presented visually, such as a map, graph or diagram are maintained and processed in the visual-sketchpad while auditory information is processed in the phonological loop. This structure allows an extension of the size of working memory. The central executive is responsible for transferring information to long-term memory and to allocate attention. Thus, if information is maintained and processed in the two slave systems, its integration in a schema should be facilitated by the use of two systems instead of one. On the contrary, if information contained in the two slave systems is not consistent or not related to the same schema, this should raise the load imposed on the central executive.

Redundancy effect

The multicomponent model was not able to explain some of the experimental results obtained in the field of cognitive load theory. For example, when studying the modality effect, it was found that presenting information in two modalities could impair learning instead of improving it. More generally, presenting more information than needed has a detrimental effect on learning, imposing more information processing with no benefits for schema construction. This result was named the redundancy effect (Sweller, Ayres, & Kalyuga, 2011). A surprising finding was observed when studying redundancy: students with low levels of expertise might benefit from more information presentation, while it might have detrimental effects on more expert students' learning.

The multicomponent model, able to explain the modality effect, is not able to describe the fact that the same information presentation might have positive or negative effects on learning, depending on the expertise level of the students. This model was helpful to explain empirical results using recent learning material such as multimedia learning, when the same information was presented in different ways. A new challenge was to describe why cognitive load changed when the same information was presented in the same manner to different learners.

Cognitive load theory and the long-term working memory model

The long-term working memory model (Ericsson & Kintsch, 1995) was advanced to take into account variations occurring in working memory performances associated with variations in expertise of participants with test material. In this model, working memory is a unitary phenomenon, meaning that there are no multiple modules and slave systems. It is defined as the activated part of the long-term memory, which implies that elements in working memory are representations held in long-term memory and activated through attentional processes. Knowledge in long-term memory can be viewed as composed of schemas that are larger and more complex with increasing expertise. The representations in working memory can thus be viewed as activated schemas, and they can vary with variations in expertise. Following Ericsson and Kintsch, this explains why people are merely able to recall 7 (+ / - 2) elements (Miller, 1956), or 4 in more recent estimations (Cowan, 2001) while they can remember a sentence of 20 words with little effort. More extensively than with Baddeley's multicomponent model, working memory is here viewed as relying on attentional resources, since elements (parts of long-term memory) are activated by attention. This meant giving up the spatial metaphor used in the multicomponent model, working memory being a mental place where information could be stored and manipulated (e.g. James, 1890; Cowan, 1988; 2014; Cowan et al., 2005). The elements held in working memory are thus defined by an activation level, which decreases over time, following a time decay hypothesis, and this decay is slower for information for which people are experts. Thus, an expert can hold large amounts of information for a longer duration at a much lower cost than a novice. What limits working memory is the level of expertise in the domain, the attentional activation of elements being dependent upon this level of expertise.

There is however no specific reference to the modality of the representation of information in long-term working memory. Since it is a unitary model and all information is part of a schema, then this information should be amodal and in isolation this model is not able to explain the modality effect observed in cognitive load theory research. On the other hand, it does explain the redundancy of information for expert learners presented information in two sensory modalities. If learners are expert enough, then this information presentation activates the same schema and thus imposes twice the processing for the same result.

Expertise reversal effect

The long-term working memory model was first incorporated into cognitive load theory to explain multiple empirical effects observed in research linked to expertise of the learners (Sweller, Ayres, & Kalyuga, 2011). On many occasions, instructional designs had beneficial effects on novice students learning while more advanced students showed no benefit at all or even adverse effect of the design. This model explains how, under certain circumstances, a beneficial effect might turn into redundancy. If different information activates the same schema with no direct benefits for the learner, imposing the need to process that information will impose a heavier load with no gain in schema formation, thus impairing learning.

Guidance fading effect

The guidance fading effect appeared when studying the worked example effect (Sweller, Ayres, & Kalyuga, 2011). A modality effect turning to a redundancy effect could be explained by the added processing for no real benefit exhibited by the expertise reversal effect. The guidance fading effect relies on a similar phenomenon to the expertise reversal effect: processing the solution of the problem has a cognitive cost with no benefit for an advanced learner and thus results in an extraneous load. Thus, after a training session on worked examples providing full guidance, it proved beneficial for learners to turn toward problem-solving exercises without guidance which constitutes guidance fading.

Pace of presentation effect

The multicomponent model describes the benefits gained from using two different sources of information for learning, at least when these sources are consistent with each other and when learners have low levels of expertise. The long-term working memory model allows us to describe the inversion in results observed with expertise increases, for example when using the modality effect. Other studies on the modality effect found that it was also sensitive to the pacing of presentation of information (Ginns, 2005; Sweller, Ayres, & Kalyuga, 2011). The modality effect, as well as the redundancy effect, are more difficult to elicit when information pace is controlled by participants than when it is system paced. Investigating this effect, Schmidt-Weigand, Kohnert and Glowalla (2010) found that when the rhythm of presentation of information was learner paced, the benefit from dual modality presentation disappeared as compared to single modality presentation. They also found that when the presentation of information was system paced, learning outcome was sensitive to the rhythm of presentation, with a slower pace associated with a better learning performance.

Transient information effect

Another effect that can be related to the rhythm of information presentation is the transient information effect. The transient information effect is found when information disappears after presentation to be replaced by new information, which is the case with, for example, spoken information. If information disappears before the student has processed it, then it must be retrieved from memory or lost if not in memory. Though expertise associated with spoken language is large enough to allow large numbers of words to be maintained in working memory, this format of instruction still imposes a heavy load on working memory capacity. When considering the transient information effect, it was found to be affected by pace of presentation and segmentation. Introducing pauses during an animation or with spoken text might help learners to appropriately process information before it vanishes from working memory (Leahy & Sweller, 2011; 2016).

These phenomena of pacing of information and of transience of information do not contradict either the multicomponent or long-term working memory models, but these models are not able to describe and explain these empirical effects. Cognitive load theory adopted a working memory model to explain why cognitive load changed when the same information was presented in different ways. It adopted a new working memory model when confronted with the fact that cognitive load changed when the same information is presented in the same way to different learners based on their prior knowledge levels. Cognitive load theory now is confronted by a new challenge that may be met by adopting a new working memory model to explain why the same information, presented the same way to the same learner might impose a different cognitive load depending on time variations in presentation.

Cognitive load theory and the Time Based Resource Sharing Model

The Time Based Resource Sharing Model (TBRS, Barrouillet, Bernardin & Camos, 2004; Barrouillet & Camos, 2015) is a recent model of working memory taking time into account to describe working memory load. It relies on four main assumptions. First, the central resource of cognition in the TBRS framework is attention (Camos & Barrouillet, 2014). Attention allows the refreshing of memory traces to prevent time related decay (Vergauwe, Dewaele, Langerock & Barrouillet, 2012). It also allows processing of information held in working memory and thus performing tasks at hand, since executive functions are deemed to rely on attention (Awh, Vogel & Oh, 2006). Second, the processes are sequential. If attentional resources are limited (e.g., Broadbent, 1958), then any cognitive system has to manage them. The most widely accepted idea is that attentional resources are sequentially attributed to the different executive functions (Salvucci & Taatgen, 2010; Barrouillet & Camos, 2015 for a review). Third, the decay of memory traces is time related. There is no consensus on the nature of forgetting in working memory, some arguing that it is interference-based (Oberauer, Lewandowsky,

Farrell, Jarrold & Greaves, 2012 for a review) and some arguing that it is time related (e.g. Baddeley, 2012; Barrouillet, Bernardin & Camos, 2004). In the TBRS model, time is considered as the main source of forgetting, and chunks held active in working memory have to be refreshed periodically to prevent forgetting (see Cowan, 1995 for a similar suggestion). Since attention is the main resource in cognition and it can only be focused on one task at any time, processing a task and maintaining chunks actively requires multitasking. Fourth, multitasking can occur due to a rapid switching between processes. Attentional focus can only be applied to one chunk after another. It follows that the more chunks are kept active, the longer it takes to refresh each chunk. When chunk activation decays too much to be retrieved, it is forgotten (Barrouillet & Camos, 2014). If two tasks have to be processed simultaneously, they share the attentional resource sequentially, on a time basis (see Salvucci & Taatgen, 2010 for a similar suggestion).

It follows from those assumptions that holding items active in working memory while performing a judgment or decision task will necessitate rapid switching between memory trace refreshing and information processing. From these conclusions, the authors infer that cognitive load can be modelled as a time ratio: the proportion of time spent to process information while not refreshing memory traces will have a direct impact on working memory span.

Following the above assumptions, the TBRS model allows us to predict working memory span. Working memory span is directly dependent on the amount of resources needed to process interfering tasks while maintaining and refreshing memory traces. Since one stored item can be refreshed at a time, the maximum number of elements in a memory span will be achieved when the time available to refresh memory traces is not enough to refresh all the chunks held actively. The remaining chunks, not refreshed, will be forgotten. From this, it follows that an additional task requiring time to be processed would linearly impair working memory capacity, shortening the time available for the refreshing cycle by the time needed to complete the task. If participants use strategies during long tasks (i.e. several seconds) to rapidly change between task processing and the refreshing cycles, short tasks requiring small amounts of attentional resources should directly impact working memory span (e.g. Barrouillet, Bernardin & Camos, 2004).

This suggestion has been tested several times, using a complex memory span protocol during which participants viewed letters to be memorised interleaved with distracting tasks, such as spatial judgment or mental calculus (Barrouillet et al., 2007). The TBRS model allows us to infer that only the ratio between the time needed to perform the distracting task and the total time available will impact the cognitive load and therefore the working memory span. Then, using harder tasks, requiring more time to be completed, or reducing the total time available should impair working memory span by increasing cognitive load. On the contrary, while freeing attentional resources by reducing the time needed to perform a second task or increasing the total time available to complete the second task and refresh items held in working memory would result in an improvement of working memory capacity.

An interesting point inferred from the model is that the number of interfering tasks one will have to process while maintaining items active will have no effect on the memory span, since only the ratio between time needed to perform one distracting task and the time available to complete it will affect cognitive load and working memory span.

Thus, cognitive load is defined as the ratio of time spent on processing information divided by the total time allowed to complete the task. Cognitive load is then defined by the equation:$C.L. = (a\ N)/T$ with "a" being the time needed to process an interfering task, "N" the number of interfering tasks to process, and "T" the available time to process the interfering tasks and refresh the memory traces. Since in a classic complex memory span protocol, participants will have N interfering tasks to process, the first equation $C.L. = (a\ N)/T$ can be transformed to:$C.L. = (a\ N)/(t\ N)$ with $tN = T$, where "t" will be the time between the onset of two consecutive interfering tasks, or the time available to complete one interfering task, and "N" will be the same number of interfering tasks to process. For only one processing task, cognitive load can be defined as$C.L. = (a)/(t)$ with "a" the time needed to process the task and "t" the time available. Considering that the time available "t" is used to both process the distracting task (Td) and refresh memory traces (Tr), cognitive load can be expressed as:$C.L. = Td/(Td+Tr)$ The TBRS model has been used in many laboratory experiments (Barrouillet & Camos, 2015 for a review). Yet, none of these experiments have evaluated its relevance to cognitive load theory. Puma, Matton, Paubel and Tricot (2018) addressed this issue. In two experiments, they used a complex span task as designed in previous studies on this model (Barrouillet et al., 2007) while replacing letters to be remembered by terms of a mental calculation to be performed. Participants had thus to maintain the terms and to perform a mental calculation while performing a spatial judgment task. In their first experiment, the time ratio was manipulated by varying the difficulty of the spatial judgment task and the authors found it affected participants' performance of the arithmetic task for the less expert participants. More expert participants showed no differences in mental calculus performance in either difficulty condition, as if they were not affected by the variation of the time ratio. In a second experiment, the time ratio was varied by changing the time available to perform the spatial judgment task. Participants had to complete the same distracting task but in one condition they had one second to process each spatial judgment task while in the other condition, they had two seconds to perform the same distracting task. This resulted in a fast condition imposing a heavier load on working memory than the slow condition. Consistent with the first experiment, the results showed that novice participants were affected by the time ratio manipulation but not the experts. By varying both time allowed to perform the relevant task and the time needed or allowed to perform the concurrent task, these experiments showed an effect of time on both the intrinsic and the extraneous cognitive loads. Rather than the absolute number of elements per se, the time and the number of distracting elements should be considered when evaluating the cognitive load imposed by a given learning task.

The results of these experiments were extended in another pilot study addressing an often underlined limit of the cognitive load theory: the lack of an objective measure of cognitive load (e.g. Paas, Tuovinen, Tabbers & van Gerven, 2003). Electroencephalography has already been suggested as a good choice for an objective measure in cognitive load theory (Antonenko, Paas, Grabner & Van Gog, 2010; Keil & Antonenko, 2017). Puma, Matton, Paubel, El-Yagoubi and Tricot (2017) used a complex span task with meaningless letters to be remembered while using the spatial judgment task used in Experiment 1 of Puma et al. (2018). During the entire study, they recorded the electro-encephalographic data of their six participants. Results showed that the theta rythm (4–8Hz) varied following both the series sizes and the time ratio imposed by the spatial judgment task. Even if replication in a larger sample is needed to confirm this result, this is an argument in favor of using a model describing dynamic variations of working memory requirements for both behavioral research on instructional design and measuring cognitive load in an objective way. Using such a model might allow the discovery of new empirical effects in cognitive load theory research as well as allowing explanations of already known effects, such as the pace of presentation effect.

Conclusion

In this chapter, working memory models were considered in relation to cognitive load theory. These models contribute to explanations of empirical effects discovered using this theory. In turn, cognitive load theory research questions and confronts empirical results related to these theoretical models. When these models were unable to explain empirical results provided by cognitive load theory, the theory has moved to another model more suitable to describe the range of results. The very first version of this theory only needed the general idea of limited cognitive resources to deal with learning tasks such as problem solving. Subsequently, in order to deal with more complex materials, e.g. multimedia documents, cognitive load theory used Baddeley's multicomponent model of working memory. Next, the long-term working memory model allowed cognitive load theory to deal with learners' expertise, i.e. the fact that learners' previous domain specific knowledge is a key issue in instructional design. Lastly, we suggest that the Time Based Resources Sharing Model allows cognitive load theory to deal with another key issue of instruction: time. According to this recent working memory model, time is a cognitive resource; more accurately, this model describes memory span as the amount of resources needed to process interfering tasks while maintaining and refreshing memory traces. With this model, we can consider extraneous load as the rate of time spent on processing irrelevant information. Therefore, when designing a learning situation, cognitive load theory allows teachers to make decisions taking into account four main aspects: learning task, learning materials, learners' expertise and time. The dialogue between cognitive load theory and working memory models has had a major consequence for cognitive load theory: it extended its practical and theoretical scope. Future research focusing on time as a cognitive resource, for example on the resource depletion effect (Chen, Castro-Alonso, Paas & Sweller, 2018), should confirm this major extension of cognitive load theory.

References

Antonenko, P., Paas, F., Grabner, R., & van Gog, T. (2010). Using electroencephalography to measure cognitive load. *Educational Psychology Review*, 22, 425–438.

Atkinson, R. C., & Shiffrin, R. M. (1968). Human memory: A proposed system and its control processes. In K. W. Spence & J. T. Spence (Eds.), *The psychology of learning and motivation* (Volume 2), (pp. 89–195). New York: Academic Press.

Awh, E., Vogel, E. K., & Oh, S. H. (2006). Interactions between attention and working memory. *Neuroscience*, 139, 201–208.

Baddeley, A. D. (1966). The influence of acoustic and semantic similarity on long-term memory for word sequences. *Quarterly Journal of Experimental Psychology*, 18, 302–309.

Baddeley, A. D. (1986). *Working memory*. Oxford: Oxford University Press.

Baddeley, A. D. (2012). Working memory: Theories, models, and controversies. *Annual Review of Psychology*, 63, 1–29.

Baddeley, A. D., & Hitch, G. (1974). Working memory. *Psychology of Learning and Motivation*, 8, 47–89.

Barrouillet, P., & Camos, V. (2014). On the proper reading of the TBRS model: Reply to Oberauer and Lewandowsky. *Frontiers in Psychology*, 5, 1–3.

Barrouillet, P., & Camos, V. (2015). *Working memory: Loss and reconstruction*. New York and London: Psychology Press.

Barrouillet, P., Bernardin, S., Portrat, S., Vergauwe, E., & Camos, V. (2007). Time and cognitive load in working memory. *Journal of Experimental Psychology: Learning, Memory, and Cognition*, 33, 570–585.

Barrouillet, P., Bernardin, S., & Camos, V. (2004). Time constraints and resource sharing in adults' working memory spans. *Journal of Experimental Psychology: General*, 133, 83–100.

Broadbent, D. E. (1958). *Perception and communication*. New York: Pergamon Press. Retrieved from: http://www.archive.org/details/perceptioncommun00broa.

Camos, V., & Barrouillet, P. (2014). Attentional and non-attentional systems in the maintenance of verbal information in working memory: The executive and phonological loops. *Frontiers in Human Neuroscience*, 8, 1–11.

Chen, O., Castro-Alonso, J. C., Paas, F., & Sweller, J. (2018). Extending cognitive load theory to incorporate working memory resource depletion: Evidence from the spacing effect. *Educational Psychology Review*, 30, 483–501.

Cowan, N. (1988). Evolving conceptions of memory storage, selective attention, and their mutual constraints within the human information processing system. *Psychological Bulletin*, 104, 163–191.

Cowan, N. (1995). *Attention and memory: An integrated framework*. New York: Oxford University Press.

Cowan, N. (2001). The magical number 4 in short-term memory: A reconsideration of mental storage capacity. *Behavioral and Brain Sciences*, 24, 87–185.

Cowan, N. (2014). Working memory underpins cognitive development, learning, and education. *Educational Psychology Review*, 26, 197–223.

Cowan, N., Elliott, E. M., Saults, J. S., Morey, C. C., Mattox, S., Hismjatullina, A., & Conway, A. R. A. (2005). On the capacity of attention: Its estimation and its role in working memory and cognitive aptitudes. *Cognitive Psychology*, 51, 42–100.

Ericsson, K. A., & Kintsch, W. (1995). Long-term working memory. *Psychological Review*, 102, 211–245.

Ginns, P. (2005). Meta-analysis of the modality effect. *Learning and Instruction*, 15, 313–331.

James, W. (1890). *Principles of psychology*. Volume 1(Chap 11). Global Grey (204). Retrieved from: www.globalgrey.co.uk.

Keil, A. ,& Antonenko, P. D. (2017). Assessing working memory dynamics with electro-encephalography implications for research on cognitive load. In R. Zheng (Ed.), *Cognitive load measurement and application: A theoretical framework for meaningful research and practice* (pp. 107–125). New York: Routledge.

Leahy, W., & Sweller, J. (2011). Cognitive load theory, modality of presentation and the transient information effect. *Applied Cognitive Psychology*, 25, 943–951.

Leahy, W., & Sweller, J. (2016). Cognitive load theory and the effects of transient information on the modality effect. *Instructional Science*, 44, 107–123.

Miller, G. A. (1956). The magical number of seven, plus or minus two. Some limits on our capacity for processing information. *Psychological Review*, 101, 343–352.

Miller, G. A., Galanter, E., & Pribram, K. H. (1960). *Plans and the structure of behaviour*. New York: Henry Holt.

Newell, A., & Simon, H. A. (1972). *Human problem solving*. Englewood Cliffs: Prentice Hall.

Oberauer, K., Lewandowsky, S., Farrell, S., Jarrold, C., & Greaves, M. (2012). Modeling working memory: An interference model of complex span. *Psychonomic Bulletin and Review*, 19, 779–819.

Paas, F., Tuovinen, J. E., Tabbers, H., & van Gerven, P. W. M. (2003). Cognitive load measurement as a means to advance cognitive load theory. *Educational Psychologist*, 38, 63–72.

Puma, S., Matton, N., Paubel, P.-V., El-Yagoubi, R., & Tricot, A. (2017). Time Based Resource Sharing model as a mean to improve cognitive load measurement. 10th International Cognitive Load Theory Conference, November 20–22. University of Wollongong, Australia.

Puma, S., Matton, N., Paubel, P.-V., & Tricot, A. (2018). Cognitive load theory and time considerations: Using the time-based resource sharing model. *Educational Psychology Review*, 30, 1199–1214.

Salvucci, D. D., & Taatgen, N. A. (2010). *The multitasking mind*. Oxford: Oxford University Press.

Schmidt-Weigand, F., Kohnert, A., & Glowalla, U. (2010). A closer look at split visual attention in system- and self-paced instruction in multimedia learning. *Learning and Instruction*, 20, 100–110.

Shah, P., & Miyake, A. (1999). Models of working memory. An introduction. In A. Miyake & P. Shah (Eds.), *Models of working memory. Mechanisms of active maintenance and executive control* (pp. 1–27). Cambridge, UK: Cambridge University Press.

Sweller, J., & Levine, M. (1982). Effects of goal specificity on means-end analysis and learning. *Journal of Experimental Psychology: Learning Memory and Cognition*, 8, 463–474.

Sweller, J. (1988). Cognitive load during problem solving: Effects on learning. *Cognitive Science*, 12, 257–285.

Sweller, J., Ayres, P., & Kalyuga, S. (2011). *Cognitive load theory*. New York: Springer.

Sweller, J., Van Merrienboer, J. J. G., & Paas, F. (1998). Cognitive architecture and instructional design. *Educational Psychology Review*, 10, 251–296.

Vergauwe, E., Dewaele, N., Langerock, N., & Barrouillet, P. (2012). Evidence for a central pool of general resources in working memory. *Journal of Cognitive Psychology*, 24, 359–366.

PART 2

Specific research advances and research procedures

5

USING ARROW-LINES TO INTEGRATE PICTORIAL AND TEXTUAL INFORMATION IN ELECTRONIC SLIDESHOW ASSISTED LECTURING[1]

Tzu-Chien Liu

DEPARTMENT OF EDUCATIONAL PSYCHOLOGY AND COUNSELING & INSTITUTE FOR RESEARCH EXCELLENCE IN LEARNING SCIENCES, NATIONAL TAIWAN NORMAL UNIVERSITY

Yi-Chun Lin

DEPARTMENT OF EDUCATIONAL PSYCHOLOGY AND COUNSELING, NATIONAL TAIWAN NORMAL UNIVERSITY

Yu-Chen Kuo

DEPARTMENT OF EDUCATIONAL PSYCHOLOGY AND COUNSELING, NATIONAL TAIWAN NORMAL UNIVERSITY

Cognitive load theory (CLT) is one of the most important theories for optimising instructional and learning materials during the last 30 years. With the development of learning technology, many instructional design principles based on CLT have also been proven to benefit the design of different types of digital learning environments, such as mobile learning (e.g., Liu, Lin, & Paas, 2013; Liu, Fan, & Paas, 2014), QR-Code assisted learning (e.g., Gao, Liu, & Paas, 2016), digital dictionary assisted language learning (e.g., Liu, Fan, & Paas, 2014), and simulation assisted learning (e.g., Lin, Liu, & Sweller, 2015).

Electronic slideshows (e.g., PowerPoint) are widely used for assisting instruction, but few studies have explored the issues of the design of electronic slideshows in terms of cognitive load theory (Liu, Lin, Gao, Yeh, & Kalyuga, 2015). Electronic slideshows are often composed of multiple information sources (such as pictures, text, audio, etc.) in which complex information is often included. In this case, students frequently confront two situations that may impede their learning: the first one is that finding the target or important information from the rich content may be difficult; the other is that the students may need to split their attention between different learning sources and have to mentally integrate relevant sources of physically separated information (i.e., split–attention effect) (Ayres & Sweller, 2014).

The classroom is where students spend the vast majority of their time each day, and the electronic slideshow is the most common technology used for assisting lectures. Since there are many unavoidable interferences in the classroom (Liu et al., 2015), finding and focusing on the target learning content presented in electronic slideshows in the classroom may be more difficult than learning in an individual learning environment. Therefore, how to help students attend to learning materials from classroom electronic slideshows is an important issue.

The cueing method is one of the techniques to draw learners' attention to essential elements of the learning materials. This method is seen as a useful way for successful multimedia learning because learners can effectively select important learning information, organise and integrate related information with the aid of cueing method (Van Gog, 2014). De Koning, Tabbers, Rikers, and Paas (2009) summarised three functions of the cueing method: (1) guiding learners to attend to important information and to distinguish particular information from unrelated information, (2) assisting learners to effectively capture the structure of complex learning material, and (3) supporting the integration of elements within one representation or between multiple representations. In addition, the use of cueing method is proven effective in reducing cognitive load and promoting learning outcomes (Xie et al., 2017). Although the cueing method has been successfully applied in assisting computer-based instructions (Kalyuga, Chandler, & Sweller, 1999) and mobile technology assisted learning (Liu et al., 2013), few studies to date have examined whether the cueing method can also successfully be applied in electronic slideshow assisted lecturing in the classroom situation.

In the current study, the arrow-line cueing method, which is applied by connecting parts from the text with the relevant parts in the picture (Liu et al., 2013),

The venation of the Green Maple is plamate-veined.

The plamate-veined includes three, five or seven veins which radiates finger-shaped from the petiole.

FIGURE 5.1 An example of the arrow-line cueing method

was selected as the method to integrate graphical and textual information in an electronic slideshow (please refer to Figure 5.1). Liu et al. (2013) found that the use of this method could enhance learning performance and learning efficiency when learning about plant leaf characteristics with or without the use of real plants. They pointed out that it is easy for learners to find the relevant elements in the text or picture with the support of arrow-line cueing.

Randomised, controlled experiments are the most common research method to examine the application of instructional effects based on cognitive load theory. However, examining the practicality of the instructional effect (e.g., the cueing method) in the classroom is not an easy task because it is difficult to simultaneously consider internal and ecological validity. In order to control internal validity, researchers often eliminate factors that may confound the results, but ecological validity thus may be neglected. A virtual classroom that simulates a normal classroom has been proved to have potential for consideration of both internal and ecological validity (Liu et al., 2015). Since the classroom is the most important place for learning and instruction, it is necessary to examine CLT instructional effects or instructional designs in the classroom.

This study aimed to examine the effects of the arrow-line cueing method on learning in electronic slideshow assisted lecturing in a classroom situation. It was hypothesised that the use of the arrow line cueing method would benefit electronic slideshow assisted lecturing in a classroom situation. It was assumed that participants who learnt with an electronic slideshow using the arrow line cueing method would have better retention, comprehension, and transfer performance, lower cognitive load in the test phase, and better instructional efficiency than participants who learnt using the electronic slideshow without the arrow line cueing method.

Method

Participants and design

A total of 70 fifth- and sixth-grade elementary school students (34 boys and 36 girls), mean age 10.99 years (SD = 0.81, range = 10–13) participated in this study. They were randomly assigned to the cued or un-cued conditions (35 participants in each condition, respectively; Figure 5.2). All students had been taught the basic concepts of plant leaf morphology in their natural science classes in third grade.

Experimental environment

Virtual Classroom Web 2.0 was selected as the experimental platform in the current study, which is the revised version of the virtual classroom developed by Liu et al. (2015). Virtual Classroom Web 2.0 presents as an authentic classroom based on a head-mounted display (HMD) VR system of Unity 4.2.3 and a set of headphones. The scenes of Virtual Classroom Web 2.0 were constructed according to an authentic classroom including projector screen, desks, chairs, etc.

FIGURE 5.2 A screenshot of the virtual classroom and the participant's location

There were one female instructor and seven students (four boys and three girls) in the virtual classroom. Each participant was located in the 4th middle row seat in the virtual classroom. Virtual students (classmates) seated around each of the participants would make some actions (e.g., yawn, turn their heads, etc.) or sounds (e.g., sneezing, chatting, etc.) that are often seen in a normal classroom.

The vividness of the virtual classroom was examined by the use of Witmer and Singer's Presence Questionnaire for measuring a person's immersive tendencies (Witmer & Singer, 1998). The questionnaire was composed of eight items based on Likert-type 7-point rating scales ranging from 1 (*very very low*) to 7 (*very very high*). A total of 27 fifth-grade elementary school students who did not participate in the current study were invited to examine the vividness of the virtual classroom. They were asked to rate the sense of reality for different components (such as virtual students, classroom environment, etc.) of the virtual classroom. The mean of the 7-item ratings was 5.56 (SD = 1.32) showing that the vividness of the virtual classroom was acceptable.

Learning material

The learning material included two parts: basic concept learning material and the primary learning material. Both parts were the revised version of what was used in the study of Liu, Lin, and Paas (2013). The topic of the learning material was "Characteristics of plant leaf morphology".

The *basic concept learning material* was composed of seven screens for introducing the basic concepts of leaf morphology, such as venation, including four types: parallel-veined, feather-veined, palmate-veined, and midrib distinct. All participants were asked to read the basic concept learning material shown on the projector screen by themselves. The reading time spent on this material was approximately one minute.

The *primary learning material* was composed of 26 slides accompanied with narrations. The first page presented the introduction of the material. The following 24 pages introduced the three characteristics of plant leaves: venation (parallel-veined, feather-veined, palmate-veined, and midrib distinct), margin (entire, dentate, palmately lobed, and sinuate) and phyllotaxy (alternate, decussate, distichous, whorled, and rosulate) with six plants as examples. The last page was used to thank the participants for their participation. The primary learning material was shown on the projector screen in the virtual classroom. Participants were guided to read the learning material on the projection screen in the front and listened to narrations by a virtual teacher. The content of the material provided to the participants in the two conditions was the same except for whether or not the arrow line cueing method was applied. The time for presenting the primary learning material was approximately 5 mins and 35 secs.

Measures

A *prior knowledge test* consisted of 10 four-item multiple-choice questions for examining the participants' prior knowledge of the basic concepts of leaf morphology. One point was given for a correct answer, so the highest and lowest possible scores were 10 and 0 respectively. The internal consistency reliability coefficient (KR-20) of the prior knowledge test was 0.79.

Retention, comprehension and transfer tests were used to examine how well the students had learnt the material, and were the revised version of the study of Liu, Lin, Gao, and Paas (2018). The *retention test* composed of 18 items to test how much the students could remember of the content they had been taught. The participants were given 12 pictures of the six plants used in the learning phase. Six of the pictures were used for testing the venation and margin of plant leaves, and the other six were used for testing the phyllotaxy of plant leaves. Participants were asked to indicate the correct characteristic of the plant leaves. One point was given for a correct answer, and the highest and lowest possible scores were 18 and 0 respectively. The internal consistency reliability (KR-20) was 0.73.

A *comprehension test* included two tasks: a drawing task and an assembling task. The drawing task was composed of eight items to examine how well the participants were able to understand the sub-types of venation (four items) and sub-types of margin (four items). An assembling task was composed of five items to test how well the participants were able to understand the sub-types of phyllotaxy (five items). One point was given for a correct answer, and the highest and lowest possible scores were 13 and 0 respectively. The internal consistency reliability (KR-20) was 0.71.

A *transfer test* consisting of 18 multiple-choice questions was used to test how well the students were able to apply what they had learnt in the learning phase to the novel plants. Similar to the retention test, the participants were given 12 pictures of six plants that were totally different from those presented in the learning phase. They were asked to indicate the correct characteristics of the leaves from multiple choice questions. One mark was given for a correct answer, and the highest and lowest possible scores were 18 and 0 respectively. The internal consistency reliability (KR-20) was 0.75.

A *cognitive load rating scale* was used to measure the perceived level of difficulty in the learning and post-test phase. The rating scale referring to the cognitive load yielded during cognitive activities, and was an adapted version of the scale originally developed by Paas and van Merriënboer, (1993). Each item used a 9-point adapted scale, 1 being *completely disagree* and 9 being *completely agree*. Accordingly, the highest level of cognitive load corresponded to 9 points and the lowest level was 1.

Instructional efficiency was used to investigate the relationship between the standardised post-test performance and standardised cognitive load perceived during the test phase. Instructional efficiency was computed for each participant using the formula:

$$E = \frac{Z_{Performance} - Z_{MentalEffort}}{\sqrt{2}}$$

(Paas & van Merriënboer, 1993; see also Van Gog & Paas, 2008)

Procedure

The experiment used the virtual classroom as the experimental platform. Each participant was assigned to learn individually with the corresponding learning material in the virtual classroom situation. The experiment had three phases.

Pre-experimental phase. There were three tasks in this phase for assisting the participants to do some preparation for the following experiment. First, they were taught to respond to the cognitive load rating scale by two math puzzles with different difficulty levels. Second, the experimenters assisted the participants to put on the Head Mounted Displays (HMDs) and do the calibration by asking them to look at the projector screen and look around the virtual classroom. Finally, the participants were asked to read the basic concept learning material presented on the projector screen in the virtual classroom, and the experimenters made sure that participants' felt comfortable with the environment. The average experiment preparation time was approximately 12 minutes.

Learning phase. After confirming that the participants felt comfortable with the environment, they were taught with different learning materials corresponding to their assigned conditions. After completing learning in this phase, they were asked to complete the cognitive load rating scale. The average time spent on the learning phase was approximately seven minutes.

Testing phase. Retention, comprehension and transfer tests were conducted to examine how well the participants learnt from the learning phase. After completing each test, participants' were asked to complete the cognitive load rating scale. The average time spent on this phase was approximately 17 minutes.

Results

In order to confirm the normality of data obtained from the cued and un-cued conditions, the Shapiro-Wilk test was conducted before the following tests. The Shapiro-Wilk test showed that the learning performance, cognitive load in responding to the comprehension test, and instructional efficiency of comprehension and transfer were normally distributed ($p > .05$). However, prior knowledge, cognitive load in learning phase, cognitive load in responding the retention and transfer tests, and instructional efficiency of retention were demonstrated to have a non-normal distribution ($p < .05$). According to the Shapiro-Wilk test results, a series of independent t tests was conducted to examine the differences of the variables normally distributed. In addition, a nonparametric Mann–Whitney U test was conducted for those variables not normally distributed. Table 5.1 lists the mean scores, standard deviations and the normality tests for each dependent variable.

Prior knowledge

The results of a nonparametric Mann–Whitney U test indicated that there were no significant differences between the conditions on the prior knowledge, $U = 573.00$, *ns*.

TABLE 5.1 Means, SDs and normality tests of the dependent variables

Measures	Cued condition			Un-cued condition		
	M	*SD*	*Shapiro-Wilk (p-value)*	*M*	*SD*	*Shapiro-Wilk (p-value)*
Prior knowledge test	7.09	1.63	.002	6.86	1.91	.027
Cognitive load in the learning phase (1–9)	4.06	1.91	.160	3.83	2.05	.021
Learning performance						
Retention test (0–18)	10.74	3.91	.145	9.11	3.25	.252
Comprehension test (0–13)	9.14	1.90	.242	6.86	2.37	.061
Transfer test (0–18)	12.91	2.58	.205	11.11	3.09	.819
Cognitive load in the test phase (1–9)						
Retention test	5.29	1.93	.200	5.83	1.56	.006
Comprehension test	5.03	1.74	.165	6.30	1.74	.096
Transfer test	5.29	1.66	.056	5.74	1.88	.004
Instructional efficiency						
Retention test	0.22	1.14	.426	-0.27	0.91	.005
Comprehension test	0.39	0.93	.121	-0.39	1.04	.238
Transfer test	0.27	0.93	.603	-0.27	0.91	.648

Cognitive load in the learning phase

A Mann–Whitney U test was conducted to examine the differences of the perceived cognitive load in the learning phase between the conditions. The results showed that there were no significant differences between the conditions, $U = 583.00$, *ns*.

Learning performance

Regarding the learning performance, the results indicated that the participants in the cued condition significantly outperformed the participants in the un-cued condition on both the comprehension test, $t(68) = 4.46$, $p < .001$, Cohen's $d = 1.06$ and the transfer test, $t(68) = 2.64$, $p < .05$, Cohen's $d = 0.63$. However, the results indicated that there was only marginally significant difference between the two conditions on the retention test, $t(68) = 1.90$, $p = .06$, Cohen's $d = 0.45$.

Cognitive load in the post-test phase

With regard to the cognitive load in the post-test phase, the results showed that a significant difference was only found in the comprehension test, $t(68) = -3.06$, $p < .01$, Cohen's $d = 0.73$, with the participants in the cued condition significantly perceiving a lower cognitive load in responding to the comprehension test. The results failed to indicate any significant difference in the perception of cognitive load of the two conditions in the retention test, $U = 506.00$, *ns*, or in the transfer test, $U = 491.50$, *ns*.

Instructional efficiency

Regarding instructional efficiency, the results indicated that the participants in the cued condition had significantly higher instructional efficiency than the participants in the un-cued condition on both the comprehension test, $t(68) = 3.35$, $p < .01$, Cohen's $d = 0.79$ and the transfer test, $t(68) = 2.50$, $p < .05$, Cohen's $d = 0.59$. However, there was no significant difference between the two conditions on the retention test, $U = 471.50$, *ns*.

Discussion and conclusions

The classroom is the most important place for providing students with knowledge and skills, and is also one of the main places for the application of learning technology. Electronic slideshows (e.g., PowerPoint) are one of the learning technologies that are often seen in the classroom. Undoubtedly, there are many advantages to using electronic slideshows; for example, it is easy for instructors to display learning materials including multiple representations (e.g., pictorial and textual information) to the students. On the one hand, the use of electronic slideshows can provide students with opportunities to understand the concept by multiple examples composed of different representations. On the other hand, finding the target information from rich content or integrating physically separated information from different learning sources within a limited time may be challenging for students. Unfortunately, the classroom situation includes a great deal of interference, making this challenge even more serious.

The arrow line cuing method has been proved to be a useful method for integrating pictorial and textual information presented in computer-based learning material (Liu et al., 2013). Differing from the individual learning situation in which the cuing method was applied in previous studies (e.g., Liu et al., 2013), the current study examined the effects of the cuing method in an environment simulated classroom situation in which all students shared one projector screen including different kinds of classroom interference. The results indicated that the use of the arrow line cuing method could benefit learning. Students who learned with this method had better learning performance and instructional efficiency (comprehension and transfer tests) than those who did not use it.

In this study, the arrow-line cueing method was applied to integrate the pictorial and textual information introducing the characteristics of plant leaves. Using this method, the characteristics of the plant leaves were marked, and the explanatory text was directly connected to the marked characteristic with arrow lines. With the assistance of arrow line cueing, the students could not only easily attend to important information (e.g., the characteristics of plant leaves), but could also efficiently integrate the graphical and textual information as well. On the contrary, those students who learned without the arrow line cuing method may not have been able to visually integrate essential but separated elements of information. Moreover, due to the lack of signaling, the un-cued condition may have processed some irrelevant information (extraneous load) from the classroom environment (e.g., yawn, turn their heads, sneezing, chatting)., resulting in a higher cognitive load, with learning negatively affected. According to Kalyuga and Singh (2016) traditional cognitive load theory claims that arrow-line cueing can be seen as a type of extraneous cognitive load because arrow-line cueing requires learners to spend extraneous working memory resources on the task unrelated to the main learning goal. However, in this study these resources were favorable because they supported learners to integrate relevant information elements (i.e., germane cognitive load) of pictorial and textual information, to optimise the schema construction and automation by reducing unnecessary visual search.

The arrow-line cueing method is a simple but useful way of integrating multiple representations. Future studies are recommended to investigate the effects of the arrow-line cuing method when integrating multiple representations in electronic slideshows with the focus on the processing of relevant information in the working memory for different learning topics.

Successfully applying a novel instructional design in a classroom situation is an important task for many educational researchers. However, examining the effects of an instructional design in a classroom situation is not easy because there are many confounding variables that might affect the experimental results. A virtual class-room, with the potential to bridge the gap between research studies in a laboratory and authentic classroom conditions, was the experimental platform in this study. In line with the previous studies (Liu et al., 2015) which used the virtual classroom as the experimental platform, the virtual classroom has been further proved to be a useful platform for examining educational issues in a classroom situation with respect to both internal and external validity. Cognitive load theory is one of the most influential theories in learning and instruction, but not all studies have investigated the instructional effects based on this theory in the classroom (Yang, Chang, Chien, Chien, & Tseng, 2013). The virtual reality technology is widely applied in education (Lin & Lan, 2015; Yeh, Lan, & Lin, 2018). The virtual class-room could be a potential platform to test the effects of instructional design prin-ciples based on cognitive load theory in the future. Virtual classroom is also an appropriate platform in which physiological instruments (e.g., eye tracker) may be used. Future research is recommended to explore the relationship between per-ceived cognitive load and visual attention in different conditions with the use of an eye tracking device.

Note

1   Some parts of this work were financially supported by the"Institute for Research Excel-lence in Learning Sciences" of National Taiwan Normal University (NTNU) from The Featured Areas Research Center Program within the framework of the Higher Education Sprout Project by the Ministry of Education (MOE) in Taiwan and Ministry of Science and Technology, Taiwan, R.O.C. under Grant no. MOST 105-2511-S-003 -026 -MY3 and MOST 106-2511-S-003 -033 -MY3.

References

Ayres, P., & Sweller, J. (2014). The split-attention principle in multimedia learning. In R. E. Mayer (Ed.), *The Cambridge handbook of multimedia learning* (2nd ed., pp. 206–226). New York: Cambridge University Press.

De Koning, B. B., Tabbers, H. K., Rikers, R. M. J. P. & Paas, F. (2009). Towards a fra-mework for attention cueing in instructional animations: guidelines for research and design. *Educational Psychology Review*, 21, 113–140.

Gao, Y., Liu, T. C., & Paas, F. (2016). Effects of mode of target task selection on learning about plants in a mobile learning environment: Effortful manual selection versus effortless QR-code selection. *Journal of Educational Psychology*, 108, 694–704.

Kalyuga, S., Chandler, P., & Sweller, J. (1999). Managing split-attention and redundancy in multimedia instruction. *Applied Cognitive Psychology*, 13, 351–371.

Kalyuga, S., & Singh, A. M. (2016). Rethinking the boundaries of cognitive load theory in complex learning. *Educational Psychology Review*, 28, 831–852.

Lin, T. J., & Lan, Y. J. (2015). Language learning in virtual reality environments: Past, present, and future. *Journal of Educational Technology & Society*, 18(4), 486–497.

Lin, Y. C., Liu, T. C., & Sweller, J. (2015). Improving the frame design of computer simulations for learning: Determining the primacy of the isolated elements or the transient information effects. *Computers & Education*, 88, 280–291.

Liu, T. C., Fan, M. H. M., & Paas, F. (2014). Effects of digital dictionary format on incidental acquisition of spelling knowledge and cognitive load during second language learning: Click-on versus key-in dictionaries. *Computers & Education*, 70, 9–20.

Liu, T. C., Lin, Y. C., Gao, Y., & Paas, F. (2018). The modality effect in a mobile learning environment: Learning from spoken text and real objects. *British Journal of Educational Technology*. doi:10.1111/bjet.12605.

Liu, T. C., Lin, Y. C., & Paas, F. (2013). Effects of cues and real objects on learning in a mobile device supported environment. *British Journal of Educational Technology*, 44, 386–399.

Liu, T. C., Lin, Y. C., Gao, Y., Yeh, S. C., & Kalyuga, S. (2015). Does the redundancy effect exist in electronic slideshow assisted lecturing? *Computers & Education*, 88, 303–314.

Paas, F., & Van Merriënboer, J. J. G. (1993). The efficiency of instructional conditions: An approach to combine mental-effort and performance measures. *Human Factors*, 35, 737–743.

Van Gog, T. (2014). The signaling (or cueing) principle in multimedia learning. In R. E. Mayer (Ed.), *The Cambridge handbook of multimedia learning* (2nd ed., pp. 263–278). Cambridge, MA: Cambridge University Press.

Van Gog, T., & Paas, F. (2008). Instructional efficiency: Revisiting the original construct in educational research. *Educational Psychologist*, 43, 16–26.

Witmer, B. G., & Singer, M. J. (1998). Measuring presence in virtual environments: A presence questionnaire. *Presence*, 7, 225–240.

Xie, H., Wang, F., Hao, Y., Chen, J., An, J., Wang, Y., & Liu, H. (2017). The more total cognitive load is reduced by cues, the better retention and transfer of multimedia learning: A meta-analysis and two meta-regression analyses. *PLoS ONE*, 12(8), e0183884.

Yang, F.-Y., Chang, C.-Y., Chien, W.-R., Chien, Y.-T., & Tseng, Y.-H. (2013). Tracking learners' visual attention during a multimedia presentation in a real classroom. *Computers & Education*, 62, 208–220.

Yeh, Y. L., Lan, Y. J., & Lin, Y. T. R. (2018). Gender-related differences in collaborative learning in a 3D virtual reality environment by elementary school students. *Journal of Educational Technology & Society*, 21(4), 204–216.

6

HOW TO MEASURE EFFECTS OF SELF-REGULATED LEARNING WITH CHECKLISTS ON THE ACQUISITION OF TASK SELECTION SKILLS

Jimmie Leppink

HULL YORK MEDICAL SCHOOL, UNIVERSITY OF YORK, UNITED KINGDOM

Fred Paas

DEPARTMENT OF PSYCHOLOGY, EDUCATION, AND CHILD STUDIES, ERASMUS UNIVERSITY ROTTERDAM, ROTTERDAM, THE NETHERLANDS; SCHOOL OF EDUCATION/EARLY START, UNIVERSITY OF WOLLONGONG, WOLLONGONG, AUSTRALIA

Tamara van Gog

ERASMUS GRADUATE SCHOOL OF SOCIAL SCIENCES AND THE HUMANITIES, ERASMUS UNIVERSITY ROTTERDAM, THE NETHERLANDS; DEPARTMENT OF EDUCATION, UTRECHT UNIVERSITY, THE NETHERLANDS

Jeroen J. G. van Merriënboer

SCHOOL OF HEALTH PROFESSIONS EDUCATION, MAASTRICHT UNIVERSITY, THE NETHERLANDS

Functioning in a society in which one must be ready to develop new knowledge and skills throughout life requires being able to *self-regulate one's learning*. Self-regulated learning is an active and constructive process in which a learner plans, monitors, and exerts control over his or her own learning process (e.g., Kostons, Van Gog, & Paas, 2012; Nelson & Narens, 1990; Pintrich, 2000; Sitzmann & Ely, 2011; Winne, 2001; Winne & Hadwin, 1998; Zimmerman, 1990; Zimmerman & Schunk, 2001). Using accurate self-assessments of one's performance on a current learning task in combination with the effort invested to reach this performance, and to use those self-assessments for selecting a new learning task that is appropriate given the current skill level in terms of the level of complexity and the degree of instructional support provided, is key to effective self-regulated learning (Corbalan, Kester, & Van Merriënboer, 2008; Kostons et al., 2012; Raaijmakers et al., 2018). For example, in the case of low performance and high mental effort, it would be sensible to select a new learning task that is of a lower level of complexity or a learning task that is of the same level of complexity but provides more instructional support. However, learners are often inaccurate in self-assessing the quality of their own performance (Bjork, Dunlosky, & Kornell, 2013; Dunning, Heath, & Suls, 2004; Dunning, Johnson, Ehrlinger & Kruger, 2003), and are unlikely to spontaneously use their performance and invested effort as input for their decision on which new learning task to select (Kostons, Van Gog, & Paas, 2010; Kostons et al., 2012). Thus, learners need instruction and guidance to develop and apply skills to accurately monitor and reflect on their own performance and effort investment, and to use that reflection for subsequent learning task selection (Aleven & Koedinger, 2002; Azevedo & Cromley, 2004; Van den Boom, Paas, & Van Merriënboer, 2007; Van den Boom, Paas, Van Merriënboer & Van Gog, 2004). At the same time, to be able to compare experimental conditions in terms of learning task selection accuracy and to provide learners with feedback on their learning task selection behavior so that they can improve their task selection skills, we need measures of task selection accuracy. This chapter proposes two measures that to our knowledge have not yet been considered: *Bias* and *Instability*. Bias refers to a tendency towards selecting learning activities that are simpler (i.e., underchallenging) or more complex (i.e., overchallenging) than considered optimal for a learner based on past learning task performance. Instability is not associated with a pronounced tendency towards underchallenge or overchallenge but is about going back and forth between underchallenge and overchallenge. In other words, Bias and Instability hint at different types of task selection behavior that have in common a tendency to select tasks that are not within the learner's zone of proximal development. Along with post-test performance, Bias and Instability can be used as outcome measures in randomiaed controlled experiments to examine the effectiveness of different methods aimed at fostering the skill of task selection.

Self-regulated learning and cognitive load theory

Adaptive instruction that is tailored to the individual learner's level of performance can stimulate learning more than one-size fits-all instruction (e.g., Anderson, Corbett, Koedinger & Pelletier, 1995; Camp, Paas, Rikers & Van Merriënboer, 2001; Koedinger, Anderson, Hadley & Mark, 1997; Salden, Paas, Broers & Van Merriënboer, 2004). Self-regulated learning can be adaptive, provided that the learning tasks selected match a learner's needs (Kostons et al., 2012). Ideally, a learning task should be in the learner's *zone of proximal development* (Vygotsky, 1978). That is, learning tasks should be challenging but not too demanding, so that learners can correctly complete them with some support. If a learning task is too demanding, it is likely that learners have insufficient working memory capacity left to develop cognitive schemas about the content or type of problem at hand (i.e., engage in learning; Sweller, 1988; Sweller, Ayres, & Kalyuga, 2011; Sweller, Van Merriënboer, & Paas, 1998). Learning tasks that are within a learner's zone of proximal development have an appropriate combination of learning task complexity and instructional support (Vygotsky, 1978). Cognitive load theory states that as learning proceeds, less instructional support is needed for learning tasks of the same level of complexity (i.e., fading guidance strategy) and that process of reducing instructional support can be repeated at subsequent levels of complexity (Renkl & Atkinson, 2003; Van Merriënboer, 1997; Van Merriënboer & Kirschner, 2018).

If learning task selection is not adaptive, the likelihood that learning tasks at some point or another are no longer in a learner's zone of proximal development increases. If the increase in complexity or fading of instructional support within a complexity level occurs too slowly, learning tasks at some point become easier than a learner can handle. If the increase in complexity or fading of instructional support within a complexity level occurs too quickly, learning tasks at some point become too complex for a learner. In either case, learning is likely to be slowed down. Cognitive load theory dictates that learning is likely to be facilitated if extraneous cognitive load is minimised and students are stimulated to allocate their available working memory resources to dealing with an optimum amount of intrinsic cognitive load (Sweller et al., 2011). A learning task that is of a too low level of complexity given a learner's cognitive schemas of the type of task at hand will contribute to very little if any intrinsic cognitive load for that learner, whereas in the case of a learning task that is too complex for that learner intrinsic cognitive load may be too high. Simultaneously, providing too little instructional support for a learner on a relatively complex learning task is likely to contribute to extraneous cognitive load through the engagement in ineffective problem-solving search, while providing instructional support that is not needed may also contribute to extraneous cognitive load through the processing of redundant information (Sweller et al., 2011; Van Merriënboer & Kirschner, 2018).

In sum, self-regulated learning can be expected to facilitate learning more than one-size-fits-all instruction provided that learners manage to select learning tasks that are in their zone of proximal development. Learning tasks in a learner's zone of proximal development provide the degree of instructional support that is needed to minimise extraneous cognitive load and are challenging enough for the learner to allocate his or her working memory resources to dealing with the intrinsic cognitive load. To be able to select learning tasks in one's zone of proximal development, accurate task selection is very important. Metacognitive prompts directed to self-assessment of one's performance on a current learning task and the effort invested to reach this performance provide a promising tool to teach self-regulation and these prompts can be presented easily in a checklist (Van den Boom et al., 2004). Under the assumption that the aforementioned metacognitive prompts on performance and effort constitute a necessary but not sufficient condition for accurate task selection, prompts to reflect on what kind of learning task to select next could be added to the checklist to practice learning task selection.

Guiding the learner through the different levels of challenge

To examine the effects of task selection training, Kostons et al. (2012) used an online learning environment in which participants freely chose eight tasks from a database comprising five tasks for each of three instructional support levels (i.e., high, low, none) at each of five complexity levels (i.e., 5 x 3 x 5 = 75 tasks). Each task presented a problem to be solved in five steps and had only one correct solution. Although Kostons et al. (2012) used learning tasks on Mendel's laws of heredity, the same kind of learning environment can be used for other topics, for example grammar or spelling rules or probability calculus. The number of complexity levels as well as the number of instructional support levels within each complexity level depend on the topic, on the learning goals in a given context as well as on the type of learning tasks used.

Probability calculus as an example

Suppose, we want students to improve their probability calculus problem solving skills. Table 6.1 presents an example of a low-complexity learning task with high instructional support.

The task in Table 6.1 is a low-complexity learning task, because the probability asked is a *marginal* or *unconditional* probability: it is found by dividing the number of people who meet a single criterion (i.e., American) by the total number of people in the population that we draw from. The task is of a high level of instructional

TABLE 6.1 A low-complexity learning task on probability calculus with high instructional support

In a population of 500 people there are 200 Americans, 160 Canadians and 140 Mexicans. None of the 500 people has a double nationality. However, within each of the three nationality groups, there are people younger than 30 years, people in the age group 30–39 years, and people of age 40 years and older. The following table presents the situation.

	< 30 years	30–39 years	40 or older	
American	50	80	70	200
Canadian	45	55	60	160
Mexican	55	45	40	140
	150	180	170	500

If we randomly draw one person from this group of 500 people, what is the probability of drawing an American?

If we randomly draw one person from this group of 500 people, what is the probability of drawing an American?

Step 1:
   Question: What number do we put in the denominator?
   Answer: 500

Step 2:
   Question: What number do we put in the numerator?
   Answer: 200

Step 3:
   Question: What is the probability?
   Answer:

support, because the first two steps are already worked out, hence the learner only needs to divide numerator (200) by denominator (500) to find the probability that is asked. Working out only the first step and asking the learner to complete the remaining two steps would constitute a low(er)-support task, and having learners do all three steps by themselves would be a conventional, no-support, problem-solving task. Some might argue that we could identify four levels of instructional support: in a full support option, all three steps could be worked out. However, when the learners who are going to practice with tasks in our environment are familiar with the concepts of numerator and denominator there is no need for a fourth, full support option.

In the context of the task presented in Table 6.1, a second level of complexity is found in entering two criteria instead of a single criterion, for instance: what is the probability of drawing an American (first criterion) who is at least 40 years old (second criterion)? Although the denominator remains the same (500), given that only 70 people are both American and at least 40 years old, the numerator is 70. At a third level, we can introduce the concept of *conditional* probability: we no longer draw from the entire population (with one or two conditions in mind), but draw from only part of that population. As an example: what is the probability of drawing an American, if the person we draw is at least 40 years old? In this example, 'at least 40 years old' is the condition and 'American' constitutes the criterion we are looking for in the subpopulation of people that meet the condition. There are further ways to increase the complexity from this third level, but for the sake of simplicity let us focus on the three levels of complexity discussed thus far and assume three levels of instructional support for each of these complexity levels: the first two steps worked out (i.e., high support), only the first step worked out (i.e., low support), and none of the steps worked out (i.e., no support). This results in the environment depicted in Table 6.2.

In this example environment, the database has learning tasks on probability calculus at each of three levels of complexity (1: easiest; 2: a bit more complex; 3: most complex) and three levels of instructional support: in the case of 'No support', the learner will have to do the learning task themself; in the case of 'Low support', the learner will get some help; in the case of 'High support', the learner will get even more help. The learner can freely choose any learning task from the database with the only restriction that s/he can choose every learning task only once. Having completed the learning task chosen, the learner is asked some

TABLE 6.2 Probability calculus learning tasks at different levels of complexity and instructional support

	High support	Low support	No support
Complexity level 1	10 tasks available	10 tasks available	10 tasks available
Complexity level 2	10 tasks available	10 tasks available	10 tasks available
Complexity level 3	10 tasks available	10 tasks available	10 tasks available

questions on how the learning task went and what kind of learning task s/he would like to choose next. Once these questions have been answered, the learner can choose the next learning task. This process is repeated until the learner has completed eight learning tasks. After completing the eighth learning task and questions on how the learning task went and what kind of learning task the learner would like to choose next, the learner will complete a short test of six learning tasks that are similar to the learning tasks in the database (two from level 1, two from level 2, two from level 3) that s/he will have to complete autonomously (no support).

Experimental manipulation

The practice stage lends itself for experimental manipulation to improve task selection skills and the post-test can yield a performance measure that can be compared across conditions. In this setup, experimental manipulations can be based amongst others on the following: feedback on task performance (e.g., showing the correct answers for each step once a task has been completed or not), a checklist that prompts learners to self-assess their performance of the task just completed and/or how much effort was needed to complete the task (e.g., Kostons et al., 2012), a checklist with questions on what kind of task one would choose next, and feedback on the accuracy of task selection (i.e., is the task chosen with previous task performance?). Table 6.3 provides an example of a checklist that comprises both types of aforementioned questions.

The checklist presented in Table 6.3 is useful for several series of experiments on task selection depending on which questions are presented, whether they are presented in the presence or absence of one of the types of feedback mentioned previously or perhaps give advice instead of or in addition to feedback. An example of the latter would be to advise a learner to take a more challenging task (i.e., higher

TABLE 6.3 Example of a checklist that prompts learners to engage in self-regulated learning

Questions with regard to the learning task you just completed	
Which of the three steps took you effort?	• Step 1: Yes / No • Step 2: Yes / No • Step 3: Yes / No
Do you think you performed the task correctly?	• Yes • No, I think I made at least one error
What kind of learning task would you choose next?	
Complexity	• Level 1 (easiest) • Level 2 (a bit more complex) • Level 3 (most complex)
Support	• High support • Low support • No support

complexity or less instructional support on the same level of complexity) if the task just completed went well and took little effort, to take the same kind of task (i.e., same complexity and same kind of support) if the task just completed went well but took effort, and to take a less challenging task (i.e., lower complexity or more instructional support on the same level of complexity) if the task just completed did not go well (i.e., one or more errors).

Outcome measures

In the context of the aforementioned manipulations, there are several useful outcome measures: time taken for practice, time needed for post-test completion, the extent of complying to task selection advice, learning task and/or post-test performance (i.e., score) as well as learning task selection *accuracy* measured during the learning stage using actual task selection and/or during post-test (i.e., asking learners after each post-test task what kind of task they would choose next). Under the evidence-based assumption that selecting learning tasks within one's zone of proximal development results in higher learning outcomes (Corbalan et al., 2008; Kostons et al., 2012), we predict that more accurate learning task selection results in better post-test performance. Therefore, in the remainder of this chapter, we focus on the aforementioned Bias and Instability as measures of task selection accuracy that can be expected to positively correlate with post-test performance.

Bias and Instability as measures of task selection accuracy

With the exception of the first learning task selected, every time a learner selects a task we can evaluate that selection given the learner's performance on the task just completed. On the one hand, if a task is completed with one or more errors, the next task chosen by the learner in question may be less challenging or perhaps equally challenging but should preferably not be more challenging (i.e., not have a higher level of complexity or less instructional support on the same level of complexity) than the task just completed. On the other hand, if a task is completed without errors, the next task chosen by the learner may be more challenging or perhaps equally challenging but should preferably not be less challenging (i.e., not have a lower level of complexity or more instructional support on the same level of complexity). Regardless of whether the last task was completed correctly or with one of more errors, it could make sense to choose the same kind of task two times in a row. Even if a task went well, it may still have taken a learner much effort, due to a relatively high intrinsic cognitive load and/or some extraneous cognitive load due to ineffective problem-solving search. Or, a learner may have made an error (s)he expects to be able to avoid in a next round. However, to remain practicing the same kind of tasks for longer sequences despite consistently high performance may hint at underchallenge, and to remain practicing the same kind of tasks for longer sequences despite consistently low performance may hint at overchallenge (i.e., too high intrinsic cognitive load and/or extraneous cognitive load

TABLE 6.4 Overchallenge (+) and underchallenge (-) in learning task selection

	Last task completed correctly	Last task completed with one or more errors
Next task is more challenging	0	+1
Next task of same kind *	0 or -1	0 or +1
Next task is less challenging	-1	0

* If two times in a row the same kind of task: 0; if a third time in a row the same kind of task despite errors on two previous tasks: +1 (overchallenge); if a third time in a row the same kind of task despite two correctly performed previous tasks: -1 (underchallenge).

due to ineffective problem-solving search). An example of underchallenge (i.e., too low intrinsic cognitive load and/or increased extraneous cognitive load due to redundant support) is a not so motivated learner who consistently chooses low complexity (level 1) tasks with high instructional support in order to get through the session as fast as possible despite all or most of these tasks being completed correctly. An example of overchallenge is found in a learner who overestimates himself and consistently chooses the same medium (level 2) or high complexity (level 3) tasks despite consistent incorrect task performance. Table 6.4 summarises this reasoning and proposes a pragmatic coding scheme for empirical testing.

Given k learning tasks, we have k minus 1 objective moments of comparison (i.e., all except the first learning task); hence, with eight learning tasks, we have seven moments of comparison. At any of these seven moments, the choice of a given learner is coded '+1' (scenario 1: more challenging next task despite one or more errors in last task; scenario 2: three times in a row the same kind of task despite one or more errors in each of the last two tasks), '-1' (scenario 1: less challenging next task despite fully correct performance of the last task; scenario 2: three times in a row the same kind of task despite fully correct performance of the two last tasks), and 0 in all other cases, where positive scores indicate a tendency towards overchallenge and negative scores are indicative of a tendency towards underchallenge.

A comparison of three hypothetical learners

By way of example, let us have a look at three hypothetical learners – A, B, and C – who each show a different somewhat undesirable task selection behavior.

There are learners who are quite skilled in a topic but lack motivation to invest a lot of effort. Learner A is such a learner. All eight tasks chosen are of level 1 (easiest) with high support. However, all eight tasks are performed correctly. Hence, the task selection behavior of this learner is coded as follows: *second task choice*: '0' (second time same kind of task despite correct performance is acceptable); *third task choice*: '-1' (both first and second task were completed correctly, hence choosing the same kind of task again raises expectation of tendency towards underchallenge); *fourth task choice*: '-1' (more evidence for the underchallenge hypothesis); *fifth task* choice: '-1' (evidence for underchallenge continues to accumulate); *sixth task* choice: '-1' (and again more evidence for tendency towards underchallenge); *seventh task* choice: '-1' (still counting); and *eighth task* choice: '-1'. Total challenge score: -6.

Learner B is a typical case of a learner who consistently chooses complex tasks despite repeated incorrect task performance. Suppose, the first task chosen by learner B is of level 3 with high support, the second task is of level 3 and low support, and the third task is of level 3 with no support. In terms of performance, only the first task is performed correctly. Hence, the task selection behavior of this learner is coded as follows: *second task* choice: '0' (since the first task was performed correctly, choosing a slightly more challenging task appears justified); *third task* choice: '0' (choosing a more challenging task despite incorrect performance of the last task is not impossible, perhaps an error was recognized after task completion and the learner wants to practice with the same kind of task again); *fourth task* choice: '+1' (choosing the same kind of task despite errors in the last two tasks hints at overchallenge); *fifth task* choice: '+1' (more evidence for overchallenge); *sixth task* choice: '+1' (evidence for overchallenge continues to accumulate); *seventh task* choice: '+1' (again seemingly a tendency towards overchallenge); and *eighth task* choice: '+1'. Total challenge score: +5.

Learner C does not really have an idea how to choose the tasks and hence takes level 1, level 2 and level 3 tasks regardless of performance of tasks just completed. Table 6.5 provides an overview of how the task behavior of this learner is coded.

Given that the first task is performed with one or more errors, choosing a more challenging second task appears to hint at overchallenge ('+1'). Likewise, given that the second task is performed with one or more errors, choosing a more challenging third task hints at overchallenge ('+1'). Next, the third task is performed with one

TABLE 6.5 Example of overchallenge/underchallenge coding for a given learner (i.e., learner C)

	Type of task	*Performance*	*Coding*
First task	Level 1, high support	With error(s)	No previous task
Second task	Level 2, high support	With error(s)	+1
Third task	Level 3, high support	With error(s)	+1
Fourth task	Level 3, low support	With error(s)	+1
Fifth task	Level 2, low support	Correct	0
Sixth task	Level 2, high support	Correct	-1
Seventh task	Level 1, low support	Correct	-1
Eighth task	Level 1, high support	Correct	-1

or more errors, yet the fourth task chosen is more challenging and that again hints at overchallenge ('+1'). The fourth task is performed with one or more errors and the choice of a less challenging fifth task therefore makes sense ('0'). Given that the fifth task is performed correctly, choosing a less challenging sixth task appears to hint at underchallenge ('-1'). Given that the sixth task is performed correctly, choosing a less challenging seventh task hints at underchallenge ('-1'). Finally, given that the seventh task is performed correctly, choosing a less challenging eighth task also hints at underchallenge ('-1'). Hence, the total challenge score is 0, but there is some instability in task behavior here.

On the computation and interpretation of Bias and Instability

A variety of measures can be computed from the aforementioned -1/0/+1 coding scheme, some of which need longer sequences of tasks than other measures. However, generally speaking, the more task selection rounds are available for coding, the more accurate the measures. Two measures that are fairly easy to use are Bias or an average tendency towards underchallenge or overchallenge and Instability or the degree of dispersion around that tendency. Bias is obtained by dividing the total challenge score (i.e., the sum of '-1', '0' and '+1' across task selection rounds) by the number of task selection rounds (i.e., the number of coding moments):$Bias$ = total challenge score/number of task selection roundsBias can range from -1 (full underchallenge) to +1 (full overchallenge) and 0 would indicate neither tendency towards underchallenge nor tendency towards over-challenge. In our example, learner A has a strong tendency towards underchallenge (Bias = -6/7 ≈ -0.857), learner B has a strong tendency towards overchallenge (Bias = +5/7 ≈ +0.714), and learner C may have a weak tendency towards over-challenge (Bias = 0/7 = 0). Values in the range of |0–0.2|, |0.2–0.5|, and |0.5–1| are indicative of weak, moderate, and strong Bias, respectively.

Instability as a measure of dispersion around Bias can be found in the *mean absolute deviation* or the average deviation of scores around the Bias:$Instability$ = (Σ | coding − Bias|) / number of task selection roundsIn our example, that results in Instability values of 0.245 for learner A, 0.408 for learner B, and 0.857 for learner C. Instability can range from 0 (no dispersion at all, the same score for all task selection rounds) to 1, with values above 0.5 indicating clear Instability. The latter is the case for learner C: '+1', '+1', '+1', '0', '-1', '-1', and '-1' is a pattern that indicates this learner has no outspoken tendency towards underchallenge or over-challenge but perhaps has no idea what criteria to use for task selection and hence more often than not makes inappropriate choices.

For illustrative purposes, learners A, B, and C constitute rather extreme examples of strong tendency towards underchallenge (A), strong tendency towards over-challenge (B), and clear Instability (C). In the ideal case, both Bias and Instability are close to zero, although they do not need to be exactly zero. For instance, take a learner who obtained the following task selection scores: '+1', '0', '0', '0', '0', '0', and '0'. This results in a weak Bias, +1/7 ≈ +0.143, and a weak Instability, 0.245.

Note that with only seven task selection rounds, the Instability value cannot be closer to 0 than it is for this learner unless it is exactly 0. This also explains the recommendation to only interpret values above 0.5 indicating clear Instability. Moreover, Bias values in the range of $|0–0.2|$ (i.e., weak Bias) may not necessarily be problematic. One the one hand, some mild positive Bias may reflect a self-confidence or self-efficacy that aids learning. On the other hand, a mild negative Bias may reflect a healthy uncertainty on the part of the learner whether s/he has understood some of the basics that are needed to perform a particular task correctly other than by sheer chance.

The more task selection rounds are available for coding, the more accurate Bias and Instability. With only a few (e.g., fewer than five) coding rounds, Bias and Instability may not provide a lot of information at the level of the individual learner. That said, Bias and Instability can also be used at group level at any given task selection round, even if there are fewer than five task selection rounds. For instance, in randomised controlled experiments or regular classroom settings, groups may well consist of 20 or more individuals. Computing these measures at group level for each task selection round may then shed light on the extent to which Bias and Instability decrease with time, which would be desirable, and – of main interest in an experimental setting – to what extent the change in Bias and Instability with time differs across conditions. Methods that are more effective in helping learners improve their task selection skills are the ones that eventually should result in the lowest Bias and Instability.

Bias and Instability as potential predictors of poor post-test performance

Based on examples discussed previously, it becomes clear that when researchers and instructors are interested in fostering self-regulated learning, Bias and Instability – at the level of the individual learner across task selection rounds as well as at the level of a group for any task selection round – may provide useful learning outcome measures of task selection accuracy along with post-test performance. The latter remains an important outcome variable. However, Bias and Instability may provide useful insights into why some methods aimed at stimulating self-regulated learning are or are not successful under certain conditions. Bias and Instability scores further away from 0 reflect a more frequent choice of tasks that are not in a learner's zone of proximal development and that should translate in deteriorated learning and hence poorer post-test performance. In other words, Bias and Instability may to some extent explain both differences in post-test performance *between groups* as well as heterogeneity in post-test performance *within groups*. As such, they could be considered as potential mediator variables (i.e., mediating effects of experimental treatments on post-test performance).

Discussion

In times where the ability to accurately select one's own learning activities is considered very important, we need to work on methods that can facilitate the development of that skill. This chapter discusses the concept of checklists that prompt learners to self-assess their current performance and to reflect on what kind of task to select next as a means to practice task selection. Additionally, we need objective measures that can help learners and instructors to monitor a learner's task selection accuracy in order to provide feedback on that task selection. This chapter proposes two such measures: Bias or a tendency towards underchallenge or over-challenge, and Instability or a tendency to go back and forth between under-challenge and overchallenge. These measures can be used along with post-test performance as outcome measures in randomised controlled experiments to examine the effectiveness of different methods aimed at fostering the skill of task selection.

Future research may also shed light on the relation between Bias and Instability on the one hand and self-efficacy and over-/under-confidence on the other hand. Although moderate or strong Bias is unlikely to have positive effects on learning, that might be different for weak Bias; slight overconfidence (i.e., mild positive Bias) might positively affect learner motivation, and mild negative Bias might reflect a healthy uncertainty on the part of the learner concerning whether s/he has understood some basic concepts or steps. Moreover, the measures proposed in this chapter consider only performance on the last two tasks and sequences of three task selection rounds. An alternative approach would be to compute Bias and Instability based on longer task sequences and give more weight to the later tasks. Although the formulae for the computation of Bias and Instability would then become considerably more complex, empirical studies can help us gain insight in the added value of more complex measures.

In educational settings which include a component of online learning such as Massive Open Online Courses (MOOCs) or blended learning courses that combine face-to-face activities with self-study or practice in online learning environments, Bias and Instability could provide students, teachers, and instructional designers with useful learning process measures that may not only help to explain current learning but also inform subsequent learning. Learners who have a moderate or strong Bias towards underchallenge (i.e., Bias values in the -0.2 to -1 range) can be stimulated to try somewhat more challenging tasks as well. Learners who demonstrate a moderate or strong Bias towards overchallenge (i.e., Bias values in the 0.2 to 1 range) can be recommended to move ahead a bit more slowly. Finally, learners who demonstrate clear Instability (i.e., Instability values in the 0.5 to 1 range) can be advised to not move back and forth across more and less challenging tasks too quickly.

References

Aleven, V. A. W. M. M., & Koedinger, K. R. (2002). An effective metacognitive strategy: Learning by doing and explaining with a computer-based cognitive tutor. *Cognitive Science, 26*, 147–179. doi:10.1016/S0364-0213(02)00061-7.

Anderson, J. R., Corbett, A. T., Koedinger, K. R., & Pelletier, R. (1995). Cognitive tutors: Lessons learned. *Journal of the Learning Sciences, 4*, 167–207. doi:10.1207/s15327809jls0402_2.

Azevedo, R., & Cromley, J. G. (2004). Does training on self-regulated learning facilitate students' learning with hypermedia? *Journal of Educational Psychology, 96*, 523–535. doi:10.1037/0022-0663.96.3.523.

Bjork, R. A., Dunlosky, J., & Kornell, N. (2013). Self-regulated learning: Beliefs, techniques, and illusions. *Annual Review of Psychology, 64*, 417–444. doi:10.1146/annurev-psych-113011-143823.

Camp, G., Paas, F., Rikers, R., & Van Merriënboer, J. J. G. (2001). Dynamic problem selection in air traffic control training: A comparison between performance, mental effort and mental efficiency. *Computers in Human Behavior, 17*, 575–595. doi:10.1016/50747-5632(01)00028-0.

Corbalan, G., Kester, L., & van Merrienboer, J. (2008). Selecting learning tasks: Effects of adaptation and shared control on learning efficiency and task involvement. *Contemporary Educational Psychology, 33*, 733–756. doi:10.1016/j.cedpsych.2008.02.003.

Dunning, D., Heath, C., & Suls, J. M. (2004). Flawed self-assessment: Implications for health, education, and the workplace. *Psychological Science in the Public Interest, 5*, 69–106. doi:10.1111/j.1529-1006.2004.00018.x.

Dunning, D., Johnson, K., Ehrlinger, J., & Kruger, J. (2003). Why people fail to recognize their own incompetence. *Current Directions in Psychological Science, 12*, 83–87. doi:10.1111/1467-8721.01235.

Koedinger, K. R., Anderson, J. R., Hadley, W. H., & Mark, M. A. (1997). Intelligent tutoring goes to school in the big city. *International Journal of Artificial Intelligence in Education, 8*, 30–43.

Kostons, D., Van Gog, T., & Paas, F. (2010). Self-assessment and task selection in learner-controlled instruction: Differences between effective and ineffective learners. *Computers & Education, 54*, 932–940. doi:10.1016/j.compedu.2009.09.025.

Kostons, D., Van Gog, T., & Paas, F. (2012). Training self-assessment and task-selection skills: A cognitive approach to improving self-regulated learning. *Learning and Instruction, 22*, 122–132. doi:10.1016/j.learninstruc.2011.08.004.

Nelson, T. O., & Narens, L. (1990). Metamemory: A theoretical framework and new findings. In G. H. Bower (Ed.), *The psychology of learning and motivation* (pp. 125–173). New York: Academic Press.

Pintrich, P. R. (2000). Multiple goals, multiple pathways: The role of goal orientation in learning and achievement. *Journal of Educational Psychology, 92*, 544–555. doi:10.1037/0022-0663.92.3.544.

Raaijmakers, S. F., Baars, M., Schaap, L., Paas, F., Van Merriënboer, J. J. G., & Van Gog, T. (2018). Training self-regulated learning skills with video modeling examples: Do task-selection skills transfer? *Instructional Science, 46*, 273–290. doi:10.1007/s11251-017-9434-0.

Renkl, A., & Atkinson, R. K. (2003). Structuring the transition from example study to problem solving in cognitive skill acquisition: A cognitive load perspective. *Educational Psychologist, 38*, 15–22. doi:10.1207/S15326985EP3801_3.

Salden, R. J. C. M., Paas, F., Broers, N. J., & Van Merriënboer, J. J. G. (2004). Mental effort and performance as determinants for the dynamic selection of learning tasks in Air Traffic Control training. *Instructional Science, 32*, 153–172. doi:10.1023/B:TRUC.000002 1814.03996.ff.

Sitzmann, T., & Ely, K. (2011). A meta-analysis of self-regulated learning in work-related training and educational attainment: What we know and where we need to go. *Psychological Bulletin, 137*, 421–442. doi:10.1037/a0022777.

Sweller, J. (1988). Cognitive load during problem solving: Effects on learning. *Cognitive Science, 12*, 257–288. doi:10.1016/0364-0213(88)90023-7.

Sweller, J., Ayres, P., & Kalyuga, S. (2011). *Cognitive load theory*. New York: Springer.

Sweller, J., Van Merriënboer, J. J. G., & Paas, F. (1998). Cognitive architecture and instructional design. *Educational Psychology Review, 10*, 251–296. doi:10.1023/A:10221937 28205.

Van den Boom, G., Paas, F., & Van Merriënboer, J. J. G. (2007). Effects of elicited reflections combined with tutor or peer feedback on self-regulated learning and learning outcomes. *Learning and Instruction, 17*, 532–548. doi:10.1016/j.learninstruc.2007.09.003.

Van den Boom, G., Paas, F., Van Merriënboer, J. J. G., & Van Gog, T. (2004). Reflection prompts and tutor feedback in a web-based learning environment: Effects on students' self-regulated learning competence. *Computers in Human Behavior, 20*, 551–567. doi:10.1016/j.chb.2003.10.001.

Van Merriënboer, J. (1997). *Training complex cognitive skills*. Englewood Cliffs, NJ: Educational Technology Publications.

Van Merriënboer, J., & Kirschner, P. (2018). *Ten steps to complex learning* (3rd Rev Ed.). New York: Routledge.

Vygotsky, L. S. (1978). *Mind in society: The development of higher psychological processes*. Cambridge, MA: Harvard University Press.

Winne, P. H. (2001). Self-regulated learning viewed from models of information processing. In B. J. Zimmerman, & D. H. Schunk (Eds.), *Self-regulated learning and academic achievement: Theoretical perspectives* (pp. 153–189). Mahwah: Erlbaum.

Winne, P. H., & Hadwin, A. F. (1998). Studying as self-regulated learning. In D. Hacker, J. Dunlosky, & A. Graesser (Eds.), *Metacognition in educational theory and practice* (pp. 279–306). Hillsdale: Erlbaum.

Zimmerman, B. J. (1990). Self-regulated learning and academic achievement: An overview. *Educational Psychologist, 25*, 3–17. doi:10.1207/s15326985ep2501_2.

Zimmerman, B. J., & Schunk, D. H. (2001). *Self-regulated learning and academic achievement: Theoretical perspectives*. Mahwah: Erlbaum.

7

THE EFFECTS OF TRANSIENT INFORMATION AND ELEMENT INTERACTIVITY ON LEARNING FROM INSTRUCTIONAL ANIMATIONS

Mona Wong

FACULTY OF EDUCATION, THE UNIVERSITY OF HONG KONG, HONG KONG, HONG KONG

Juan C. Castro-Alonso

CENTER FOR ADVANCED RESEARCH IN EDUCATION (CIAE), UNIVERSIDAD DE CHILE, SANTIAGO, CHILE

Paul Ayres

SCHOOL OF EDUCATION, UNIVERSITY OF NEW SOUTH WALES, SYDNEY, AUSTRALIA

Fred Paas

DEPARTMENT OF PSYCHOLOGY, EDUCATION, AND CHILD STUDIES, ERASMUS UNIVERSITY ROTTERDAM, ROTTERDAM, THE NETHERLANDS; SCHOOL OF EDUCATION/EARLY START, UNIVERSITY OF WOLLONGONG, WOLLONGONG, AUSTRALIA

Animations, or dynamic visualisations, depict change in a visual format directly, which is potentially a major advantage over their equivalent static visualisations. However, animations may also have a negative learning effect, which has been termed the *transient information effect* in cognitive load theory. In brief, learning from a transient format (e.g. spoken text, animations, etc.) where information quickly disappears often demands more cognitive resources than learning from a permanent format (e.g. written text, static pictures, etc.). Any increases in cognitive load may be even higher if the learning materials are high in element interactivity. The main aim of this chapter is to discuss the potential influence of element interactivity on learning from transient visualisation formats (i.e., animations), and as a consequence provide more guidance on designing effective instructional animations.

There are four main sections to the chapter. First, a brief description of the transient information effect and animation as a source of transience is provided. Second, the definition of, and relationship between, element interactivity and information complexity is described. Third the inter-relationship between the transient information effect and element interactivity will be discussed. Fourth, the chapter will finish with suggestions and further directions in studying the intricate relationship between element interactivity and the transient information effect when learning from animations.

Animations and the transient information effect

As defined by Ayres, Castro-Alonso, Wong, Marcus, and Paas (2019), animations are visualisations composed of a series of static pictures shown in sequence at a high speed. They have great flexibility in depicting continuous physical and temporal changes, especially those relating to the learning of human movement (see, Ayres et al., 2019; Castro-Alonso, Ayres, & Paas, 2015; Paas & Sweller, 2012). Animations can enhance a learner's mental animation constructions as they do not require the transitions between static pictures to be mentally filled. By reducing the amount of extracting or imagining the changes (i.e. information extraction), animations can therefore lower a learner's cognitive load, leading to better schema construction and more understanding (Chandler, 2004; Paas, van Gerven, & Wouters, 2007; see also Bétrancourt & Tversky, 2000).

However, the dynamic nature of animations can lead to the transient information effect, which is detrimental to students' learning (Ayres & Paas, 2007; Castro-Alonso, Ayres, & Paas, 2014; Castro-Alonso, Ayres, Wong, & Paas, 2018). The transient information effect, as defined by Sweller, Ayres, and Kalyuga (2011, p. 220), is 'a loss of learning due to information disappearing before the learner has time to adequately process it or link it with new information'. In the case of animations, information on one frame will soon roll over to another frame and can be lost. Learners, when processing animations, are required to deal with a larger amount of information within a designated time limit in comparison to static pictures which are more permanent. Learners have to attend and identify changes, to store and process the information in their working memory, and to integrate the continuous stream of new information with the old information simultaneously (Ayres & Paas, 2007; Castro-Alonso et al., 2014; van Gog, Paas, Marcus, Ayres, & Sweller, 2009). According to cognitive load theory (see Sweller et al., 2011), such processing creates extraneous cognitive load (see Sweller, van Merriënboer, & Paas, 1998), which puts a heavy burden on our highly limited working memory. In other words, it takes precious working memory resources away from learning (schema construction) to deal with difficulties generated by the instructional design, and consequently inhibits learning. Evidence of transient effects has been found in modality research (see Leahy & Sweller, 2011) as well as studies comparing spoken text (a fundamental form of transient information) with the more permanent written text (Singh, Marcus, & Ayres, 2017).

Moreover, van Gog et al. (2009) proposed that the negative transient information effect from instructional animations may be reduced when learning about human movements, as such tasks tap into our innate motion-learning ability (human movement effect, for details see Paas & Sweller, 2012). This argument has been supported by a number of studies (e.g. Castro-Alonso et al., 2015; Marcus,

Cleary, Wong, & Ayres, 2013; Wong, Leahy, Marcus, & Sweller, 2012). It is argued that these human movement conditions might be a key factor in explaining why instructional animations are sometimes superior to their static equivalents (Paas & Sweller, 2012; Sweller et al., 2011, p. 222).

We believe the human movement argument is rather compelling, however, other explanations have been made. For example, Boucheix and Forestier (2017) proposed that the seemingly positive human movement effect might actually be a result of a negative *static-presentation effect*, in which participants expend extra cognitive load integrating the movement gap between each static picture. In other words, the negative transient information effect is not reduced by the human movement effect but overwhelmed by the negative static–presentation effect. Furthermore, Ganier and de Vries (2016) compared the effectiveness of picture + text, video + text, and video + audio in teaching sutures to medical students. The results showed that the video + text group outperformed the picture + text group only in earlier trials (trial 1–3) and starting from the fourth trial, the picture + text group outperformed the video + text group. It was concluded that animations only foster shallow mimicking without any deep processing engagement when learning complex human movement tasks.

Consequently, more studies are needed on human movement tasks to provide a clearer picture of the reasons why instructional animations may or may not be effective.

Information complexity and element interactivity

The complexity of a problem or a learning task depends on two factors: the nature of the information being processed and an individuals' prior knowledge. With respect to prior knowledge, as an example, for an expert mathematician, solving a differential equation is straightforward but for a school student who is learning basic algebra, it is extremely complex, if not impossible. In cognitive load theory, task difficulty/information complexity is determined by element interactivity. From a learning perspective, an element is the simplest form of a single learning item that needs to be learned or processed, or has been learned or processed (Chandler & Sweller, 1996; Sweller et al., 2011). Element interactivity (Sweller et al., 2011; Sweller & Chandler, 1994; Sweller et al., 1998) can be determined by counting the number of interacting elements that a person has to process simultaneously in working memory when dealing with new information. Indeed, some cognitive load theory studies have measured task complexity by counting the number of elements that are required to be memorised/learned in the learning tasks (e.g. Hanham, Leahy, & Sweller, 2017; van Gog & Sweller, 2015). Sometimes the elements can be learned or processed in isolation from each other, for example learning an alphabet, where element interactivity is considered low. However, if a large number of elements needs to be processed simultaneously (e.g. solving an advanced mathematics equation), then element interactivity is considered high, and the learning process becomes more demanding of working memory resources.

Learning tasks high in element interactivity are considered to have a high *intrinsic cognitive load* whereas those low in element interactivity have a low intrinsic cognitive load.

Consideration of element interactivity can explain why some new materials are more difficult to learn than others (Sweller & Chandler, 1994). Moreover, after a new schema is created consisting originally of a number of sub-elements that were previously treated individually but now form an integrated whole, retrieval of such information can be treated as one element in working memory rather than a series of individual items. Hence, element interactivity depends not only on the nature of the information being processed but also on learners' prior knowledge, which dictates how complex learners find the learning tasks (Sweller et al., 2011). As a result, it is essential to consider element interactivity when designing effective instructional materials such as animations.

Learning complex materials from animations

The transient nature of animations and the element interactivity of the task generate two different kinds of cognitive load. The former is extraneous cognitive load because it results from the instructional design and the latter is intrinsic cognitive load because it depends on the intrinsic nature of the learning tasks. Despite being independent of each other, the two loads will interact with each other and impact on working memory. Working memory resources will have to be expended on dealing with both the intrinsic and extraneous loads. If the information is low in element interactivity, learners may still be able to process and link the new information on the current frame with that in their existing schema thus dealing successfully with transient information. However, if the information is high in element interactivity, learners might need to expend excessive cognitive resources to process, or even fail to process, the information before it disappears, thus possibly not dealing successfully with transient information.

In comparison, a static picture may facilitate learning with high element interactivity materials because of its permanent nature which provides opportunities for learners to revisit the learning material and consequently lowers extraneous cognitive load. Leahy and Sweller (2011) tested the impact of transient information (transient spoken text format vs. permanent written text format) on complex information. They found a reversed modality effect when learning complex materials with a transient format (i.e. spoken form) but a normal modality effect (see Low & Sweller, 2014) with less transient information (i.e. written form). Leahy and Sweller (2011) argued that the load imposed by the transient nature of the presentation mode combined with complex learning materials was so large that it prevented the modality effect from occurring.

In regards to research investigating the interplay between element interactivity and the transient information effect, most of the studies have compared instructions using different modalities rather than only visualisation (e.g. Irrazabal, Saux, & Burin, 2016; Leahy & Sweller, 2011). Khacharem, Zoudji, and Kalyuga (2015) examined the effect of element interactivity (low vs. high) when learning soccer activity patterns using visualisations (animated vs. static). The results showed that there was a significant interaction effect where the static pictures group (i.e. low transient level) outperformed those in the animation group, when the learning materials were high in element interactivity. However, when the learning materials were low in element interactivity, there were no significant differences between the presentation formats.

Similarly, Boucheix and Forestier (2017) conducted two experiments with the aim to examine the impact of transiency levels when learning motor-related tasks (i.e. knot tying). Various factors were examined including visualisation formats (dynamic vs. static), section length (long vs. short) and levels of complexity (simple vs. complex). The results showed that participants learned more effectively using animations than static pictures with short sections rather than long sections. Furthermore, the interaction effect between the visualisation format and section length was stronger for the complex task than the simple task.

The studies reported in this section have shown that animations were inferior to their equivalent static visualisations when learning complex information despite the nature of the learning tasks (activity patterns or motor-related tasks). For less complex information, animations had a positive effect. These studies suggest that the level of transience of the instructional format and the element interactivity of the learning topics are both vital factors in animation studies.

Many studies investigating learning complex information from animations have tried to improve the presentation format by adding external features, such as cueing (e.g. de Koning, Tabbers, Rikers, & Paas, 2010), pedagogical agent/models (e.g. Hoogerheide, van Wermeskerken, Loyens, & van Gog, 2016; Lusk & Atkinson, 2007), or employing a segmentation strategy (e.g. Biard, Cojean, & Jamet, 2018; Wong et al., 2012). Some, but not all, have used such strategies deliberately to compensate for the transient nature of animations. Nevertheless, the focus has been on improving the effectiveness of the animations rather than dealing with high element interactivity, which has to some extent been ignored.

Educational implications and future research

Although the impact of an interaction between the transient information effect and element interactivity is still uncertain, a number of educational implications flow from the research dealing separately with the transient information effect and element interactivity.

As frequently pointed out in cognitive load theory research, instructional animations are not always effective as they contain transient information. Extraneous cognitive load can be generated by transient information and therefore additional strategies must be introduced to avoid this load, and the associated loss of working memory resources due to dealing with it. As suggested above, segmentation is one of the common strategies, where practitioners or material developers can divide the learning material into smaller segments to allow learners to process the transient information (Spanjers, van Gog, Wouters, & van Merriënboer, 2012). Also, adding spatial cues (e.g. pointing arrows), temporal cues or signals (e.g., highlighting) have been found to be effective strategies as they can guide learners' attention to important information at the right moment (de Koning et al., 2009, 2010, 2011). Practitioners should be cautious of these strategies when selecting suitable instructional animations, especially for learners who have lower spatial ability. Castro-Alonso, Ayres, Wong, and Paas (In press), have argued that learners' spatial ability also plays a role when learning from animations. In brief, learners with higher spatial ability have an advantage in extracting visual information from dynamic visualisations and as a consequence are able to construct better mental animations. Low spatial ability learners experience more problems with processing of transient information from dynamic visualisations, and consequently their learning is more likely to be negatively affected by transient information and positively affected by appropriately designed animations.

In addition, when learning complex materials (i.e. high in element interactivity), a high intrinsic cognitive load may be experienced, also leading to a loss of learning. Cognitive load theory has tested a number of strategies that can deal with a high intrinsic load. There is the isolating elements strategy (see Ayres, 2006, 2013; Pollock, Chandler, & Sweller, 2002), where the material is initially reduced to a smaller number of elements before the full interacting number of elements are introduced. Or there is pre-training, where prior-knowledge is built up before the more complex concepts are introduced (see Clarke, Ayres, & Sweller, 2005; Mayer, Mathias, & Wetzell, 2002). Instructional designers can apply both strategies to be implemented into an animated environment. A situation where a learner is faced with high extraneous and intrinsic load simultaneously, must be avoided at all costs.

In considering the potential interaction effect between the transient information effect and element interactivity, it is clear from our examination of the literature that there is little animation research that has varied the complexity of the learning materials. As shown in the interactions reported (see Boucheix & Forestier, 2017; Khacharem et al., 2015), task complexity impacts on the effectiveness of animations, as well as static pictures. If, as some studies suggest, animations are more helpful for low element interactivity materials, but not high element interactivity, then element interactivity must be a major design consideration. Certainly, more studies are needed to investigate this potential significant interaction. It is encouraging that strategies have been identified to deal with the transient nature of animations, but it may be equally important to reduce intrinsic cognitive load as well. A further discussion of the factors that impact the effectiveness of animations, can be found in Chapter 15.

Conclusion

To conclude, learning complex tasks (i.e., tasks that are high in element inter-activity) using animations, which are high in transience, is not an ideal condition, as it puts exceptionally high demands onto our limited working memory. Although animations have an advantage depicting changes, such advantage can easily be negated by the transient information effect. Equally, problem complexity can interfere with the effectiveness of animations. Both the transient information effect and element interactivity should be considered when using instructional animations. Furthermore, more research is required to investigate this crucial interaction.

References

Ayres, P. (2006). Using subjective measures to detect variations of intrinsic cognitive load within problems. *Learning and Instruction*, 16, 389–400.

Ayres, P. (2013). Can the isolated-elements strategy be improved by targeting points of high cognitive load for additional practice? *Learning and Instruction*, 23, 115–124. doi:10.1016/j.learninstruc.2012.08.002.

Ayres, P., Castro-Alonso, J. C., Wong, M., Marcus, N., & Paas, F. (2019). Factors that impact on the effectiveness of instructional animations. In S. Tindall-Ford, J. Sweller, & S. Agostinho (Eds.), *Advances in cognitive load theory: Rethinking teaching*. Australia: Routledge.

Ayres, P., & Paas, F. (2007). Making instructional animations more effective: A cognitive load approach. *Applied Cognitive Psychology*, 21, 695–700. doi:10.1002/acp.1343.

Bétrancourt, M., & Tversky, B. (2000). Effect of computer animation on users' performance: A review. *Le Travail Humain*, 63(4), 311–329.

Biard, N., Cojean, S., & Jamet, E. (2018). Effects of segmentation and pacing on procedural learning by video. *Computers in Human Behavior*, 89, 411–417. doi:10.1016/j.chb.2017.12.002.

Boucheix, J.-M., & Forestier, C. (2017). Reducing the transience effect of animations does not (always) lead to better performance in children learning a complex hand procedure. *Computers in Human Behavior*, 69, 358–370. doi:10.1016/j.chb.2016.12.029.

Castro-Alonso, J. C., Ayres, P., & Paas, F. (2014). Learning from observing hands in static and animated versions of non-manipulative tasks. *Learning and Instruction*, 34, 11–21. doi:10.1016/j.learninstruc.2014.07.005.

Castro-Alonso, J. C., Ayres, P., & Paas, F. (2015). The potential of embodied cognition to improve STEAM instructional dynamic visualizations. In X. Ge, D. Ifenthaler, & J. M. Spector (Eds.), *Emerging technologies for STEAM education: Full STEAM ahead* (pp. 113–136). New York, NY: Springer.

Castro-Alonso, J. C., Ayres, P., Wong, M., & Paas, F. (2018). Learning symbols from permanent and transient visual presentations: Don't overplay the hand. *Computers & Education*, 116, 1–13. doi:10.1016/j.compedu.2017.08.011.

Castro-Alonso, J. C., Ayres, P., Wong, M., & Paas, F. (2019). Visuospatial tests and multimedia learning: The importance of employing relevant instruments. In J. Sweller, S. Tindall-Ford, & S. Agostinho (Eds.), *Advances in cognitive load theory: Rethinking teaching*. Australia: Routledge.

Chandler, P. (2004). The crucial role of cognitive processes in the design of dynamic visualizations. *Learning and Instruction*, 14, 353–357.

Chandler, P., & Sweller, J. (1996). Cognitive load while learning to use a computer program. *Applied Cognitive Psychology*, 10(2), 151–170. doi:10.1002/(SICI)1099-0720(199604)10:2-151:AID-ACP380-3.0.CO;2-U.

Clarke, T., Ayres, P., & Sweller, J. (2005). The impact of sequencing and prior knowledge on learning mathematics through spreadsheet applications. *Educational Technology Research and Development*, 53(3), 15–24. doi:10.1007/bf02504794.

de Koning, B. B., Tabbers, H. K., Rikers, R. M. J. P., & Paas, F. (2009). Towards a framework for attention cueing in instructional animations: Guidelines for research and design. *Educational Psychology Review, 21*(2), 113–140. doi:10.1007/s10648-009-9098-7.

de Koning, B. B., Tabbers, H. K., Rikers, R. M. J. P., & Paas, F. (2010). Attention guidance in learning from a complex animation: Seeing is understanding? *Learning and Instruction, 20*(2), 111–122. doi:10.1016/j.learninstruc.2009.02.010.

de Koning, B. B., Tabbers, H. K., Rikers, R. M. J. P., & Paas, F. (2011). Attention cueing in an instructional animation: The role of presentation speed. *Computers in Human Behavior, 27*(1), 41–45. doi:10.1016/j.chb.2010.05.010.

Ganier, F., & de Vries, P. (2016). Are instructions in video format always better than photographs when learning manual techniques? The case of learning how to do sutures. *Learning and Instruction, 44*, 87–96. doi:10.1016/j.learninstruc.2016.03.004.

Hanham, J., Leahy, W., & Sweller, J. (2017). Cognitive load theory, element interactivity, and the testing and reverse testing effects. *Applied Cognitive Psychology, 31*, 265–280. doi:10.1002/acp.3324.

Hoogerheide, V., van Wermeskerken, M., Loyens, S. M. M., & van Gog, T. (2016). Learning from video modeling examples: Content kept equal, adults are more effective models than peers. *Learning and Instruction, 44*, 22–30. doi:10.1016/j.learninstruc.2016.02.004.

Irrazabal, N., Saux, G., & Burin, D. (2016). Procedural multimedia presentations: The effects of working memory and task complexity on instruction time and assembly accuracy. *Applied Cognitive Psychology, 30*(6), 1052–1060. doi:10.1002/acp.3299.

Khacharem, A., Zoudji, B., & Kalyuga, S. (2015). Perceiving versus inferring movements to understand dynamic events: The influence of content complexity. *Psychology of Sport and Exercise, 19*, 70–75. doi:10.1016/j.psychsport.2015.03.004.

Leahy, W., & Sweller, J. (2011). Cognitive load theory, modality of presentation and the transient information effect. *Applied Cognitive Psychology, 25*(6), 943–951. doi:10.1002/acp.1787.

Low, R., & Sweller, J. (2014). The modality principle in multimedia learning. In R. E. Mayer (Ed.), *The Cambridge handbook of multimedia learning* (2nd ed., pp. 227–246). New York, NY: Cambridge University Press.

Lusk, M. M., & Atkinson, R. K. (2007). Animated pedagogical agents: Does their degree of embodiment impact learning from static or animated worked examples? *Applied Cognitive Psychology, 21*, 747–764. doi:10.1002/acp.1347.

Marcus, N., Cleary, B., Wong, A., & Ayres, P. (2013). Should hand actions be observed when learning hand motor skills from instructional animations? *Computers in Human Behavior, 29*, 2172–2178.

Mayer, R. E., Mathias, A., & Wetzell, K. (2002). Fostering understanding of multimedia messages through pre-training: evidence for a two-stage theory of mental model construction. *Journal of Experimental Psychology: Applied, 8*(3), 147–154.

Paas, F., & Sweller, J. (2012). An evolutionary upgrade of cognitive load theory: Using the human motor system and collaboration to support the learning of complex cognitive tasks. *Educational Psychology Review, 24*, 27–45. doi:10.1007/s10648-011-9179-2.

Paas, F., van Gerven, P. W. M., & Wouters, P. (2007). Instructional efficiency of animation: Effects of interactivity through mental reconstruction of static key frames. *Applied Cognitive Psychology, 21*, 783–793. doi:10.1002/acp.1349.

Pollock, E., Chandler, P., & Sweller, J. (2002). Assimilating complex information. *Learning and Instruction, 12*, 61–86. doi:10.1016/S0959-4752(01)00016-0.

Singh, A.-M., Marcus, N., & Ayres, P. (2017). Strategies to reduce the negative effects of spoken explanatory text on integrated tasks. *Instructional Science, 45*(2), 239–261. doi:10.1007/s11251-016-9400-2.

Spanjers, I. A. E., van Gog, T., Wouters, P., & van Merriënboer, J. J. G. (2012). Explaining the segmentation effect in learning from animations: The role of pausing and temporal cueing. *Computers & Education, 59*(2), 274–280. doi:10.1016/j.compedu.2011.12.024.

Sweller, J., Ayres, P., & Kalyuga, S. (2011). *Cognitive load theory*. New York, NY: Springer.

Sweller, J., & Chandler, P. (1994). Why some material is difficult to learn. *Cognition and Instruction, 12*(3), 185–233.

Sweller, J., van Merriënboer, J. J. G., & Paas, F. (1998). Cognitive architecture and instructional design. *Educational Psychology Review, 10*, 251–296. doi:10.1023/A:1022193728205.

van Gog, T., Paas, F., Marcus, N., Ayres, P., & Sweller, J. (2009). The mirror neuron system and observational learning: Implications for the effectiveness of dynamic visualizations. *Educational Psychology Review, 21*, 21–30. doi:10.1007/s10648-008-9094-3.

van Gog, T., & Sweller, J. (2015). Not new, but nearly forgotten: The testing effect decreases or even disappears as the complexity of learning materials increases. *Educational Psychology Review, 27*(2), 247–264. doi:10.1007/s10648-015-9310-x.

Wong, A., Leahy, W., Marcus, N., & Sweller, J. (2012). Cognitive load theory, the transient information effect and e-learning. *Learning and Instruction, 22*(6), 449–457. doi:10.1016/j.learninstruc.2012.05.004.

8

VISUOSPATIAL TESTS AND MULTIMEDIA LEARNING

The importance of employing relevant instruments

Juan C. Castro-Alonso

CENTER FOR ADVANCED RESEARCH IN EDUCATION (CIAE), UNIVERSIDAD DE CHILE, SANTIAGO, CHILE

Paul Ayres

SCHOOL OF EDUCATION, UNIVERSITY OF NEW SOUTH WALES, SYDNEY, AUSTRALIA

Mona Wong

FACULTY OF EDUCATION, THE UNIVERSITY OF HONG KONG, HONG KONG, HONG KONG

Fred Paas

DEPARTMENT OF PSYCHOLOGY, EDUCATION, AND CHILD STUDIES, ERASMUS UNIVERSITY ROTTERDAM, ROTTERDAM, THE NETHERLANDS; SCHOOL OF EDUCATION/EARLY START, UNIVERSITY OF WOLLONGONG, WOLLONGONG, AUSTRALIA

According to the multicomponent model of working memory (see Baddeley, 1992) there is a *visuospatial* subprocessor in working memory. This component allows visual and spatial information to be recognised, generated, and transformed (see McGrew, 2009; Ness, Farenga, & Garofalo, 2017), and is therefore fundamental to learning from multimedia and instructional visualisations (e.g., Höffler, 2010; Schüler, Scheiter, & van Genuchten, 2011). Consequently, students' ability to learn in demanding instructional multimedia environments is positively related to their visuospatial skill (e.g., Bartholomé & Bromme, 2009; Castro-Alonso, Ayres, Wong, & Paas, 2018).

There are five main aims of this review chapter. Firstly, to show that there are different tests to measure the different processing abilities of the visuospatial component of working memory. Secondly, to provide evidence testing the hypothesis that these visuospatial processing abilities help learning from visualisations and multimedia materials. Thirdly, to show that these abilities are particularly important in multi-media learning conditions imposing a high load on working memory (i.e., high cognitive load). Fourthly, to provide examples of studies based on the match between the chosen visuospatial tests and the actual multimedia learning tasks. Lastly, to argue for the need to investigate direct links between different visuospatial abilities and particular multimedia learning tasks, and to present a battery of visuospatial tests that could help in investigating these links.

Visuospatial processing

Two different research traditions have measured performance of the visuospatial processor of working memory: (a) the psychometric tradition using standard spatial ability tests (e.g., Michael, Guilford, Fruchter, & Zimmerman, 1957), and (b) the working memory tradition with tests employing visuospatial stimuli (e.g., Milner, 1971). We consider both traditions in this chapter as examples of *visuospatial processing*.

Psychometric tradition

From the psychometric approach, we found the *mental rotation* and *mental folding* tasks as the most investigated measures related to multimedia learning studies. Mental rotation is the ability to perceive an object or figure and being capable of rotating it mentally (e.g., Ekstrom, French, Harman, & Dermen, 1976). The instruments that measure mental rotation involve 2D (two-dimensional) or 3D (three-dimensional) tasks. A standard test measuring 2D mental rotations is the *Card Rotations Test*, originally developed by Ekstrom et al. (1976). It includes items where one abstract shape must be compared to eight different depictions positioned alongside, to determine which are rotated and which are rotated and reflected (mirror images) versions. Two common instruments to measure 3D mental rotations are the *Mental Rotations Test* and the *Cube Comparisons* Test. The Mental Rotations Test was originally developed by Vandenberg and Kuse (1978). For every item of the test, an abstract 3D shape as a "Tetris block" must be compared to four different versions positioned alongside, to determine which are rotated and which are rotated and reflected. The Cube Comparisons Test, produced by Ekstrom et al. (1976), requires the comparison of two cubes with different letters on their faces, to gauge whether both cubes are rotated depictions of each other or if they are different cubes.

Mental folding, also known as spatial visualisation, is an ability that relies partially on mental rotation but also uses the additional resources of mental restructuring and serial operations (e.g., Ekstrom et al., 1976). Two standard instruments that measure mental folding are the *Paper Folding Test* and the *Surface Development Test*, and both are included in the tests developed by Ekstrom et al. (1976). The Paper Folding Test contains items showing a sequence of folds made to a sheet of paper and then a puncture hole made to this folded sheet. It must then be judged how the holes would look when the paper is completely unfolded. For every item of the Surface Development Test, the participants must imagine how a 2D figure would fold into a given 3D volumetric shape.

Working memory tradition

The customary measure of the working memory tradition uses a *dual task methodology* (see Britton & Tesser, 1982), which requires a memorisation of a primary task interrupted by a secondary processing task. In the case of visuospatial dual complex tasks, visuospatial elements must be memorised in the order shown, while answering visuospatial processing questions that hinder recalling the memorised stimuli. Two examples are the *Symmetry Span Test* and the *Rotation Span Test*. In the Symmetry Span Test (e.g., Kane et al., 2004), the memory task involves remembering the location of a filled square from a pattern of remaining empty squares. The processing task requires deciding if other shape patterns are symmetrical or asymmetrical. For the Rotation Span Test (e.g., Shah & Miyake, 1996), the memory stimuli are arrows indicating different rotations, sometimes of different lengths. The processing task involves determining if rotated capital letters are in their normal positions or mirror reversed.

Both the psychometric and the working memory traditions include visuospatial processing tests whose scores tend to be correlated with each other (e.g., Hegarty & Waller, 2004; Miyake, Friedman, Rettinger, Shah, & Hegarty, 2001). As such, all these abilities can be beneficial when learning from instructional visualisations and multimedia, as described next.

Multimedia learning and visuospatial processing

As defined by Mayer (2001), multimedia learning involves processing verbal and visuospatial information in working memory. This implies that both verbal and visuospatial contents are integrated in working memory to comprehend the learning material (see *referential connections* of dual coding theory in Clark & Paivio, 1991). The visuospatial part of multimedia can be presented as instructional static or dynamic visualisations (e.g., animations, videos, simulations). Learning from these visual components (visualisations) of multimedia demands visuospatial processing (see Schüler et al., 2011). Therefore, as indicated in the introduction, we can test the hypothesis that when learning from visualisations alone or multimedia materials, students with higher visuospatial processing abilities would outperform their lower visuospatial peers. Independent of verbal abilities, higher visuospatial processing would allow students to manage better the visualisations included in multimedia presentations. The following examples provide evidence for this hypothesis.

Bartholomé and Bromme (2009) investigated 84 university participants (77% females) learning from a multimedia presentation about botany. A total spatial ability was calculated by combining the scores of several instruments, including a mental rotation test. This aggregated score was significantly correlated with multimedia learning performance. Loftus, Jacobsen, and Wilson (2017) investigated 29 adult participants (35% females) learning anatomy through different visualisations. A median split of the sample was based on the scores of the Mental Rotations Test.

The higher scorers in this 3D mental rotation test outperformed their lower counterparts in solving different human anatomy tasks. Castro-Alonso, Ayres, Wong, and Paas (2018) assessed the performance of 104 university students (50% females) on memory location tasks with coloured symbols, in both static and animated formats. Multiple regression analyses showed that mental rotation could predict performance on both static and animated presentations, and that there was a close to significant trend of visuospatial working memory predicting performance on the animated task.

Altogether, these findings support the given hypothesis, as students with lower visuospatial processing tend to be challenged by learning from multimedia materials. Hence, a careful design of the visuospatial elements in instructional multimedia is needed to benefit learning, particularly for low visuospatial students. Cognitive load theory provides some guidelines on how to effectively design multimedia materials to assist all learners, including those with low visuospatial processing abilities.

Cognitive load theory and visuospatial processing

Cognitive load theory (see Sweller, Ayres, & Kalyuga, 2011) is an instructional theory that employs knowledge of human cognitive architecture to design effective instructional procedures and materials. One critical foundation assumption of the theory is that working memory is limited in capacity and unable to deal with many elements of novel information, shown simultaneously or sequentially (e.g., Cowan, 2001). There is a distinction between *intrinsic cognitive load* and *extraneous cognitive load* (see Sweller, 2010). Intrinsic cognitive load depends on how many essential simultaneous or sequential learning elements the task involves while extraneous cognitive load depends on the number of non-essential learning elements involved where non-essential elements are determined by instructional design. The more learning elements, the higher the intrinsic or extraneous cognitive load of the task. Consequently, learning is often impeded in these cases of high cognitive load in which too much information needs to be processed at the same time (see Chandler & Sweller, 1991). In the specific case of visuospatial processing, the same situation arises: it is difficult for learners to cope with the simultaneous or sequential processing of too many visuospatial elements (e.g., Luck & Vogel, 1997). Moreover, those learners showing less visuospatial processing capacity would be unable to process as many elements as those with a higher processing capacity, and thus would be disadvantaged (e.g., Castro-Alonso, Ayres, Wong, & Paas, 2018).

As indicated above, the extraneous load depends on how the educational material was designed. Research based on cognitive load theory has identified some strategies that can reduce the extraneous cognitive load of multimedia materials (see also Chapter 15), which are particularly helpful for the more disadvantaged lower capacity visuospatial students. For example, (a) diagrams and text are integrated together to avoid *split-attention* effects (see Ayres & Sweller,

2014), (b) different sources of information do not repeat the same information to avoid *redundancy* (see Kalyuga & Sweller, 2014), and (c) *signalling* of key information makes it easier for learners to find important information (see van Gog, 2014).

As described, there are some clear strategies to avoid raising cognitive load in multimedia presentations, which could be particularly suitable for low visuospatial ability learners (see also Chapter 7). This again shows a link between visuospatial processing abilities and multimedia learning. We argue next that this link needs further investigation, as not all visuospatial processing tests seem to be equally fitted to measure all visualisation and multimedia learning tasks.

Relations between visuospatial tests and multimedia learning tasks

The diversity of tests presented above suggests that there are a number of instruments that can identify different visuospatial aspects that influence multimedia learning. However, there is a research gap in how these aspects relate to the different learning tasks or cognitive load of multimedia materials (cf. Kirschner, Ayres, & Chandler, 2011). For example, there is no conclusive answer yet to explain why scoring high on the Card Rotations Test specifically helps learning from multimedia materials. The following examples from the multimedia learning literature show cases in which the standard tests of mental rotation, mental folding, and dual complex tasks were poorly related to learning tasks. In contrast, we also provide examples of a more direct link between specific tests and multimedia learning tasks.

Visuospatial tests poorly related to the learning tasks

In their second experiment, Mayer and Sims (1994) investigated 97 university participants studying animations about the human respiratory system. Findings indicated that higher spatial ability students outperformed lower spatial participants on a transfer test. Münzer, Seufert, and Brünken (2009) investigated 94 students (77% females) learning about the synthesis of the ATP macromolecule from different multimedia conditions. In the design with static images and motion arrows, spatial ability predicted gains in process knowledge about this biology topic. In these two examples, a 2D mental rotation instrument (the Card Rotations Test) and a mental folding instrument (the Paper Folding Test) were used to calculate an aggregated score of spatial ability. In these studies, which both found positive correlations between visuospatial ability and performance, it is difficult to explain why there is a direct link between mentally rotating 2D images, mentally folding papers, and understanding the biological processes of human respiration and molecule syntheses. As such, following the air movement from the nose to the lungs (Mayer & Sims, 1994) or the visual processes to develop the ATP macromolecule (Münzer et al., 2009) are not the same processes as those involved in rotating and folding abstract shapes.

In the third experiment of Kozhevnikov, Motes, and Hegarty (2007), university students with higher mental folding scores outperformed students with lower mental folding scores in solving kinematic graph problems of velocity. Similarly, an experiment with 198 university participants (76% females) by Kühl, Stebner, Navratil, Fehringer, and Münzer (2018) showed the importance of mental folding for learning about the velocity of planets orbiting the sun from static visualisations. Paik and Schraw (2013) investigated 65 psychology undergraduates (75% females) learning a toilet flushing system from different static and animated depictions. For all types of visualisations, mental folding had a significant effect on the overall retention scores. In these three reports, mental folding was measured with the Paper Folding Test. It is not evident how the ability to imagine folding and unfolding papers can be related to understanding distance vs. time graphs (Kozhevnikov et al., 2007), planetary velocity in elliptical orbits (Kühl et al., 2018), and the movement of water in a toilet tank (Paik & Schraw, 2013).

Hambrick et al. (2012) reported a study with 67 adult participants (46% females) attempting to determine the structure of a mountain area. Participants were assessed in six tests of visuospatial processing, including 3D mental rotation, mental folding, and dual complex tasks with visuospatial stimuli. An aggregated visuospatial score was calculated from these tests. It was observed that, for novices in geological knowledge, the visuospatial composite score was a significant predictor of their performance. However, it is again difficult to find a direct link between the abilities to mentally rotate, fold, and perform dual tasking with visuospatial stimuli, and being able to cope with tasks involving maps and geological instruments.

Visuospatial tests more related to the learning tasks

In a study with 54 university students (78% females), Münzer, Fehringer, and Kühl (2018) investigated the relationship between a 3D mental rotation instrument (the Mental Rotations Test) and an architecture task involving the mental rotations of single-floor blueprints. Both tasks were largely correlated ($r = .50$, $p < .001$), and the test explained 20% of the variance for the architecture task. The study by Nguyen, Nelson, and Wilson (2012) compared 60 adult participants (52% females) learning anatomical structures through either a video or six static images. The participants were assessed in 3D mental rotation with a computer version of the Mental Rotations Test. To measure anatomy learning, a computer instrument was developed, which involved identification of 2D cross-sections and mental rotation of the anatomical structures. The participants scoring high in the Mental Rotations Test outperformed lower mental rotators in the computer anatomy tests, but this effect was only observed in the video condition, as there were no differences in anatomy performance after studying the static images. In a follow-up work, Nguyen, Mulla, Nelson, and Wilson (2014) reported that 42 university students (57% females) showed a large positive correlation ($r = .72$, $p < .001$) between the computer anatomy test scores and the Mental Rotation Test scores. As can be observed in these three examples, the spatial ability instrument, which measures 3D mental rotation, is aligned with the learning tasks, which also relied on mental rotations.

Garland and Sanchez (2013) studied 80 undergraduates learning three knots from different visualisations. 3D mental rotation was measured with the Cube Comparisons Test, and mental folding was measured with the Surface Development Test. However, spatial abilities failed to predict performance in the knot tasks. Despite this lack of significant results, this is another example of a direct connection of the processing requirements for the visuospatial tests and the learning tasks, as both the tests and knot tying involved mental rotation and mental folding.

Discussion

As presented above, the various instruments used to measure visuospatial processing do not always have a direct relation to the processes depicted in the instructional presentations. It is difficult to align paper folding tasks, for example, with the learning of various science topics from instructional visualisations. Researchers may have assumed that these measures tap into general visuospatial processing that is relevant to the learning content, but this argument is generally not made and future research could investigate with a higher detail what aspect of visuospatial processing is better aligned with certain multimedia and visuospatial content.

Main educational implications

Due to the relationship between visuospatial processing and multimedia learning, an important educational implication is that multimedia designers and teachers need to carefully align their materials with the visuospatial abilities of the learners. For example, lowering cognitive load by avoiding split-attention (e.g., Huff & Schwan, 2011) and redundancy (e.g., Korbach, Brünken, & Park, 2016) can be particularly effective for low visuospatial processing students. In addition, multimedia could be adaptive (cf. Plass, Homer, & Kinzer, 2015) and adjust its cognitive load to the visuospatial processing levels of the learners. Alternatively, some remedial strategies could be geared towards raising the ability of learners with low levels, such as spatial training (see Stieff & Uttal, 2015; Uttal et al., 2013). As another alternative, a more tailored approach of developing specific visuospatial processing abilities that are highly relevant to learning certain tasks could be used. Multimedia designers and teachers could concentrate on training only this specific ability for the intended learning purpose, thus optimising learning time and resources. As all these solutions involve measuring visuospatial processing, we describe next a battery of tests that could help in these assessments.

A flexible approach to measure visuospatial processing

We have showed that not all studies displaying connections between multimedia learning and visuospatial processing can predict which aspects of visuospatial processing support learning in these scenarios. However, a battery of computer-based visuospatial tests has been recently developed (see Castro-Alonso, Ayres, & Paas, 2018) which may enable closer matching between visuospatial ability testing and the content of instructional presentations. In general, computer instruments (unlike pen-and-paper designs), allow different versions of the tests to be produced (see Berch, Krikorian, & Huha, 1998), so changing different aspects of a test can be investigated. Two examples of this versatility, provided in the battery by Castro-Alonso, Ayres, and Paas (2018), are: (a) the 2D mental rotation test can incorporate novel shapes that can be altered in their rotation; and (b) there are six different dual complex tasks, which can be formed by combining two different visuospatial memory tasks (Rotated Arrows and Matrix Positions) and three different visuospatial processing tasks (Letter Rotations, Symmetry Patterns, and Visual Equations). We argue that this flexible battery and similar future efforts with multiple tests of visuospatial processing could lead to a better understanding of the links between certain visuospatial abilities and different multimedia learning tasks and designs.

Conclusion

Visuospatial processing is part of working memory processing. It is not a single construct but includes many different visuospatial abilities, such as mental rotation, mental folding, dual complex tasking, and multimedia learning. Due to these relationships, we hypothesise that students showing lower scores in standard tests of visuospatial processing will also be disadvantaged when learning from multimedia modules and visualisations. In particular for these learners, more effective multimedia designs, such as those following cognitive load theory principles, should be pursued. Furthermore, evidence exists that researchers have not always applied the most appropriate visuospatial tests when investigating the impact of visuospatial processing on learning outcomes. Future research could develop more appropriate tests which could inform researchers and practitioners which specific visuospatial tests should be used in a certain multimedia learning environment.

References

Ayres, P., & Sweller, J. (2014). The split-attention principle in multimedia learning. In R. E. Mayer (Ed.), *The Cambridge handbook of multimedia learning* (2nd ed., pp. 206–226). New York, NY: Cambridge University Press. doi:10.1017/CBO9781139547369.011.

Baddeley, A. (1992). Working memory. *Science*, 255(5044), 556–559.

Bartholomé, T., & Bromme, R. (2009). Coherence formation when learning from text and pictures: What kind of support for whom? *Journal of Educational Psychology*, 101(2), 282–293. doi:10.1037/a0014312.

Berch, D. B., Krikorian, R., & Huha, E. M. (1998). The Corsi block-tapping task: Methodological and theoretical considerations. *Brain and Cognition*, 38(3), 317–338. doi:10.1006/brcg.1998.1039.

Britton, B. K., & Tesser, A. (1982). Effects of prior knowledge on use of cognitive capacity in three complex cognitive tasks. *Journal of Verbal Learning and Verbal Behavior, 21*(4), 421–436. doi:10.1016/S0022-5371(82)90709-90705.

Castro-Alonso, J. C., Ayres, P., & Paas, F. (2018). Computerized and adaptable tests to measure visuospatial abilities in STEM students. In T. Andre (Ed.), *Advances in human factors in training, education, and learning sciences: Proceedings of the AHFE 2017 International Conference on Human Factors in Training, Education, and Learning Sciences* (pp. 337–349). Cham, Switzerland: Springer. doi:10.1007/978-3-319-60018-5_33.

Castro-Alonso, J. C., Ayres, P., Wong, M., & Paas, F. (2018). Learning symbols from permanent and transient visual presentations: Don't overplay the hand. *Computers & Education*, 116, 1–13. doi:10.1016/j.compedu.2017.08.011.

Chandler, P., & Sweller, J. (1991). Cognitive load theory and the format of instruction. *Cognition and Instruction*, 8(4), 293–332.

Clark, J., & Paivio, A. (1991). Dual coding theory and education. *Educational Psychology Review*, 3(3), 149–210. doi:10.1007/bf01320076.

Cowan, N. (2001). The magical number 4 in short-term memory: A reconsideration of mental storage capacity. *Behavioral and Brain Sciences*, 24(1), 87–185. doi:10.1017/S0140525X01003922.

Ekstrom, R. B., French, J. W., Harman, H. H., & Dermen, D. (1976). *Kit of factor-referenced cognitive tests*. Princeton, NJ: Educational Testing Service.

Garland, T. B., & Sanchez, C. A. (2013). Rotational perspective and learning procedural tasks from dynamic media. *Computers & Education*, 69, 31–37. doi:10.1016/j.compedu.2013.06.014.

Hambrick, D. Z., Libarkin, J. C., Petcovic, H. L., Baker, K. M., Elkins, J., Callahan, C. N., … LaDue, N. D. (2012). A test of the circumvention-of-limits hypothesis in scientific problem solving: The case of geological bedrock mapping. *Journal of Experimental Psychology: General*, 141(3), 397–403. doi:10.1037/a0025927.

Hegarty, M., & Waller, D. (2004). A dissociation between mental rotation and perspective-taking spatial abilities. *Intelligence*, 32(2), 175–191. doi:10.1016/j.intell.2003.12.001.

Höffler, T. N. (2010). Spatial ability: Its influence on learning with visualizations—a meta-analytic review. *Educational Psychology Review*, 22(3), 245–269. doi:10.1007/s10648-10010-9126-9127.

Huff, M., & Schwan, S. (2011). Integrating information from two pictorial animations: Complexity and cognitive prerequisites influence performance. *Applied Cognitive Psychology*, 25(6), 878–886. doi:10.1002/acp.1762.

Kalyuga, S., & Sweller, J. (2014). The redundancy principle in multimedia learning. In R. E. Mayer (Ed.), *The Cambridge handbook of multimedia learning* (2nd ed., pp. 247–262). New York, NY: Cambridge University Press. doi:10.1017/CBO9781139547369.013.

Kane, M. J., Hambrick, D. Z., Tuholski, S. W., Wilhelm, O., Payne, T. W., & Engle, R. W. (2004). The generality of working memory capacity: A latent-variable approach to verbal and visuospatial memory span and reasoning. *Journal of Experimental Psychology: General*, 133(2), 189–217. doi:10.1037/0096-3445.133.2.189.

Kirschner, P. A., Ayres, P., & Chandler, P. (2011). Contemporary cognitive load theory research: The good, the bad and the ugly. *Computers in Human Behavior*, 27(1), 99–105. doi:10.1016/j.chb.2010.06.025.

Korbach, A., Brünken, R., & Park, B. (2016). Learner characteristics and information processing in multimedia learning: A moderated mediation of the seductive details effect. *Learning and Individual Differences*, 51, 59–68. doi:10.1016/j.lindif.2016.08.030.

Kozhevnikov, M., Motes, M. A., & Hegarty, M. (2007). Spatial visualization in physics problem solving. *Cognitive Science, 31*(4), 549–579. doi:10.1080/15326900701399897.

Kühl, T., Stebner, F., Navratil, S. C., Fehringer, B. C. O. F., & Münzer, S. (2018). Text information and spatial abilities in learning with different visualizations formats. *Journal of Educational Psychology*, 110(4), 561–577. doi:10.1037/edu0000226.

Loftus, J. J., Jacobsen, M., & Wilson, T. D. (2017). Learning and assessment with images: A view of cognitive load through the lens of cerebral blood flow. *British Journal of Educational Technology*, 48(4), 1030–1046. doi:10.1111/bjet.12474.

Luck, S. J., & Vogel, E. K. (1997). The capacity of visual working memory for features and conjunctions. *Nature, 390*(6657), 279–281. doi:10.1038/36846.

Mayer, R. E. (2001). *Multimedia learning*. New York, NY: Cambridge University Press.

Mayer, R. E., & Sims, V. K. (1994). For whom is a picture worth a thousand words? Extensions of a dual-coding theory of multimedia learning. *Journal of Educational Psychology, 86*(3), 389–401. doi:10.1037/0022-0663.86.3.389.

McGrew, K. S. (2009). CHC theory and the human cognitive abilities project: Standing on the shoulders of the giants of psychometric intelligence research. *Intelligence*, 37(1), 1–10. doi:10.1016/j.intell.2008.08.004.

Michael, W. B., Guilford, J. P., Fruchter, B., & Zimmerman, W. S. (1957). The description of spatial-visualization abilities. *Educational and Psychological Measurement, 17*(2), 185–199. doi:10.1177/001316445701700202.

Milner, B. (1971). Interhemispheric differences in the localization of psychological processes in man. *British Medical Bulletin*, 27(3), 272–277.

Miyake, A., Friedman, N. P., Rettinger, D. A., Shah, P., & Hegarty, M. (2001). How are visuospatial working memory, executive functioning, and spatial abilities related? A latent-variable analysis. *Journal of Experimental Psychology: General*, 130(4), 621–640. doi:10.1037//0096-3445.130.4.621.

Münzer, S., Fehringer, B. C. O. F., & Kühl, T. (2018). Specificity of mental transformations involved in understanding spatial structures. *Learning and Individual Differences*, 61, 40–50. doi:10.1016/j.lindif.2017.11.004.

Münzer, S., Seufert, T., & Brünken, R. (2009). Learning from multimedia presentations: Facilitation function of animations and spatial abilities. *Learning and Individual Differences*, 19(4), 481–485. doi:10.1016/j.lindif.2009.05.001.

Ness, D., Farenga, S. J., & Garofalo, S. G. (2017). *Spatial intelligence: Why it matters from birth through the lifespan*. New York, NY: Routledge.

Nguyen, N., Mulla, A., Nelson, A. J., & Wilson, T. D. (2014). Visuospatial anatomy comprehension: The role of spatial visualization ability and problem-solving strategies. *Anatomical Sciences Education*, 7(4), 280–288. doi:10.1002/ase.1415.

Nguyen, N., Nelson, A. J., & Wilson, T. D. (2012). Computer visualizations: Factors that influence spatial anatomy comprehension. *Anatomical Sciences Education*, 5(2), 98–108. doi:10.1002/ase.1258.

Paik, E. S., & Schraw, G. (2013). Learning with animation and illusions of understanding. *Journal of Educational Psychology*, 105(2), 278–289. doi:10.1037/a0030281.

Plass, J. L., Homer, B. D., & Kinzer, C. K. (2015). Foundations of game-based learning. *Educational Psychologist*, 50(4), 258–283. doi:10.1080/00461520.2015.1122533.

Schüler, A., Scheiter, K., & van Genuchten, E. (2011). The role of working memory in multimedia instruction: Is working memory working during learning from text and pictures? *Educational Psychology Review*, 23(3), 389–411. doi:10.1007/s10648-10011-9168-9165.

Shah, P., & Miyake, A. (1996). The separability of working memory resources for spatial thinking and language processing: An individual differences approach. *Journal of Experimental Psychology: General*, 125(1), 4–27. doi:10.1037/0096-3445.125.1.4.

Stieff, M., & Uttal, D. H. (2015). How much can spatial training improve STEM achievement? *Educational Psychology Review*, 27(4), 607–615. doi:10.1007/s10648-10015-9304-9308.

Sweller, J. (2010). Element interactivity and intrinsic, extraneous, and germane cognitive load. *Educational Psychology Review*, 22(2), 123–138. doi:10.1007/s10648-10010-9128-9125.

Sweller, J., Ayres, P., & Kalyuga, S. (2011). *Cognitive load theory*. New York, NY: Springer.

Uttal, D. H., Meadow, N. G., Tipton, E., Hand, L. L., Alden, A. R., Warren, C., & Newcombe, N. S. (2013). The malleability of spatial skills: A meta-analysis of training studies. *Psychological Bulletin*, 139(2), 352–402. doi:10.1037/a0028446.

van Gog, T. (2014). The signaling (or cueing) principle in multimedia learning. In R. E. Mayer (Ed.), *The Cambridge handbook of multimedia learning* (2nd ed., pp. 263–278). New York, NY: Cambridge University Press. doi:10.1017/CBO9781139547369.014.

Vandenberg, S. G., & Kuse, A. R. (1978). Mental rotations, a group test of three-dimensional spatial visualization. *Perceptual and Motor Skills*, 47(2), 599–604. doi:10.2466/pms.1978.47.2.599.

PART 3

Human movement, pointing, tracing and gesturing

9

EMBODYING LEARNING THROUGH PHYSICAL ACTIVITY AND GESTURES IN PRESCHOOL CHILDREN

Myrto Mavilidi

PRIORITY RESEARCH CENTRE FOR PHYSICAL ACTIVITY AND NUTRITION, SCHOOL OF EDUCATION, UNIVERSITY OF NEWCASTLE, NEWCASTLE, AUSTRALIA; EARLY START, UNIVERSITY OF WOLLONGONG, WOLLONGONG, AUSTRALIA

Kim Ouwehand

DEPARTMENT OF PSYCHOLOGY, EDUCATION AND CHILD STUDIES, ERASMUS SCHOOL OF SOCIAL AND BEHAVIOURAL SCIENCES, ERASMUS UNIVERSITY ROTTERDAM, ROTTERDAM, THE NEDERLANDS

Anthony D. Okely

EARLY START, UNIVERSITY OF WOLLONGONG, WOLLONGONG, AUSTRALIA

Paul Chandler

EARLY START, UNIVERSITY OF WOLLONGONG, WOLLONGONG, AUSTRALIA

Fred Paas

DEPARTMENT OF PSYCHOLOGY, EDUCATION, AND CHILD STUDIES, ERASMUS UNIVERSITY ROTTERDAM, ROTTERDAM, THE NETHERLANDS; SCHOOL OF EDUCATION/EARLY START, UNIVERSITY OF WOLLONGONG, WOLLONGONG, AUSTRALIA

Bodily movement is undoubtedly a fundamental tool for learning throughout human life. From an early age, different motor experiences, such as reaching and grasping movements (Daum, Vuori, Prinz, & Aschersleben, 2009), gross motor patterns of varying complexity learned in the context of sports and physical activity (Cross, Hamilton, & Grafton, 2006), and gesturing (Goldin-Meadow & Beilock, 2010), are omnipresent throughout life, helping children act upon and understand the environment (Thelen, Schöner, Scheier, & Smith, 2001). Interestingly, research has shown a tight connection between action (bodily movements), perception (sensory processes) and cognition (Barsalou, 2008). The studies of Piaget (1968, 1970), previously demonstrated that the expansion of a child's repertoire of motor skills is based on developmental changes in perception, cognition, and behavior. More recent examples of this tight relationship between sensorimotor processes and cognition can be found in research showing positive effects of bodily movements on learning cognitive tasks.

In this book chapter, we use cognitive load theory (e.g., Paas, Renkl, & Sweller, 2003; Sweller, Ayres, & Kalyuga, 2011), along with the incorporation of an evolutionary approach to learning (Paas & Sweller, 2012, based on Geary, 2008), and the theoretical framework of embodied cognition (e.g., Barsalou, 2008) in our approach to learning. These theories nicely complement each other, in the sense that cognitive load theory focuses on the origins of learning mechanisms using human movement (which are largely based on sensorimotor processes), thereby providing evidence from educational research. The second approach focuses on the mechanisms derived from fundamental and brain research to explain how this grounding of sensorimotor processes occurs in cognition. In the first part of this chapter, recent upgrades of cognitive load theory and embodied cognition theory will be briefly introduced, followed by empirical evidence from the 2018 cognitive load theory conference and a general discussion.

Upgrade of cognitive load theory

Cognitive load theory takes human cognitive architecture into account in the design of instruction and is particularly focused on characteristics of the physical learning environment (e.g., noisy or silent classroom), the learners (e.g., low or high working memory capacity), the learning tasks (e.g., visual or verbal learning task), and the interactions between these factors (see, Choi, Van Merrienboer, & Paas, 2014). Geary's evolutionary theory makes a distinction between biologically primary and secondary knowledge, with this categorisation heavily influencing cognitive load theory (Geary, 2008; Geary & Berch, 2016). Biologically primary knowledge is considered information that we have evolved to acquire; it consequently can be processed and acquired without much effort (e.g., native language, movement, tool use). Obtaining and using this knowledge largely occurs unconsciously and, therefore, does not require limited working memory capacity. On the other hand, biologically secondary knowledge is related to information that has become culturally important and needs to be learned explicitly requiring conscious processing (e.g., mathematics or science). Because conscious processing relies on our limited working memory capacity, it is much harder and requires more effort to acquire secondary knowledge than primary knowledge. Using Geary's ideas, Paas and Sweller (2012) suggested that biologically primary knowledge can be used to assist in acquiring biologically secondary knowledge. This claim is supported by research showing that studying animations led to superior learning of complex procedural tasks including human movement (e.g., how to bandage a hand) than studying static representations (Ayres & Paas, 2007a, 2007b; Höffler & Leutner, 2007). Furthermore, Paas and Sweller (2012) and Sweller (2011) used this approach to explain why gesture observation and production can facilitate formal learning. For example, it has been found that pre-schoolers understand the principle of symmetry faster from teachers who gestured during instruction than from teachers who did not gesture (Valenzeno, Alibali, & Klatzky, 2003). Similar results were found when kindergarten and first grade children learned the Piagetian conservation of quantity principle (Ping & Goldin-Meadow, 2008) and third and fourth graders learned mathematical equations (Singer & Goldin-Meadow, 2005). Producing gestures has also proven beneficial for learning. For example, Goldin-Meadow, Nusbaum, Kelly, and Wagner (2001) showed that performing two tasks simultaneously, i.e., remember a list of words while explaining how to solve a math problem, is easier when people are allowed to gesture about the math problem. The performance results on the secondary memory task indicated that performing these gestures lightened the cognitive load needed for the math problems thereby freeing up mental resources to memorise the list of words.

Embodied cognition

According to the theoretical framework of embodied cognition, action and perception are considered to be inextricably bound and bi-directionally influence each other, with cognitive processes being profoundly grounded in the physical environment (Barsalou, 2008). From this viewpoint, cognition is shaped through interactions with the world (Wilson, 2002), in which the physical environment can be processed via observation and manipulation (Gelman & Brenneman, 2004; Zacharia, Loizou, & Papaevripidou, 2012). Human movement especially can be considered as a part of the cognitive system (Paas & Sweller, 2012; Pouw, de Nooijer, Van Gog, Zwaan, & Paas, 2014).

The bidirectional influence of action on perception is evidenced by co-activation of a specific set of neurons in the brain (the putative mirror neuron system) when performing an action or simply observing an action (Chong, Cunnington, Williams, Kanwisher, & Mattingley, 2008; Gazzola & Keysers, 2008). Research showed that only perceiving manageable objects, irrespective of the intention of the participants, leads to a partial activation of the motor areas that are involved when actually using these objects (Grèzes & Decety, 2002). Similar support for embodied cognition comes from language research showing that words are represented in the brain by their perceptual features (Glenberg & Robertson, 2000; Zwaan & Madden, 2005). For example, Hauk, Johnsrude, and Pulvermüller (2004) demonstrated that an embodied representation of action words related to arm movements activate pre-motor areas representing the hand, while action words related to leg movements activate pre-motor areas representing the leg.

Interestingly, not only concrete sensorimotor experiences but also abstract concepts can be represented by perceptual properties. For example, research has shown that an abstract concept, such as "power" is associated with an attentional bias toward "looking up" (Zanolie et al., 2012). Note that in the western world, power hierarchy is usually depicted as a pyramid, with the most powerful on top and the least on the bottom; abstract concepts can be internalised through such tangible examples.

As such, embodying knowledge in addition to listening or seeing a cognitive task can lead to the construction of more enriched mental representations in long-term memory (Lindgren & Johnson-Glenberg, 2013), because the to-be-learned information is not only seen and/or heard, but also connected with information from the physical environment. Mental representations that consist of multimodal resources (i.e., auditory, visual, kinaesthetic) are closely intertwined with our sensorimotor functions (e.g., movements, perception, tactility, vision, and sound reception and production; Radford, 2014), resulting in the construction of higher-quality mental representations or cognitive schemas (Goldin-Meadow, et al., 2001; Ping & Goldin-Meadow, 2010). Through these schemas, in which information from different modalities is chunked together, the working memory can deal with more information at the same time (Ginns, 2005; Kalyuga, Chandler, & Sweller, 2000; Risko & Gilbert, 2016). Thus, the richer cognitive schemas promote memory performance while imposing lower demands on working memory resources (i.e., low cognitive load; Madan & Singhal, 2012; Paas & Sweller, 2012).

The idea of schema enrichment through students' engagement in perceptual tasks and actions is consistent with the Dual-Coding Theory, which stresses that students who engage in motions and perceptions, are able to connect the kinaesthetic "imagery" with visual and verbal cues (Clark & Paivio, 1991). For example, a mental image for the word "bunsen burner" includes a visual image of the object, auditory and olfactory images for the sound and smell of gas, and motor images for adjusting the flow of gas (Clark & Paivio, 1991). Also, this process of mental simulation can facilitate learners to link incomprehensible concepts with sensorimotor metaphors (e.g., interactive simulation of planetary astronomy; Lindgren, Tscholl, Wang, & Johnson, 2016). Besides decreasing the working memory load, kinaesthetic and tactile cues automatically draw attention, also evidenced by studies showing that information around the hand position is processed longer and deeper than information presented further away from the hand (Cosman & Vecera, 2010; Reed, Grubb, & Steele, 2006). For instance, the index fingers can be used when reading a textbook to mark positions in sequential tasks. Including areas around the hand that automatically receive more attention when designing instructions might have a positive effect on learning (Risko & Gilbert, 2016).

Empirical evidence

Overall, various theoretical frameworks linked to or extending cognitive load theory suggest the cognitive benefits of movements on learning (Agostinho, Ginns, Tindall-Ford, Mavilidi, & Paas, 2016). In the following, five experimental studies investigating possible effects of task-relevant movements (physical activities and gestures) on preschool children's learning in different domains will be described.

Summary of methodology

The five studies were conducted in childcare centres. The centres were randomly assigned to the experimental conditions of each study. The instructions were presented to the children by the research team, and the teachers' role was merely supportive. The learning sessions were conducted in small groups (max. 10 children), whereas the instruction in Study 3 took place individually (children one by one). Pre-tests, where included, were used to assess children's prior knowledge. Post-tests were individually assessed and administered immediately after the intervention and again 5–6 weeks later (Study 1 had no follow-up test).

Each study used a different method regarding the way learning performance was assessed. However, evaluation ratings were similar in all studies (Study 2 had no evaluation rating): Children evaluated how much they liked the type of instruction they had received ("Did you like this game") and whether they would like to be taught in the same way again in the future ("Would you like to play it again in the future"), answering on a 5-point Likert scale with smiley faces as anchors. The two ratings were aggregated resulting in one evaluation score.

The summary of the methods is presented in Table 9.1, whereas the means and standard deviations for performance and evaluation scores per study are found in Table 9.2.

Study 1*(Foreign language).* In a quasi-experimental design, children were assessed on vocabulary through physical activity and gestures (Toumpaniari, Loyens, Mavilidi, & Paas, 2015). In the physical activity and gesturing condition, children acted out animal movements. In the gesturing condition, children acted out the same animal movements with gestures without moving from their position. In both conditions, children imitated the movements of animals called out by the instructor. In the control condition, children only repeated the animal names in both languages.

During the learning phase, static pictures with words depicting the various animals (e.g., pig, horse, cow, dog) were shown to children, adjusted from the "On the farm" activity of the Energizers classroom-based physical activity program (Mahar et al., 2006). Children were administered a cued-recall test, in which the research team said the word in Greek and children had to say the word in English.

Results showed that children who could enact the words through physical activity and gesturing or only gesturing outperformed the children in the control condition, $t(64) = 2.77$, $p < .01$. Also, the children who enacted the words through physical activity and gesturing performed better than the children who enacted the words through gesturing only, $t(64) = 3.17$, $p < .01$. Finally, the condition in which children embodied the words through physical activity and gestures was preferred over the other two instructional conditions (both $p < .05$).

Study 2*(Foreign language).* In the second study, whether enacting words through whole-body movements (i.e., physical activity) or part-body movements (i.e., gestures) would improve foreign vocabulary learning was investigated (Italian; Mavilidi, Okely, Chandler, Cliff, & Paas, 2015). Children's performance was assessed across three different time points (two weeks, four weeks, and ten weeks). The children were randomly assigned to one of the four experimental conditions. In the integrated condition, children enacted the words with physical activity. For example, when the word was "dance", children actually danced for a few seconds. In the non-integrated condition, children were engaged in physical activity at the

TABLE 9.1 Summary of methods of experimental studies

Study	Learning domain	Condition	Participants (N, Age) No. of childcare centres	Subject matter of learning	Performance assessment	Duration of learning	No. of learning sessions per week – Total duration
1	Foreign language	Embodied words through physical activity and gestures (N = 23) Embodied words through gestures (N = 23) Control: no movements involved (N = 21)	67 4–5 years old 2	Learning 20 animal words (translation from Greek to English)	Immediate post-test Type: Cued-recall	1 hour	2 lessons 4 weeks
2	Foreign language	Integrated: task-relevant physical activity (N = 31) Non-integrated: task-irrelevant physical activity (N = 23) Gesturing: task-relevant gesture (N = 31) Control: no movements involved (N = 26)	111 4–5 years old 15	Learning 14 words (translation from English to Italian)	Immediate post-test 6-week delayed post-test Type: Free-recall Cued-recall	15–20 min	2 lessons 4 weeks

Study	Learning domain	Condition	Participants (N, Age) No. of childcare centres	Subject matter of learning	Performance assessment	Duration of learning	No. of learning sessions per week – Total duration
3	Geography	Integrated: task-relevant physical activity (N = 28)	87 4–5 years old 8	Learning the continents and characteristic animals	Pre-test Immediate post-test 5-week delayed post-test Type: Free & cued- recall	10 min	1–2 lessons 2 weeks
		Non-integrated: task-irrelevant physical activity (N = 29)					
		Control: no movements involved (N = 30)					
4	Science	Integrated: task-relevant physical activity (N = 30)	86 4–5 years old 7	Learning the planets	Pre-test Immediate post-test 6-week delayed post-test Type: Free & cued- recall	10 min	2 lessons 4 weeks
		Non-integrated: task-irrelevant physical activity (N = 27)					
		Control: no movements involved (N = 29)					

Study	Learning domain	Condition	Participants (N, Age) No. of childcare centres	Subject matter of learning	Performance assessment	Duration of learning	No. of learning sessions per week – Total duration
5	Mathematics	Integrated: task-relevant physical activity (N = 30)	115	Learning numeracy skills (counting, number line estimation, numerical comparison and identification)	Pre-test	15 mins	2 lessons
			3.5–5 years old				4 weeks
		Observing integrated: observing task-relevant physical activity of peers in the integrated condition (N = 29)	9		Immediate post-test 6-week delayed post-test		
		Non-integrated: task-irrelevant physical activity (N = 29)					
		Control: no movements involved (N = 27)					

same intensity as the integrated condition, but the physical activity was not related to the task. For example, for the word "dance", children ran around the room and repeated the word "dance". In the gesturing condition, children enacted the words with pantomime gestures while remaining seated. For the word "dance", children moved their hands rhythmically. Finally, in the control condition, children verbally repeated the words while remaining seated.

In the learning phase, the research team pronounced each Italian action word along with a picture depicting that action to the children. Children also verbally repeated the words after the instructor. Children had to remember as many Italian words as they could (free-recall), and were asked to say the relevant Italian word after being shown the same static picture used during instruction (cued-recall).

Results revealed that the children in the integrated condition outperformed all other children in the free-recall test (compared to non-integrated, $p = .006$; gesturing, $p = .049$, control, $p < .001$). No differences were observed between children in the non-integrated and gesturing condition, $p = .327$, non-integrated and control condition, $p = .473$, and gesturing and control condition, $p = .076$. In the cued-recall test, the children in the integrated condition outperformed the children in the gesturing, $p = .044$, and control condition, $p = .012$. No differences were found between children in the integrated and non-integrated condition, $p = .073$. The children in the gesturing condition remembered more words than those in the control condition, $p = .012$, and children in the non-integrated condition remembered more than those in the control condition, $p = .017$.

Study 3(*Geography*). In the third study, whether learning using physical movements could improve geography learning was investigated (Mavilidi, Okely, Chandler, & Paas, 2016). The children looked at a world map on the floor displaying the names of the continents and characteristic animals living there. The instructor called aloud the name of the continents and showed the animal movements to the children. In the integrated physical activity condition, children moved from one continent to the other, imitating the animal movements they were representing. For example, they hopped like a kangaroo while moving from Oceania to Asia. In the non-integrated condition, children ran in a circle around the map. In the control condition, children stood still and looked at the map. The learning test consisted of both free-recall (e.g., name the continents) and cued-recall (e.g., What is the continent of the kangaroo?) questions.

Results demonstrated that children in the integrated condition outperformed those in the control condition, $p < .001$, and children in the non-integrated condition outperformed those in the control condition, $p < .001$. Also, children in the integrated and non-integrated conditions enjoyed the active conditions more than children in the control condition, $p < .001$ and $p = .019$, respectively. There were no differences between the integrated and non-integrated condition in terms of learning, $p = .095$ and evaluation of the instructional method, $p = .084$.

Study 4(*Science*). In the fourth study, the possible effects of integrated whole-body movements (i.e., physical activity) on learning were investigated when children learned about the planetary system (Mavilidi, Okely, Chandler, & Paas, 2017).

TABLE 9.2 Means and standard deviations of performance and evaluation as a function of condition

| | Performance | | Evaluation | |
| | | Time of testing | | |
Condition	Immediate post-test M (SD)	Delayed post-test M (SD)	Immediate post-test M (SD)	Delayed post-test M (SD)
Study 1				
Physical activity and gesturing	16.96 (1.49)		4.17 (0.44)	
Gesturing	15.13 (2.01)		3.87 (0.41)	
Control	14.62 (2.31)		3.78 (0.49)	
Study 2 (Free-recall)				
Integrated	2.63 (1.81)	1.58 (1.41)		
Non-integrated	1.65 (1.15)	1.13 (1.55)		
Gesturing	1.71 (1.40)	1.61 (1.93)		
Control	1.19 (0.98)	0.81 (1.10)		
Study 2 (Cued-recall)				
Integrated	5.61 (2.79)	4.58 (2.58)		
Non-integrated	4.30 (1.67)	4.24 (2.16)		
Gesturing	4.37 (2.22)	4.00 (2.81)		
Control	3.15 (1.77)	2.40 (1.56)		
Study 3				
Integrated	17.07 (3.42)	15.14 (4.02)	4.61 (0.52)	4.75 (0.48)
Non-integrated	15.38 (3.45)	13.62 (4.35)	4.36 (0.71)	4.34 (0.87)
Control	12.50 (3.64)	10.23 (4.38)	4.07 (1.11)	3.77 (1.17)
Study 4				
Integrated	15.53 (4.91)	12.63 (5.08)	4.35 (1.05)	4.37 (0.82)
Non-integrated	11.07 (5.04)	8.97 (4.14)	3.98 (0.91)	3.91 (1.00)
Control	5.52 (4.37)	5.14 (3.36)	3.67 (1.17)	3.31 (0.88)
Study 5				
Integrated	41.83 (11.56)	40.03 (12.87)	4.70 (0.46)	4.48 (0.87)
Observing physical activity	30.48 (13.72)	30.41 (14.28)	4.43 (0.46)	4.21 (0.71)

	Performance		Evaluation	
	Time of testing			
	Immediate post-test	Delayed post-test	Immediate post-test	Delayed post-test
Condition	M (SD)	M (SD)	M (SD)	M (SD)
Non-integrated physical activity	27.72 (12.90)	26.55 (11.95)	3.53 (1.19)	3.29 (0.86)
Control	22.59 (10.90)	23.11 (11.45)	3.87 (0.85)	3.61 (1.08)

Units measured

Performance: Study 1 = 0–20; Study 2 = 0–14; Study 3 = 0–24; Study 4 = 0–28; Study 5 = 0–61

Evaluation: 1 = "Did not like it at all" - 5 = "I liked it a lot"

The learning material consisted of a picture of the solar system (i.e., sun and the planets in space) and soft toy planets placed in a straight line on the floor in the same order as shown in the picture. The instructor called aloud the names of the planets in the right order. Children had to learn the names of the planets and their order based on their distance from the sun.

In the integrated condition, children started from the sun, moved to the planet Mercury, returned back to the sun, and then continued the same process for each other planet. It was assumed that this would enable children to make a conceptual representation of the planets and their relative distance to the sun. In the non-integrated condition, children performed movements that were not related to the learning task. Children ran around in a circle shape in the room. In the control condition, children observed the planets. In the free-recall test, children were asked to name the planets and place the soft toy planets in a straight line on the floor based on their relative distance from the sun. In the cued-recall test, children were asked the same questions as in the free-recall test but they were assisted with hints (e.g., pictures or planets shown, soft toy planets placed on the floor).

Results showed that the learning scores in the integrated condition were higher than those in the non-integrated and control conditions, both $p < .001$. Also, the non-integrated condition was better than the control condition, $p < .001$. The integrated condition was rated as more enjoyable compared to the control condition, $p < .001$. No differences were found between the non-integrated, $p < .075$, and the control condition, $p < .053$) in terms of evaluation ratings.

Study 5 *(Mathematics).* In this study, the possible effects of integrated whole-body movements (i.e., physical activity) on learning numeracy skills were investigated (Mavilidi, Okely, Chandler, Domazet, & Paas, 2018). The learning content involved counting skills and the order of the numbers when they were presented in a straight line from 1–20, using foam blocks of numbers. The instructor called out the numbers after which children in all experimental conditions repeated the numbers. In the integrated condition, children ran to the right side when the numbers increased, or to the left side when the numbers decreased. In the observing integrated condition, children remained seated and looked at their peers in the integrated condition performing the movements. In the non-integrated condition, children ran in a circle around in the room. In the control condition, children remained seated. The math test consisted of counting, number line estimation, numerical magnitude comparison and identification.

Results showed that the children whose movements were integrated with the learning material (integrated condition) outperformed children in the observing integrated condition, $p = .006$, the non-integrated condition, $p = .034$; and control condition, $p < .001$. Performance of the children in the non-integrated condition did not differ from those in the observing integrated condition, $p = .999$, or the control condition, $p = .485$. Also, no difference in performance was found between children in the observing integrated condition and the control condition, $p = .999$. In terms of evaluation ratings, children in the integrated condition enjoyed the instructional method more than children in the observing integrated condition and the control condition, both $p < .001$. In addition, children in the non-integrated condition rated the instructional method higher than children in the observing integrated condition, $p < .001$ and the control condition, $p = .002$. The integrated and non-integrated conditions did not differ from each other, $p = .128$, as well as the observing integrated condition and the control condition, $p = .076$.

Discussion

This chapter has synthesised an interdisciplinary approach combining the evolutionary account of cognitive load theory and embodied cognition theory, providing evidence about the effectiveness and success of embodied learning (Kontra, Goldin-Meadow, & Beilock, 2012; Madan & Singhal, 2012). The current work explored cognitive load theory from a relatively new perspective stressing the beneficial role of movement on learning, extending it beyond gestures that predominantly have been investigated so far. A series of studies used whole-body movements in the form of physical activity. The results of these studies consistently confirmed the notion that the task-relevance of movements is influential for inducing learning effects (Mavilidi et al., in press). More specifically, all studies included a condition of task-relevant movements (integrated condition), compared to a condition involving non-relevant movements (non-integrated condition), and a control condition which represented the usual sedentary practice with no movements. Additional conditions examined the gesturing effect and the potential advantage of learning through looking at others' movements. The most pronounced learning effects were observed in the integrated condition. The experimental studies conducted demonstrated that the effects were prominent for different learning domains (e.g., language, geography, mathematics, science). Interestingly, the effects of whole-body movements (i.e., physical activity) were more pervasive than part-body movements (i.e., gestures). However, one could argue that children have a natural urge to move around in the *gesture only* and *no movement* conditions, and inhibiting this urge might have increased the extraneous load of the task (i.e., the effort needed to stay seated could not be dedicated to learning). In line with this idea, studies revealed that response inhibition is more effortful for young children (Diamond, Kirkham & Amso, 2002) because frontal brain areas associated with this function are still underdeveloped (e.g., Bunge, Dudukovic, Thomason, Vaidya, & Gabrieli, 2002). On the other hand, the studies presented here also clearly show that the *integrated physical activity* groups (whose movements were related to the task) outperformed the *non-integrated* groups (whose movements were irrelevant to the task). This suggests that the combination of full-body movements, the freedom to run around and the association with the task content provides a superior learning strategy.

Besides higher learning outcomes, the physical activity conditions also promoted enjoyment (reflected in the scores on the question "Did you like this game?") and satisfaction (reflected in the scores on the question "Would you like to play it again in the future?") during the instruction. These findings suggest that learning through physical activity was also a motivating learning strategy. Motivation (which literally means "to move") is an important factor for learning outcomes (e.g., Steinmayr & Spinath, 2009) and is considerable in cognitive load theory as well (Paas, Tuovinen, van Merriënboer & Darabi 2005). Especially intrinsic motivation, which is the enjoyment of the learning activity itself, has positive effects on learning and creativity (Ryan & Deci, 2000). Therefore, we suggest that physical activity, regardless of the content, improves learning because of its positive effects on intrinsic motivation. The additional positive effect on the learning outcomes in the *integrated physical activity* conditions on top of the *non-integrated* conditions is in line with research depicting that multimodal learning can lead to the construction of more enriched mental representations in long-term memory than unimodal learning (Lindgren & Johnson-Glenberg, 2013).

In terms of instructional design, asking children to enact movements can facilitate learning. However, this seem to be true especially for movements that are meaningfully related to the content of the learning task. The sensorimotor information received can be processed simultaneously but through different sub-systems (Risko & Gilbert, 2016), reducing the inherent intrinsic complexity of the task (Sweller, 1994). The physical action can be used to alter the information processing requirements of a task by decreasing its cognitive demand, known as "cognitive offloading" (Risko & Gilbert, 2016). Moreover, the act of physical activity was enjoyed more by the children. As such, the instructional material responds to an interactive process of learning with minimal cognitive demand promoting germane cognitive load (Sweller, 2010) and (intrinsic) motivation (Ryan & Deci, 2000).

References

Agostinho, S., Ginns, P., Tindall-Ford, S., Mavilidi, M. F., & Paas, F. (2016). "Touch the screen": Linking touch-based educational technology with learning – a synthesis of current research. In L. Lin and R. Atkinson (Eds.), *Educational technologies: Challenges, applications and learning outcomes* (pp. 33–57). New York: Nova Science Publishers.

Ayres, P., & Paas, F. (2007a). Making instructional animations more effective: A cognitive load approach. *Applied Cognitive Psychology*, 21, 695–700.

Ayres, P., & Paas, F. (2007b). Can the cognitive-load approach make instructional animations more effective? *Applied Cognitive Psychology*, 21, 811–820.

Barsalou, L. W. (2008). Grounded cognition. *Annual Review of Psychology*, 59, 617–645.

Bunge, S. A., Dudukovic, N. M., Thomason, M. E., Vaidya, C. J., & Gabrieli, J. D. (2002). Immature frontal lobe contributions to cognitive control in children: Evidence from fMRI. *Neuron*, 33(2), 301–311.

Choi, H. H., Van Merriënboer, J. J., & Paas, F. (2014). Effects of the physical environment on cognitive load and learning: towards a new model of cognitive load. *Educational Psychology Review*, 26(2), 225–244.

Chong, T. T. J., Cunnington, R., Williams, M. A., Kanwisher, N., & Mattingley, J. B. (2008). fMRI adaptation reveals mirror neurons in human inferior parietal cortex. *Current Biology*, 18(20), 1576–1580.

Clark, J. M., & Paivio, A. (1991). Dual coding theory and education. *Educational Psychology Review*, 3(3), 149–210.

Cosman, J. D., & Vecera, S. P. (2010). Attention affects visual perceptual processing near the hand. *Psychological Science*, 21(9), 1254–1258.

Cross, E. S., Hamilton, A. F. D. C., & Grafton, S. T. (2006). Building a motor simulation de novo: Observation of dance by dancers. *Neuroimage*, 31(3), 1257–1267.

Daum, M. M., Vuori, M. T., Prinz, W., & Aschersleben, G. (2009). Inferring the size of a goal object from an actor's grasping movement in 6-and 9-month-old infants. *Developmental Science*, 12(6), 854–862.

Diamond, A., Kirkham, N., & Amso, D. (2002). Conditions under which young children can hold two rules in mind and inhibit a prepotent response. *Developmental Psychology*, 38 (3), 352–362.

Gazzola, V., & Keysers, C. (2008). The observation and execution of actions share motor and somatosensory voxels in all tested subjects: single-subject analyses of unsmoothed fMRI data. *Cerebral Cortex*, 19(6), 1239–1255.

Geary, D. C. (2008). An evolutionarily informed education science. *Educational Psychologist*, 43(4), 179–195.

Geary, D. C., & Berch, D. B. (2016). Evolution and children's cognitive and academic development. In *Evolutionary perspectives on child development and education* (pp. 217–249). Springer, Cham.

Gelman, R., & Brenneman, K. (2004). Science learning pathways for young children. *Early Childhood Research Quarterly*, 19(1), 150–158.

Ginns, P. (2005). Meta-analysis of the modality effect. *Learning and Instruction*, 15(4), 313–331.

Glenberg, A. M., & Robertson, D. A. (2000). Symbol grounding and meaning: A comparison of high-dimensional and embodied theories of meaning. *Journal of Memory and Language*, 43(3), 379–401.

Goldin-Meadow, S., & Beilock, S. L. (2010). Action's influence on thought: The case of gesture. *Perspectives on Psychological Science*, 5(6), 664–674.

Goldin-Meadow, S., Nusbaum, H., Kelly, S. D., & Wagner, S. (2001). Explaining math: Gesturing lightens the load. *Psychological Science*, 12(6), 516–522.

Grèzes, J., & Decety, J. (2002). Does visual perception of object afford action? Evidence from a neuroimaging study. *Neuropsychologia*, 40(2), 212–222.

Hauk, O., Johnsrude, I., & Pulvermüller, F. (2004). Somatotopic representation of action words in human motor and premotor cortex. *Neuron*, 41(2), 301–307.

Höffler, T. N., & Leutner, D. (2007). Instructional animation versus static pictures: A meta-analysis. *Learning and Instruction*, 17(6), 722–738.

Kalyuga, S., Chandler, P., & Sweller, J. (2000). Incorporating learner experience into the design of multimedia instruction. *Journal of Educational Psychology*, 92(1), 126–136.

Kontra, C., Goldin-Meadow, S., & Beilock, S. L. (2012). Embodied learning across the life span. *Topics in Cognitive Science*, 4(4), 731–739.

Lindgren, R., & Johnson-Glenberg, M. (2013). Emboldened by embodiment: Six precepts for research on embodied learning and mixed reality. *Educational Researcher*, 42(8), 445–452.

Lindgren, R., Tscholl, M., Wang, S., & Johnson, E. (2016). Enhancing learning and engagement through embodied interaction within a mixed reality simulation. *Computers & Education*, 95, 174–187.

Madan, C. R., & Singhal, A. (2012). Using actions to enhance memory: effects of enactment, gestures, and exercise on human memory. *Frontiers in Psychology*, 3, 1–4.

Mahar, M. T., Murphy, S. K., Rowe, D. A., Golden, J., Shields, A. T., & Raedeke, T. D. (2006). Effects of a classroom-based program on physical activity and on-task behavior. *Medicine and Science in Sports and Exercise*, 38(12), 2086–2094.

Mavilidi, M. F., Okely, A. D., Chandler, P., & Paas, F. (2016). Infusing physical activities into the classroom: Effects on preschool children's geography learning. *Mind, Brain, and Education*, 10(4), 256–263.

Mavilidi, M. F., Okely, A. D., Chandler, P., & Paas, F. (2017). Effects of integrating physical Activities into a science lesson on preschool children's learning and enjoyment. *Applied Cognitive Psychology*, 31(3), 281–290.

Mavilidi, M. F., Okely, A. D., Chandler, P., Cliff, D. P., & Paas, F. (2015). Effects of integrated physical exercises and gestures on preschool children's foreign language vocabulary learning. *Educational Psychology Review*, 27(3), 413–426.

Mavilidi, M. F., Okely, A., Chandler, P., Domazet, S. L., & Paas, F. (2018). Immediate and delayed effects of integrating physical activity into preschool children's learning of numeracy skills. *Journal of Experimental Child Psychology*, 166, 502–519.

Mavilidi, M. F., Ruiter, M., Schmidt, M., Okely, A. D., Loyens, S., Chandler, P., & Paas, F. (in press). A narrative review of school-based physical activity for enhancing cognition and learning: The importance of relevancy and integration. *Frontiers in Psychology*, 9. doi:10.3389/fpsyg.2018.02079.

Paas, F., & Sweller, J. (2012). An evolutionary upgrade of cognitive load theory: Using the human motor system and collaboration to support the learning of complex cognitive tasks. *Educational Psychology Review*, 24(1), 27–45.

Paas, F., Tuovinen, J. E., Van Merrienboer, J. J., & Darabi, A. A. (2005). A motivational perspective on the relation between mental effort and performance: Optimizing learner involvement in instruction. *Educational Technology Research and Development*, 53(3), 25–34.

Paas, F., Renkl, A., & Sweller, J. (2003). Cognitive load theory and instructional design: Recent developments. *Educational Psychologist*, 38(1), 1–4.

Piaget, J. (1968). Quantification, conservation, and nativism. *Science*, 162, 976–979.

Piaget, J. (1970). *Science of education and the psychology of the child*. Trans. D. Coltman. Oxford: Orion.

Ping, R. M., & Goldin-Meadow, S. (2008). Hands in the air: Using ungrounded iconic gestures to teach children conservation of quantity. *Developmental Psychology*, 44(5), 1277–1287.

Ping, R., & Goldin-Meadow, S. (2010). Gesturing saves cognitive resources when talking about nonpresent objects. *Cognitive Science*, 34(4), 602–619.

Pouw, W. T., De Nooijer, J. A., Van Gog, T., Zwaan, R. A., & Paas, F. (2014). Toward a more embedded/extended perspective on the cognitive function of gestures. *Frontiers in Psychology*, 5, 1–14.

Radford, L. (2014). Towards an embodied, cultural, and material conception of mathematics cognition. *ZDM*, 46(3), 349–361.

Reed, C. L., Grubb, J. D., & Steele, C. (2006). Hands up: Attentional prioritization of space near the hand. *Journal of Experimental Psychology: Human Perception and Performance*, 32(1), 166–177.

Risko, E. F., & Gilbert, S. J. (2016). Cognitive offloading. *Trends in Cognitive Sciences*, 20(9), 676–688.

Ryan, R. M., & Deci, E. L. (2000). Self-determination theory and the facilitation of intrinsic motivation, social development, and well-being. *American Psychologist*, 55(1), 68–78.

Singer, M. A., & Goldin-Meadow, S. (2005). Children learn when their teacher's gestures and speech differ. *Psychological Science*, 16(2), 85–89.

Steinmayr, R., & Spinath, B. (2009). The importance of motivation as a predictor of school achievement. *Learning and Individual Differences*, 19(1), 80–90.

Sweller, J. (1994). Cognitive load theory, learning difficulty, and instructional design. *Learning and Instruction*, 4(4), 295–312.

Sweller, J. (2010). Element interactivity and intrinsic, extraneous, and germane cognitive load. *Educational Psychology Review*, 22(2), 123–138.

Sweller, J. (2011). Cognitive load theory. In *Psychology of learning and motivation* (Vol. 55, pp. 37–76). Academic Press.

Sweller, J., Ayres, P., & Kalyuga, S. (2011). *Cognitive load theory*. New York, NY: Springer.

Thelen, E., Schöner, G., Scheier, C., & Smith, L. B. (2001). So what's a modeler to do? *Behavioral and Brain Sciences*, 24(1), 70–80.

Toumpaniari, K., Loyens, S., Mavilidi, M. F., & Paas, F. (2015). Preschool children's foreign language vocabulary learning by embodying words through physical activity and gesturing. *Educational Psychology Review*, 27(3), 445–456.

Valenzeno, L., Alibali, M. W., & Klatzky, R. (2003). Teachers' gestures facilitate students' learning: A lesson in symmetry. *Contemporary Educational Psychology*, 28(2), 187–204.

Wilson, M. (2002). Six views of embodied cognition. *Psychonomic Bulletin & Review*, 9(4), 625–636.

Zacharia, Z. C., Loizou, E., & Papaevripidou, M. (2012). Is physicality an important aspect of learning through science experimentation among kindergarten students? *Early Childhood Research Quarterly*, 27(3), 447–457.

Zanolie, K., Dantzig, S. V., Boot, I., Wijnen, J., Schubert, T. W., Giessner, S. R., & Pecher, D. (2012). Mighty metaphors: Behavioral and ERP evidence that power shifts attention on a vertical dimension. *Brain and Cognition*, 78(1), 50–58.

Zwaan, R. A. & Madden, C. J. (2005). Embodied sentence comprehension. In D. Pecher & R. A. Zwaan (Eds.), *Grounding cognition: The role of perception and action in memory, language, and thinking* (pp. 224–246). Cambridge: Cambridge University Press.

10

LEARNING HUMAN PHYSIOLOGY BY POINTING AND TRACING

A cognitive load approach

Paul Ginns and Amy Kydd

SYDNEY SCHOOL OF EDUCATION AND SOCIAL WORK, THE UNIVERSITY OF SYDNEY, SYDNEY, AUSTRALIA

Cognitive load theory (Sweller, Ayres, & Kalyuga, 2011) holds that when learning about something unfamiliar, a student's working memory – the conscious part of the human mind – will often be at risk of overload, especially when the lesson is complicated and/or designed in ways that distract from learning. However, Paas and Sweller (2012), adopting Geary's (2008) evolutionary perspective, proposed working memory limitations may only be critical when dealing with culturally constructed knowledge or biologically secondary knowledge. They speculate, "if biologically primary knowledge is less affected by working memory limitations, it may be advantageous to use primary information to assist in the acquisition of secondary information" (Paas & Sweller, 2012, p. 27). One of the forms of biologically primary knowledge proposed by Paas and Sweller that might support learning biologically secondary knowledge is gesture. While a range of gestures are typically produced in mid-air as part of speech-based communication, tracing gestures typically involve moving the pointed index finger against a surface; instructions to trace have been found to support understanding and learning across a range of contexts (Agostinho, Tindall-Ford, Ginns, Howard, Leahy, & Paas, 2015; Ginns, Hu, Byrne, & Bobis, 2016; Hu, Ginns, & Bobis, 2014, 2015; Macken & Ginns, 2014).

One context in which the efficacy of pointing and tracing has been demonstrated is learning human physiology from expository text and diagrams. Macken and Ginns (2014) found participants who were instructed to point and trace performed significantly better on terminology and comprehension tests than those who were instructed not to gesture. However, the study was unable to provide cognitive load-related explanations for the results; single-item ratings of intrinsic, extraneous and germane cognitive load based on measures developed by Cierniak, Scheiter, and Gerjets (2009) did not differ across conditions. Participants who were instructed to gesture did not report significantly lower intrinsic extraneous load or higher germane cognitive load than participants who were instructed not to gesture. The present study aims to replicate and extend Macken and Ginns's study, using an alternative method of cognitive load measurement to investigate the effects of tracing and pointing while learning.

Literature review

Across the human lifespan, people are capable of learning a vast amount of knowledge, but the ease with which we construct our knowledge of ourselves, others, and the world varies considerably. Geary (2008) proposed a fundamental distinction between biologically primary and secondary knowledge. Biologically primary knowledge is learned effortlessly as humans have evolved to acquire it (Geary, 2008). Facial recognition and learning a native language are examples of this form of knowledge (Sweller & Sweller, 2006). In contrast, humans are limited in their ability to acquire biologically secondary knowledge, which is usually taught in an educational context (Geary, 2008). Paas and Sweller (2012) suggested that, under some conditions, biologically primary knowledge might assist in the construction of biologically secondary knowledge. Evidence for this is seen in a study conducted by Ayres, Marcus, Chan, and Qian (2009). Students who were presented with an animation of a knot construction or puzzle ring deconstruction outperformed the students who received static diagrams. Examining the results of this study, Paas and Sweller (2012) argued that observing human movement and copying it is a form of biologically primary knowledge, as observing the animation did not place an extra burden on working memory resources.

Pointing appears to be another human movement that supports construction of both biologically primary and secondary knowledge. The physical skill of configuring the hand to point also appears to be biologically primary, emerging naturally in the course of development at around 12 months (Liszkowski, Brown, Callaghan, Takada, & de Vos, 2012). Research has been conducted into the importance of pointing to language development in children. In their meta-analysis study, Colonessi, Stams, Koster, and Noon (2010) found a strong relation between pointing gestures and language development in infants and found evidence to support the idea that pointing gestures support the development of language. These studies provide strong evidence to suggest that pointing aids early word learning.

Besides pointing, the finger can also be used to trace while learning. Maria Montessori (e.g., Montessori, 1912) developed a multisensory method of learning that uses tracing, known as Sandpaper Letters. This method involves the teacher saying the sound of the letter as the child traces their finger over the sandpaper letter. Montessori (1912) argued that "touching the letters and looking at them at the same time fixes the image more quickly through the cooperation of the senses" (p. 266). There have been a number of experimental investigations into this method of tracing that support its effectiveness. Tracing around the letter was found to improve memory for the name of the letter (Bara, Gentaz, Cole, & Sprenger-Charolles, 2004; Hulme, Monk, & Ives, 1987) and the corresponding letter sound (Bara et al., 2004). Similarly, when abstract shapes are traced there is also an improvement in recall (Hulme et al., 1987) and a clearer understanding of shape categories (Kalenine, Pinet, & Gentaz, 2010). These studies reveal that Montessori's method of learning can improve the recall of shapes and letters.

The potential for a variety of human movements and gestures, including pointing, to enhance communication and learning has been revealed across a range of topics and ages (Goldin-Meadow, 2005; Hostetter, 2011). Goldin-Meadow (2005) suggests gestures can play two different roles in learning – they can reveal understanding that is not shown in speech, and they can lighten cognitive load. An emerging body of research supports the arguments of Goldin-Meadow around the impact of our hands on cognitive processing. This research has shown that close hand positioning has a number of benefits for learning including faster target detection (Reed, Grubb, & Steele, 2006), directing attention to objects close to the hands (Cosman & Vecera, 2010), and shielding attention from interferences (Davoli & Brockmole, 2012). Pointing also appears to affect fundamental cognitive processes. In their study, Dodd and Shumborski (2009) instructed participants to memorise the location of two arrays of objects. They were required to passively view one array and tap each object on the other. Participants had better memory for the arrays they pointed to compared with the ones they passively viewed. Taken together, these findings from basic cognitive science research imply that hand position and activity, including pointing and tracing, fundamentally shape cognitive processing.

The experiment presented here followed the design of Macken and Ginns's (2014) experiment, in which students in the experimental condition were instructed to use pointing and tracing gestures while studying, or sit on their hands while studying for the control condition. There were two key changes to Macken and Ginns' protocol. First, a more relaxed control condition than that used by Macken and Ginns was designed, requiring students to place their hands next to the study materials. Such a control condition aimed to represent a more typical study posture, allowing effects of pointing and tracing to be assessed in a more ecologically valid design. Second, self-reports of difficulty as a measure of cognitive load were collected after each page. Van Gog, Kirschner, Kester, and Paas (2012) found this method of measuring cognitive load provided more valid indications of cognitive load during a learning phase than a single post-learning phase rating.

Hypotheses were as follows:

1. The pointing and tracing gesture group will report lower cognitive load than participants in the non-gesture group.
2. The pointing and tracing gesture group will outperform participants in the non-gesture group on subsequent tests of learning.

Method

Participants

Thirty university students (20 females, 10 males) with a mean age of 21.47 years (SD = 1.55) participated in the study. Participants were a convenience sample of students from a range of disciplines including Education, Arts, Science, Economics and Engineering, who were randomly assigned to one of two conditions: gesturing and non-gesturing.

Materials

Participants were presented with a number of paper-based materials required for the experiment. These included the prior knowledge rating scale, learning instruction sheet, 12 pages of information about the human heart, an ease of learning and understanding rating scale, and two multiple choice tests.

Prior knowledge rating scale. Prior knowledge is widely recognised as an important influence on subsequent learning (Shing & Brod, 2016). In the present study we evaluated whether the two groups were equivalent in prior knowledge using a prior knowledge rating scale developed by O'Reilly, Symons, and MacLatchy-Gaudet (1998), assessing participants' prior knowledge of four different aspects of the human circulatory system: the structure and function of the human heart, the function and composition of the human blood vessels, the function and structure of human blood, and the pattern of blood circulation in the human body. Participants rated their understanding of the above aspects of the circulatory system using a Likert rating scale ranging from 1 (very low) to 7 (very high). The estimated internal consistency (Cronbach's alpha) of responses to this rating scale was 0.96.

Learning instructions. An instruction sheet was provided to each participant on how to learn the heart materials. There were two different types of instruction sheets; one for the gesture group, and one for the non-gesture group. Both sheets informed the participant that they would have 25 minutes "to read through, understand and learn about some aspects of human anatomy".' The gesture group was instructed that they must use their hands to make a link between the text and the associated part of the diagram, through the following instructions:

"Please use your hands where you need to make a link between text and an associated part of the diagram. Some ways you may like to do this:

- Point at the word in the text, then point at the corresponding location on the diagram
- Leave your finger on the diagram as you read about the corresponding element in the text
- Use more than one finger/hand to simultaneously point to parts of text and the diagram that are related
- Where you see arrows indicating blood flow, use your hands to trace along the arrows."

The non-gesture group were instructed not to use their hands while learning the material and to only use their hands to turn the page, as follows:

"Please do not use your hands while you learn this material. To assist you keeping in your hands still, please:

- Place your hands next to the materials you will be studying
- Only use your hands to turn the page."

At the bottom of the instruction sheet both groups were provided with an example of human physiology instructional materials on the eye to practice learning with or without their hands.

Learning materials. Dwyer (1972) developed the 12 pages of information about the human heart used in this experiment. The 12-page document was about 2,000 words long and each page contained a black and white diagram accompanying the text. The text was integrated with the diagrams and was placed closed to the corresponding aspect of the diagram. Given word count differences across the 12 pages, time allowed for studying was standardised based on similarities in word count. Thus, 1 minute was given for pages 6 and 7 (ranging from 41–61 words); 2 minutes were given for pages 2–5 and pages 9–12 (ranging from 78–174 words); 2.5 minutes were given for page 8 (187 words); and 3 minutes were given for page 1 (388 words).

Cognitive load rating scale. Following each page of instruction, participants were asked to rate how easy or difficult the content of that page was to understand and learn using a Likert scale ranging from 1 (extremely easy) to 9 (extremely difficult). Van Gog, Kirschner, Kester, and Paas (2012) found this multiple-rating method of measuring cognitive load provided a more effective indication of cognitive load during learning than a single rating after learning the materials, as was used by Macken and Ginns (2014). In order to account for differences in study time per page, each cognitive load rating was weighted by the proportion of the total study time (total: 23.5 minutes) taken by that page. For example, ratings of the first page, with 3 minutes study time, received a weighting of 3/23.5 = .128. The estimated internal consistency (Cronbach's alpha) of responses to this rating scale was 0.97.

Learning performance tests. Effects of gesturing on learning were assessed by two 20-item criterion-referenced multiple-choice tests developed by Dwyer (1972). The first test assessed participants' learning of heart structure and function terminology; an example item is "Vessels that allow the blood to flow from the heart are called the _____". The second test assessed comprehension of the heart's structure and function; an example question is "Which valve is most like the tricuspid in function?". The reliability of the Terminology and Comprehension tests was assessed using the Kuder-Richardson (KR-20) measure of internal consistency for dichotomously scored items. For the Terminology test, KR-20 = .87, and for the Comprehension test, KR-20 = .82. The two tests were chosen to allow effects of pointing and tracing to be evaluated across different levels of required cognitive processing. Thus, the Terminology test required recall of specific terms, while the Comprehension test required participants to have both understood the instructions, and to use that information to explain other phenomena (Dwyer, 1972).

Procedure

The experiment was conducted one-on-one in a quiet office. Participants were provided with a Participant Information Statement and were given a participant consent form to read and sign. After being randomly assigned to one of two conditions (Gesture or Non-Gesture), participants rated their prior knowledge of the structure and function of the human heart using the rating scale developed by O'Reilly et al. (1998). Participants then studied the 12 pages on heart structure and function appropriate to their experimental condition. The study time per page was standardised, ranging from 1 minute (pages 6, 7) to 3 minutes (page 1) depending on the complexity of the instructions given on the page. Prior to beginning studying each page, the researcher told the participant how long they would have to study that page, then asked the participant to turn the page and begin studying. After studying each page, participants rated how easy or difficult the page was to understand and learn. After completing studying the 12 pages, participants completed the terminology and comprehension tests; participants were given a maximum of 12 minutes to complete each test. On completion of the tests, participants were debriefed about the purpose of the study.

Results

Assumptions of normality and homogenous variances for the independent groups t-test were tested using the Anderson-Darling test and Levene's test respectively; these analyses did not indicate any substantial violation of assumptions. Group differences were evaluated using independent groups t-tests accompanied with the standardised mean difference effect size, Cohen's d, with its 95% confidence interval. In the present study, benchmarks recommended by Hattie (2009) are adopted: (small $d = .20$, medium $d = .40$, and large $d = .60$). For each of the tests of statistical significance reported below, the Type 1 error rate was controlled at .05.

Were the groups equivalent in prior knowledge?

A preliminary analysis investigated whether the gesturing and non-gesturing conditions were equivalent in self-reported prior knowledge of structure and function of the human heart. The difference in self-reported prior knowledge between the gesture condition ($M = 2.93$, $SD = 1.38$) and the non-gesture condition ($M = 3.20$, $SD = 1.52$) was not statistically significant, $t(28) = -.51$, $p = .617$, $d = -.18$, 95% CI [-0.902, 0.532]; thus, random assignment of participants to conditions was effective in distributing levels of self-reported prior knowledge across conditions.

Does the instruction to gesture affect self-reported cognitive load?

Students in the gesture condition reported lower cognitive load (M = 4.09, SD = 1.65) than the non-gesture condition (M = 5.15, SD = 1.63) using a one-tailed test, $t(28)$ = 1.76, p = .046 (one-tailed), d = .64, 95% CI [-.091, 1.377]. We tested the effect of not weighting cognitive load ratings by time spent studying a specific page through a follow-up analysis; not weighting cognitive load ratings by study time resulted in a somewhat less sensitive test of the effect of gesturing, $t(28)$ = 1.69, p = .051 (one-tailed), d = .62, 95% CI [-.12, 1.350].

Do instructions to point and trace improve learning?

For the Terminology test, students in the gesture condition achieved higher average test scores (M = 14.47, SD = 4.41) than students in the non-gesture condition (M = 9.73, SD = 4.77), $t(28)$ = 2.82, p = .009, d = 1.03, 95% CI [0.268, 1.791]. For the Comprehension test, students in the gesture condition also achieved higher average test scores (M = 13.40, SD = 3.04) than the non-gesture condition (M = 10.00, SD = 5.14), $t(28)$ = 2.20, p = .036, d = 0.80, 95% CI [0.061, 1.549].

Discussion

This study builds on the results of Macken and Ginns (2014) to investigate effects of pointing and tracing gestures on learning from expository text and diagrams. The foundation of this study is theory and research suggesting pointing and tracing gestures are a form of biologically primary knowledge that might assist in the acquisition of biologically secondary knowledge (Paas & Sweller, 2012). Results were consistent with this hypothesis. Across a test of heart structure terminology and a test of comprehension of materials, large effects (cf. Hattie, 2009) of pointing and tracing were found (terminology test: d = 1.03; comprehension test: d = 0.80). The instructional materials used in this study were designed to reduce extraneous cognitive load; thus, across both conditions, text and diagrams were presented in a spatially contiguous format, and numbering and arrows were used wherever possible, in order to reduce search and match processes as a source of extraneous cognitive load (Ginns, 2006). Students' self-reported cognitive load, in the form of difficulty ratings made after studying each page in the lesson, provides evidence that pointing and tracing gestures act to reduce cognitive load (d = .64).

These results replicate and extend those of Macken and Ginns (2014) in several ways. Effects of tracing and pointing on learning were generated in the present study using a more natural hand position ("Place your hands next to the materials you will be studying") than the instructions to control group participants used by Macken and Ginns ("Sit on your hands"). These latter instructions were used to maximise the difference in potential hand use by the two conditions, but might be criticised as not reflecting a typical studying posture; it is even possible that maintaining such a posture might result in extraneous cognitive load, as students have to consciously remind themselves to keep sitting on their hands. The present study thus demonstrates tracing and pointing enhances learning when compared to a more naturalistic control group.

As noted above, this study also provides evidence that pointing and tracing effects can be understood through their effects on cognitive load. The current form of cognitive load theory distinguishes between intrinsic and extraneous cognitive load. Drawing on the information packaging hypothesis (cf. Alibali, Kita, & Young, 2000), Ping and Goldin-Meadow (2010) hypothesised gestures "can provide an overarching framework that serves to organize ideas conveyed in speech, in effect chunking mental representations to reduce the load on working memory" (p.616). According to cognitive load theory, chunking multiple elements of information into a single element acts to reduce intrinsic cognitive load, supporting schema construction and/or automation. Under this analysis, gestures such as tracing might also enhance schema construction. Hu et al. (2015) used difficulty ratings of test scores as evidence of effects of intrinsic cognitive load, but subsequent studies (Agostino et al., 2015; Ginns et al., 2016) failed to replicate these results. The present study's findings using intra-lesson difficulty ratings as measures of cognitive load are more consistent with an extraneous cognitive load explanation for these effects; under this analysis, effects of pointing and tracing and learning are likely due to their effects on attentional resources (cf. Cosman & Vecera, 2010; Davoli & Brockmole, 2012), including assisting with search and match processes. Future research should incorporate measures of both intrinsic and extraneous cognitive load (e.g., Leppink, Paas, Van der Vleuten, Van Gog, & Van Merriënboer, 2013) to support tests of these competing hypotheses. Beyond subjective measures, cognitive load theorists (e.g., Brünken, Seufert, & Paas, 2010; Korbach, Brünken, & Park, 2017) have identified a range of objective measures that might support a deeper understanding of cognitive processes associated with pointing and tracing, such as eye-tracking methodologies (see Chapter 12 for a discussion), secondary tasks (e.g., Korbach et al., 2017; Park & Brünken, 2015, 2018), and electroencephalography (EEG; Antonenko, Paas, Grabner, & Van Gog, 2010).

Some aspects of the present study's design could potentially be strengthened in future research. First, the sample was relatively small ($n = 30$); thus, while large group differences were statistically significant, confidence intervals for effect sizes were wide. Replicating these findings with larger samples is desirable. Second, in the present study the measure of prior knowledge used to establish initial group equivalence was self-reported. While self-reports of prior knowledge and academic achievement are strongly correlated with actual achievement (see Hattie, 2009; Kuncel, Credé, & Thomas, 2005), the use of such measures could be criticised as subjective. Future studies might supplement self-reports with more objective measures of prior knowledge. In summary, this experiment found that instructions to point and trace while learning from expository text and diagrams improved learning. Cognitive load remains a potential explanation for the benefits of these gestures. Further research is required to more effectively measure cognitive load when students point and trace during learning.

Educational implications

The results of this study and others focusing on pointing and tracing with the index finger may be used by teachers and instructional designers to assist students to learn more effectively while studying. According to our theorising, pointing and tracing gestures are biologically primary; that is, such gestures should not generate any cognitive load when incorporated into lessons. At the same time, the results of these studies are based on clear instructions to students about what parts of the instructional materials to point at and trace. Thus, in the present study, students in the gesture condition received explicit instructions prior to the lesson to encourage them to make links between the text and associated parts of the diagrams, such as "Point at the word in the text, then point at the corresponding location on the diagram" and "Where you see arrows indicating blood flow, use your hands to trace along the arrows". In contrast, Hu et al.'s (2015) instructions to trace out elements of geometry worked examples were incorporated into each step towards solving a problem, e.g. "Step 1: There are two parallel lines here. They are crossed by a transversal. [Trace out the parallel lines and the transversal with your finger.]"

While these two examples of instructions to use the index finger to learn are quite different in their surface features, in both cases, the key elements and processes to be learnt were first identified, and were then highlighted in the tracing instructions. Teachers and instructional designers who wish to incorporate pointing and tracing gestures into lessons will likewise need to be clear to students in their instructions to point or trace. For novice learners, more generic instructions (e.g., "Use your hands to help you learn" without more specific guidance) may result in students failing to focus on key aspects of to-be-learnt information.

References

Agostinho, S., Tindall-Ford, S., Ginns, P., Howard, S., Leahy, W., & Paas, F. (2015). Giving learning a helping hand: Finger tracing of temperature graphs on an iPad. *Educational Psychology Review*, 27, 427–443. doi:10.1007/s10648-10015-9315-9315.

Alibali, M. W., Kita, S., & Young, A. J. (2000). Gesture and the process of speech production: We think, therefore we gesture. *Language and Cognitive Processes, 15*, 593–613. doi:10.1080/016909600750040571.

Antonenko, P., Paas, F., Grabner, R., & Van Gog, T. (2010). Using electroencephalography to measure cognitive load. *Educational Psychology Review*, 22, 425–438. doi:10.1007/s10648-10010-9130-y.

Ayres, P., Marcus, N., Chan, C., & Qian, N., (2009). Learning hand manipulative tasks: When instructional animations are superior to equivalent static representations. *Computers in Human Behavior*, 25, 348–353. doi:10.1016/j.chb.2008.12.013.

Bara, F., Gentaz, E., Cole, P., & Sprenger-Charolles, L. (2004). The visuo-haptic and haptic exploration of letters increases the kindergarten-children's understanding of the alphabetic principle. *Cognitive Development*, 19, 433–499. doi:10.1016/j.cogdev.2004.05.003.

Brünken, R., Seufert, T., & Paas, F. (2010). Measuring cognitive load. In J. L. Plass, R. Moreno, & R. Brünken (Eds.), *Cognitive load theory* (pp.181–202). New York: Cambridge University Press.

Cierniak, G., Scheiter, K., & Gerjets, P. (2009). Explaining the split-attention effect: Is the reduction of extraneous cognitive load accompanied by an increase in germane cognitive load? *Computers in Human Behavior*, 25, 315–324. doi:10.1016/j.chb.2008.12.020.

Colonessi, C., Stams, G. J. J. M., Koster, I., & Noon, M. J. (2010). The relation between pointing and language development: A meta-analysis. *Developmental Review*, 30, 352–366. doi:10.1016/j.dr.2010.10.001.

Cosman, J. D., & Vecera, S. P. (2010). Attention affects visual perceptual processing near the hand. *Psychological Science*, 21, 1254–1258. doi:0.1177/0956797610380697.

Davoli, C. C., & Brockmole, J. R. (2012). The hands shield attention from visual interference. *Attention, Perception, & Psychophysics*, 74, 1386–1390. doi:10.3758/s13414-13012-0351-0357.

Dodd, M. D., & Shumborski, S. (2009). Examining the influence of action on spatial working memory: The importance of selection. *The Quarterly Journal of Experimental Psychology*, 62, 1236–1247. doi:10.1080/17470210802439869.

Dwyer, F. M. (1972). *A guide for improving visualized instruction*. State College, PA: Learning Services.

Geary, D. C. (2008). An evolutionarily informed education science. *Educational Psychologist*, 43, 179–195. doi:10.1080/00461520802392133.

Ginns, P. (2006). Integrating information: Meta-analyses of the spatial contiguity and temporal contiguity effects. *Learning and Instruction*, 16, 511–525. doi:10.1016/j.learninstruc.2006.10.001.

Ginns, P., Hu, F. T., Byrne, E., & Bobis, J. (2016). Learning by tracing worked examples. *Applied Cognitive Psychology*, 30, 160–169. http://doi.org/10.1002/acp.3171.

Goldin-Meadow, S. (2005). *Hearing gesture: How our hands help us think*. Cambridge, MA: The Belknap Press of Harvard University Press.

Hattie, J. (2009). *Visible learning: A synthesis of over 800 meta-analyses relating to achievement*. New York, NY: Routledge.

Hostetter, A. B. (2011). When do gestures communicate? A meta-analysis. *Psychological Bulletin*, 137, 297–315. doi:10.1037/a0022128.

Hu, F.-T., Ginns, P., & Bobis, J. (2014). Does tracing worked examples enhance geometry learning? *Australian Journal of Educational & Developmental Psychology*, 14, 45–49.

Hu, F.-T., Ginns, P., & Bobis, J. (2015). Getting the point: Tracing worked examples enhances learning. *Learning and Instruction*, 35, 85–93. doi:10.1016/j.learninstruc.2014.10.002.

Hulme, C., Monk, A., & Ives, S. (1987). Some experimental studies of multi-sensory teaching: The effects of manual tracing on children's paired-associate learning. *British Journal of Developmental Psychology*, 5, 299–307.

Kalenine, S., Pinet, L., & Gentaz, E. (2010). The visual and visuo-haptic exploration of geometrical shapes increases their recognition in pre-schoolers. *International Journal of Behavioural Development*, 35, 18–26. doi:10.1177/0165025410367443.

Korbach, A., Brünken, R., & Park, B. (2017). Differentiating different types of cognitive load: A comparison of different measures. *Educational Psychology Review*, 30, 503–529. doi:10.1007/s10648-017-9404-8.

Kuncel, N. R., Credé, M., & Thomas, L. L. (2005). The validity of self-reported grade point averages, class ranks, and test scores: A meta-analysis and review of the literature. *Review of Educational Research*, 75, 63–82. doi:10.3102/00346543075001063.

Leppink, J., Paas, F., Van der Vleuten, C. P., Van Gog, T., & Van Merriënboer, J. J. (2013). Development of an instrument for measuring different types of cognitive load. *Behavior Research Methods*, 45, 1058–1072. doi:10.3758/s13428-13013-0334-0331.

Liszkowski, U., Brown, P., Callaghan, T., Takada, A., & de Vos, C. (2012). A prelinguistic gestural universal of human communication. *Cognitive Science*, 36, 698–713. doi:10.1111/j.1551-6709.2011.01228.x.

Macken, L., & Ginns, P. (2014). Pointing and tracing gestures may enhance anatomy and physiology learning. *Medical Teacher, 36*, 569–601. doi:10.3109/0142159X.2014.899684.

Montessori, M. (1912). *The Montessori method* (Revised ed.). New York, NY: Frederick Stokes.

O'Reilly, T., Symons, S., & MacLatchy-Gaudet, H. (1998). A comparison of self-explanation and elaborative interrogation. *Contemporary Educational Psychology*, 23, 434–445. doi:10.1006/ceps.1997.0977.

Paas, F., & Sweller, J. (2012). An evolutionary upgrade of Cognitive Load Theory: Using the human motor system and collaboration to support the learning of complex cognitive tasks. *Educational Psychology Review*, 24, 27–45. doi:10.1007/s10648–10011–9179–9172.

Park, B., & Brünken, R. (2018). Secondary task as a measure of cognitive load. In R. Zheng (Ed.), *Cognitive load measurement and application: A theoretical framework for meaningful research and practice*. Routledge.

Park, B., & Brünken, R. (2015). The rhythm method: A new method for measuring cognitive load – an experimental dual-task study. *Applied Cognitive Psychology*, 29, 232–243. doi:10.1002/acp.3100.

Ping, R., & Goldin-Meadow, S. (2010). Gesturing saves cognitive resources when talking about nonpresent objects. *Cognitive Science*, 34, 602–619. doi:10.1111/j.1551-6709.2010.01102.x.

Reed, C. L., Grubb, J. D., & Steele, C. (2006). Hands up: Attentional prioritization of space near the hand. *Journal of Experimental Psychology: Human Perception and Performance, 32*, 166–177. doi:10.1037/0096-1523.32.1.166.

Shing, Y. L., & Brod, G. (2016). Effects of prior knowledge on memory: Implications for education. *Mind, Brain, and Education*, 10, 153–161. doi:10.1111/mbe.12110.

Sweller, J., Ayres, P., & Kalyuga, S. (2011). *Cognitive load theory*. New York: Springer.

Sweller, J., & Sweller, S. (2006). Natural information processing systems. *Evolutionary Psychology*, 4, 434–458. doi:10.1177/147470490600400135.

Van Gog, T., Kirschner, F., Kester, L., & Paas, F. (2012). Timing and frequency of mental effort measurement: Evidence in favour of repeated measures. *Applied Cognitive Psychology*, 26, 833–839. doi:10.1002/acp.2883.

11

GESTURE-BASED LEARNING WITH ICT

Recent developments, opportunities
and considerations

Stoo Sepp

SCHOOL OF EDUCATION/EARLY START, UNIVERSITY OF WOLLONGONG, WOLLONGONG, AUSTRALIA

Shirley Agostinho

SCHOOL OF EDUCATION/EARLY START, UNIVERSITY OF WOLLONGONG, WOLLONGONG, AUSTRALIA

Sharon Tindall-Ford

SCHOOL OF EDUCATION/EARLY START, UNIVERSITY OF WOLLONGONG, WOLLONGONG, AUSTRALIA

Fred Paas

DEPARTMENT OF PSYCHOLOGY, EDUCATION, AND CHILD STUDIES, ERASMUS UNIVERSITY ROTTERDAM, ROTTERDAM,
THE NETHERLANDS; SCHOOL OF EDUCATION/EARLY START, UNIVERSITY OF WOLLONGONG, WOLLONGONG, AUSTRALIA

A recent increase in technologies that allow for tactile or embodied experiences presents an opportunity to explore the effect of movement on learning within a cognitive load theory framework. One of the first ICT tools that provided tactile or embodied experiences for students was the interactive whiteboard (for a review see Smith, Higgins, Wall, & Miller, 2005) with more recent examples being smartphones and tablets (Sheu & Chen, 2014). As these touch-based technologies become more readily available in schools, the opportunity to investigate their effects on learning can provide valuable insights to educators.

This chapter first provides an overview of research into gestures within the context of ICT, followed by a study currently in progress that illustrates how research is being conducted to capture hand gestures on touch-based devices. Possibilities for future inquiry within the framework of the human motor system and cognitive load theory are then discussed, as well as implications for the integration of gesture-based ICT tools into instructional practice.

Cognitive load theory and gesture research

Cognitive load theory has identified several empirically supported effects that can inform instructional interventions to support learning (Kalyuga, Ayres, Chandler, &

Sweller, 2003; Mousavi, Low, & Sweller, 1995; Sweller, Ayres, & Kalyuga, 2011; Tindall-Ford, Chandler, & Sweller, 1997). Research has demonstrated that certain approaches to the design of learning materials and the associated activities derived from the design, can enhance learning due to learners' efficient use of limited cognitive resources. For example, one effect, the modality effect, has shown that when students are given learning materials containing diagrams and corresponding audio narrations in the place of expository written text, this dual-modality presentation can provide learning benefits. A key study that demonstrated this effect was Mousavi, Low, and Sweller (1995), where children were provided with worked examples in geometry. The first group was given worked examples with diagrams and written statements describing them, the second group was given the same diagrams and written statements and also listened to a corresponding audio statement played through a tape recorder. The third group was presented with a diagram and audio statement alone, but no written text. Results suggested that students presented the diagram with audio and no written statements completed questions faster than the other two groups. Tindall-Ford, Chandler, and Sweller (1997) found a similar effect with electrical apprentices studying electrical engineering materials. This study found that test scores were higher in a mixed mode condition. Similar to the modality effect, Mayer's Theory of Multimedia Learning (Mayer, 2009; Mayer & Moreno, 1998) applied the same principle of combining visual and auditory materials to multimedia animations, further informing the use of audio-visual technology to support learning.

The effectiveness of using audio-visual instructions is explained within a cognitive load theory framework by dual modality presentations using both auditory and visual channels in working memory rather than just the visual channel. Over the last ten years there has been a shift in cognitive load theory research exploring the use of learning strategies that incorporate the human motor system. This research has extended beyond learners being presented with audio and visual instruction to leverage the use of gestures in support of working memory processes. While it is argued that audio-visual instructions support learning through the use of co-reinforcement of novel information across modalities, using movements like gestures may also provide similar support by freeing up, or more efficient allocating of limited working memory resources. A synthesis of this research will be provided next to illustrate the key findings and highlight areas of emerging research in how the human motor system can support learning.

Human movement effect

Within cognitive load theory research, the human movement effect refers to the benefits of observing human movements when learning to perform motor tasks. This effect was identified after a series of experiments exploring the use of instructional animations found evidence that animations related to procedural motor tasks proved more effective for learning than the equivalent static materials. Two studies were critical in highlighting the efficacy of human movement for learning. Wong et al. (2009) presented learners with an animation depicting origami being folded from a first-person perspective, without showing hands. When compared with learners who were given static images to guide their paper folding, the learners who watched the animation demonstrated higher learning outcomes. Ayres, Marcus, Chan, and Qian (2009) found similar results in a study exploring the learning of knot-tying, with one group of learners looking at static images, and the other at animations of hands tying the knot, with the latter demonstrating increased learning outcomes. From a cognitive load theory perspective, this may suggest that observing human movement may free up, or more efficiently allocate, limited working memory resources that can be used to focus on other task-relevant goals. This theoretical advancement provided some insights into why the observation and physical replication of motor tasks may be beneficial for learning.

Given that human movement like gestures may free up limited working memory resources when learning procedural motor tasks, it may be hypothesised that self-gesturing may support mental simulation of a task when learning to solve a problem. In one recent study, when participants were given the Tower of Hanoi puzzle to solve, results showed that those who gestured had lower saccadic eye movement counts when compared to those who did not gesture (Pouw, Mavilidi, van Gog, & Paas, 2016). Eye movements have been found to provide a support mechanism for visually indexing information during visuospatial problem-solving tasks, with the quantification of saccadic eye movements indicating a measure of cognitive processing. It is thought that gesturing can assist in problem solving by externalising working memory processes, and as a result reduces cognitive load. The research showed that observing and making gestures may play an important role in learning and problem solving in certain contexts. While research within the confines of cognitive load theory has contributed to advancing our understanding of the human motor system's role in learning, other areas of research have also provided an understanding of the benefits of human movement for learning, albeit from different theoretical perspectives. The next section provides an overview of key findings of the benefit of movement for learning from different theoretical perspectives and how these research findings can contribute to cognitive load theory research and increase our understanding of how gestures affect educational experiences.

Embodied cognition

After the human movement effect provided theoretical grounding for the benefit of gestures within cognitive load theory research, Paas and Sweller (2012) identified a separate field of psychology, Embodied Cognition (Foglia & Wilson, 2013), as a framework for future studies investigating human movement. Embodied cognition posits that all cognition, including information processing, learning and problem solving is integrated with all types of sensory input including visual, auditory and human movement. When traditionally explored modalities such as visual and auditory information are coupled with physical experiences, cognition and schema acquisition is also supported (Barsalou, 1999). By assuming that a learner's body movements, including gestures, tactile and touch experiences, as well as their motion through an environment may support learning, subsequent studies within cognitive load theory began to incorporate embodied cognition as a supporting source of knowledge.

Through an examination of learning environments such as classrooms and early learning centers, a body of literature has grown around exploring the use of gestures in more traditional educational contexts. Research by Goldin-Meadow and others (Cook, Duffy, & Fenn, 2013; Cook, Mitchell & Goldin-Meadow, 2008; Goldin-Meadow & Cook, 2009; Goldin-Meadow, & Cook, 2009; Goldin-Meadow et al., 2012; Montessori, 1912/1964) has explored the role of pointing and gestures that represent concepts or processes in children's learning of math and language. This research has provided evidence that gestures can support learners' understanding of novel concepts, which is evidenced through increased learning outcomes. Though this work is not firmly grounded in an embodied cognition framework, the findings may be interpreted as such, while at the same time providing further evidence for the positive role of gestures in classroom-based learning.

Hand gestures have also been shown to benefit foreign languages learners in the classroom (Macedonia & Klimesch, 2014; Mavilidi, Okely, Chandler, Cliff, & Paas, 2015). When participants produced gestures representing an action associated with a novel word or phrase in foreign language learning, such as acting out the word for "swim" while learning the word in Italian, increased recall of these novel words was demonstrated. Further, when full-body movement was compared with arm and hand gesturing while sitting, the learners that engaged in full-body movement benefitted further (Mavilidi, et al., 2015). This study situated within the Embodied Cognition literature used iconic gestures (pretending to act on non-present objects) for learning novel vocabulary. This same type of gesturing can support mimicry. Novack, Goldin-Meadow, & Woodward (2015) showed that when an infant observed an adult demonstrate how a toy worked through an iconic gesture, an infant's ability to successfully operate a toy increased. Within the framework of cognitive load theory and embodied cognition, research into the cognitive function of gestures is presenting many interesting advances. With the increased use of touch-based technologies in classrooms, research that examines gestures facilitated through technology may provide evidence to inform how gestures and ICT may be integrated effectively to support student learning. The section that follows, discusses current research into gesture-based ICT and argues that further exploration of gesturing within ICT may provide important insights into learning, as technological affordances continue to advance.

Gesturing and ICT

While the modality effect and Mayer's Theory of Multimedia Learning (Mayer & Moreno, 1998; Mayer 2009) describe the benefits of simultaneous visual and auditory learning materials, these frameworks for multimodal learning experiences historically did not explore gestures. This may be due to a lack of exploration involving gestures at the time, as well as an absence of the technologies required to accurately record these movements. Recent studies exploring the use of pointing and tracing gestures may serve as foundational work for extending these frameworks by leveraging touch-based technologies to investigate more active physical engagement with ICT-based learning materials.

Macken and Ginns (2014) investigated the relationship between gesturing and learning. This foundational study demonstrated that learners who pointed to particular key medical terms on a paper-based diagram of a heart, benefited from increased learning outcomes, when compared with those who did not point. Additionally, the research showed that learners who traced along paths of blood flow on a diagram of a heart demonstrated greater understanding of the content, compared to those that did not trace. Research by Hu, Ginns, & Bobis (2015) showed the practical use of self-gesturing by having learners trace worked examples of angles in geometry. Results showed that students who traced angles outperformed those students who did not, a finding supported by related research in the area of experimental psychology. Multiple studies investigating child development have suggested that attention is prioritised near the hands, suggesting that the hands provide a joint attention mechanism tied to the early language acquisition in the early years of life (Abrams, Davoli, Du, Knapp, & Paull, 2008; Liszkowski, Carpenter, Henning, Striano, & Tommasello, 2004).

A number of studies have expanded upon pointing and tracing to leverage the affordances of touch-based ICT tools. Agostinho et al. (2015) extended Hu and Ginns' work in a study that investigated the effect of children tracing on an iPad while learning how to understand temperature line graphs. Results demonstrated that those who traced scored higher in transfer tests than those who did not. The results from this study are supported by Lee's (2015) research that found students' learning about the heart using a touch-based device who tapped the screen to focus attention on specific structures performed better on a post-test identification task than students who used a traditional keyboard and mouse-based PC to learn the same information about the heart. Similar benefits of hand gestures were found for a basic mathematics estimation task using iPads (Dubé & McEwen, 2015). In this study students were either asked to point on a line or drag along a slider to estimate quantities. The research shows that the dragging condition led to higher learning outcomes when compared to simply pointing. While these gestures function primarily as a means to control the user interface to specify quantity, they could also be interpreted as interactions that reinforce the relationships between concepts in that a sliding movement better aligns with estimating quantity than pointing. When considering previous research that has focused on pointing and tracing on paper, these ICT-based studies are of interest given that they provide learners the opportunity to directly interact with dynamic multimedia learning materials, a learning experience not possible prior to the advent of tablets and smartphones. Though additional research is needed, studies investigating gesture-based ICT tools in educational contexts have suggested that gestures related to reinforcing and establishing relationships between concepts can benefit learning. The underlying explanation of these results is still yet to be firmly established, though it is possible that attentional and embodied experiences can act as a form of reinforcement, much like an audio narration which reinforces the content of visual learning materials.

Incorporating gestures to support learning has consistently demonstrated benefits through the embodiment of concepts and objects, attention guidance and problem-solving simulation, but in the context of ICT use, there are questions that remain to be answered. Given that the investigation of hand gestures and how they affect learning is still a growing area of research, we still do not understand how the different types of gestures such as pointing and tracing, may affect learning in different ways. It is also important to consider the cognitive function that these gestures play, as previous studies have explored both conceptually linked gestures, and gestures that merely guide attention, such as pointing. As stated by Sheu and Chen (2014, p.276) in their review of research in gesture-based computing, "innovative cross-disciplinary research and related publications that document specific gesture-based learning systems and their associated designs are now vital". In the next section we outline a novel study in gesture-based ICT-supported research that may provide further insight into the benefits of gesturing coupled with educational technologies.

Exploring gestures with the use of ICT

A study to explore multiple types of gestures through touch-based ICT materials has been recently undertaken by Sepp, Tindall-Ford, Agostinho, and Paas. This research investigates how high school students' learning performance and cognitive load is affected by observing and making different finger-based gestures while working through an audiovisual geometry lesson on an iPad. The iPad is a multi-touch tablet device increasingly ubiquitous in educational contexts. The lesson presented on an iPad focuses on learning to solve for angles on a parallel line by presenting a number of worked examples to demonstrate the steps involved. Students watched different versions of the multimedia lesson corresponding to one of four conditions:

1. no animated cues and no gestures performed.
2. animated hands shown tracing along key angles and no gestures performed.
3. animated hands shown pointing on key angles and pointing gestures performed.
4. animated hands shown tracing along key angles and tracing gestures performed.

For the purposes of this study, pointing gestures are considered to focus attention for the learner, whereas tracing gestures (or "embodied" gestures) are considered to physically embody aspects of the problem-solving strategy, in this study the relationship between angles. This study's primary goal was to:

i   isolate attentional gestures which focus learner's attention to these angles (e.g. pointing at two equal angles). (Groups 1 & 2)

ii   isolate "embodied" gestures that physically represent aspects of the problem-solving strategy (e.g. tracing along two equal angles). (Groups 3 & 4)

A secondary goal of the research was to explore how observation and performance of these gestures affected learning in different ways.

While this study is continuing, the methods presented below may provide a foundation for future studies in gesture-based research. A custom ICT tool was developed which displayed interactive worked example lessons, and also served as the primary means of collecting gesture-based data. During the experiment, participants worked through a custom-designed application or "app" created specifically for the iPad. The app (called Geometry Touch) included audiovisual lessons on geometry, specifically focusing on learning how to solve for angles on a parallel line, along with test questions on concept recall, and near and far transfer of knowledge. Each lesson was presented as a video, which included integrated worked example diagrams, and accompanying audio explanations. Diagrams and worked examples were visually presented as static learning materials, with specific animated hands overlaid for each condition (See Figure 11.1).

While participants worked through the lessons and test questions, their interactions with the touch screen were recorded through the software. Leveraging touch-based technologies provided the researchers with invaluable insight into how students physically engaged with the lesson, including which gestures were performed and when, whether they complied with instructions and how they gestured outside of expected norms, such as touching the screen to aid solving maths problems or simply tapping to focus their concentration. It was critical the students not be distracted or supported by any lines digitally drawn on the screen and so, as they worked through each lesson, every touch registered on the iPad's screen was

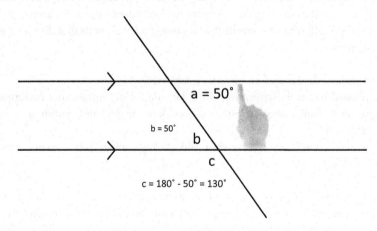

FIGURE 11.1 Animated hand shown during lesson on Geometry Touch iPad App

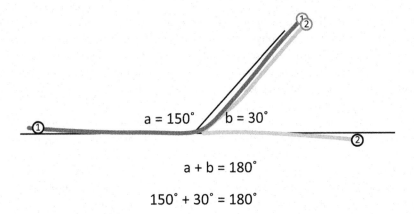

FIGURE 11.2 Tracing gestures captured from Geometry Touch iPad app

recorded, but not displayed. These touches were then rendered and saved by the app for later analysis as visual and quantitative data. As shown in Figure 11.2, the app takes a "picture" of each participant's gesture performance for every screen they are asked to interact with. The lines in the image along with the numbered circles indicate the path and sequence tracing gestures along with their direction with green circles indicating the start of a trace and red circles indicating the end. The color of the line (represented by yellow to red shading) represents the speed of the gesture from slow to fast. In addition, the maximum, minimum and average of any sustained touches such as traces were recorded as numerical data. This study provides a novel methodology for observing the physical interactions participants have with ICT learning materials. In the next section, a discussion of how this study may inform future research is presented, including integration with emerging technologies such as Virtual, Augmented and Mixed realities, and how these technologies may affect learning.

Discussion: possibilities and considerations

The integration of gesture-based learning materials and apps is already taking place in many classrooms and other educational contexts. Digital learning environments including web apps, mobile apps and other emerging technologies are blurring the line between physical and screen-based learning. It may be argued that within these environments, the human motor system may support learning, with further research providing insights into the cognitive benefits that these physical actions provide.

Historically, ICT tools within the context of educational research have been used for the unidirectional presentation of information and indirect interaction with learning materials through a mouse or keyboard. The aforementioned study leverages novel research methods for the capturing of participants' direct physical engagement with learning materials beyond direct observation or video recordings.

This is significant because technologies now exist that allow researchers and educators alike to capture the physical movements of learners as they interact with virtual objects and learning materials while working to solve problems. This capturing of physical interactions may constitute an expansion of available learning analytics to provide "physical learning analytics", which can inform the future design of learning materials and experiences.

With regards to gesture-based research within the framework of cognitive load theory, leveraging the affordances of new technologies presents exciting opportunities for future research. Our study presented a method for isolating the effects of different types of gestures by capturing the physical interactions that the participants had on a touch-screen with two-dimensional learning materials focusing on geometry. There are, however many technologies that are available that now support tracking movement in three-dimensional space: Virtual Reality (VR), Mixed Reality (MR) and Augmented Reality (AR). These technologies immerse the user in computer-generated virtual worlds or overlay digital images, objects or information over real world environments. These technologies push beyond the presentation of learning materials on a screen, to immerse the learner in real or virtual applications of concepts. This is accomplished by tracking their hand, head, eye and even full body movement through a confined physical space, with the learning environment responding to their physical actions. Having access to this tracking information opens many doors for future studies within cognitive load theory and embodied cognition research, especially with regards to how it can inform our understanding of attention and embodiment. By capturing how learners are physically engaging with these environments, we can gain a unique understanding of how these actions may support learning.

Before taking a leap of faith into virtual worlds (VR), researchers should consider that results for studies conducted in the real world may not apply in virtual ones. Ongoing studies in psychology and other areas are continuing to investigate how cognition and motor function differ in VR, so it is important to first replicate existing studies in these environments to confirm that the same rules for perception and cognition apply. By reaffirming that cognitive load effects still apply in VR, we can start exploring new areas with a robust foundation, confident in our assumption that the modality effect, human movement effect and the benefits that gestures make to learning, may translate into the virtual world. Though emerging technologies including VR, MR and AR may not currently be present in every classroom, the next section provides important implications for more ubiquitous gesture-based technologies and how they may best support learning and instruction.

Implications for educational practice

Touch-based technologies such as smart phones, tablets and other portable computing devices present unique opportunities for instructional practice. When considering the use of these technologies for teaching, findings within gesture-based research can inform decisions regarding how they may be implemented effectively. Presented below are two recommendations for considering the use of apps and touch-based ICT tools.

Apps that encourage gestures that are not conceptually aligned with the learning materials may not offer the same benefits as those that do.

Questions remain around the cognitive function of gestures, with regard to their support of attention guidance and conceptual reinforcement. When choosing apps for use in the classroom, the ways in which they encourage human movement and gesturing should be a primary factor in that choice. Apps that encourage gestures for attention guidance and clarification of information related to learning, may provide cognitive supports that lead to increased outcomes whereas apps that only include gestures for navigation and other superfluous tasks may not. As gesture-based technologies become more common, research that investigates how these tools affect cognition can provide important insights into how the human motor system can enhance learning. As we continue to experiment in the classroom, and to investigate through research, it is important to think critically about how our bodies interact with technology, because while there may be an app for everything, an app may not always be the best solution.

ICT Tools that provide opportunities for observing and making gestures can support learning and problem solving.

Whether it be for presentation of content, learning motor tasks or assessment and reflection, giving students opportunities to both observe and actively perform gestures and other movements while using ICT should be leveraged whenever possible. In early learning contexts, games and play are a common strategy, but as students age, it is generally assumed that they are relegated to seated rows and note taking. Current studies demonstrate that even with the use of ICT tools, the human motor system may play an important role in facilitating the learning process, regardless of age. Instructional strategies may include embedding hand gestures in an online lecture to bring attention to key points, leveraging the physical sensors in smartphones to play games in the classroom, or simply to encourage the use of pointing and tracing when engaging with digital learning materials. Given that an array of ICT tools are now available to many learners, instructors should consider the advantages that movement can bring to their students' learning experiences, beyond those of being motivating and different. If using a certain tool results in students being less physically active, or if they are passively engaging with materials that do not take advantage of the benefits that movement can bring, that tool may not encourage learning in the ways that another tool, or even a more traditional approach might. It is important then, to consider how educational technologies can build upon traditional teaching by incorporating gestures and other movements to benefit learning.

Conclusion

This chapter has provided an overview of the current state of gesture-based research within cognitive load theory, along with an emerging area of inquiry around the use of touch-based ICT tools. An in-progress study, which uses ICT to present learning materials while simultaneously collecting gesture data was discussed in terms of future directions for cognitive load theory research. Instructional implications for the use of gesture-based apps and ICT tools were then presented to ground current findings in educational practice. As research into the benefits of hand gestures and movement continues to provide important insights for learning, the incorporation of gesture-based ICT tools into this research can build upon existing findings to inform future educational practice.

References

Abrams, R. A., Davoli, C. C., Du, F., Knapp, W. H.III, & Paull, D. (2008). Altered vision near the hands. *Cognition*, 107(3), 1035–1047. http://doi.org/10.1016/j.cognition.2007.09.006.

Agostinho, S., Tindall-Ford, S., Ginns, P., Howard, S. J., Leahy, W., & Paas, F. (2015). Giving learning a helping hand: Finger tracing of temperature graphs on an iPad. *Educational Psychology Review*, 27(3), 427–443. http://doi.org/10.1007/s10648-015-9315-5.

Ayres, P., Marcus, N., Chan, C., & Qian, N. (2009). Learning hand manipulative tasks: When instructional animations are superior to equivalent static representations. *Computers in Human Behavior*, 25(2), 348–353. http://doi.org/10.1016/j.chb.2008.12.013.

Barsalou, L. W. (1999). Perceptions of perceptual symbols. *Behavioral and Brain Sciences*, 22 (04), 637–660. http://doi.org/10.1017/S0140525X99532147.

Cook, S. W., Duffy, R. G., & Fenn, K. M. (2013). Consolidation and transfer of learning after observing hand gesture. *Child Development*, 84(6), 1863–1871. http://doi.org/10.1111/cdev.12097.

Cook, S. W., Mitchell, Z., & Goldin-Meadow, S. (2008). Gesturing makes learning last. *Cognition*, 106(2), 1047–1058. http://doi.org/10.1016/j.cognition.2007.04.010.

Dubé, A. K., & McEwen, R. N. (2015). Do gestures matter? The implications of using touchscreen devices in mathematics instruction. *Learning and Instruction*, 40(C), 89–98. http://doi.org/10.1016/j.learninstruc.2015.09.002.

Foglia, L., & Wilson, R. A. (2013). Embodied cognition. *Wiley Interdisciplinary Reviews: Cognitive Science*, 4(3), 319–325. http://doi.org/10.1002/wcs.1226.

Goldin-Meadow, S., & Cook, S. W. (2009). Gesturing gives children new ideas about math. *Psychological Science*, 20(3), 267–272. http://doi.org/10.1086/659964?ref=search-gateway:4d5c7866182d0f01d9bef79f563ad121.

Goldin-Meadow, S., Levine, S. C., Zinchenko, E., Yip, T. K., Hemani, N., & Factor, L. (2012). Doing gesture promotes learning a mental transformation task better than seeing gesture. *Developmental Science*, 15(6), 876–884. http://doi.org/10.1111/j.1467-7687.2012.01185.x.

Hu, F. T., Ginns, P., & Bobis, J. (2015). Getting the point: Tracing worked examples enhances learning. *Learning and Instruction*, 35(C), 85–93. http://doi.org/10.1016/j.learninstruc.2014.10.002.

Kalyuga, S., Ayres, P., Chandler, P. A., & Sweller, J. (2003). The expertise reversal effect. *Educational Psychologist*, 38(1), 23–31. http://doi.org/10.1207/S15326985EP3801_4.

Lee, H. W. (2015). Does touch-based interaction in learning with interactive images improve students' learning? *The Asia-Pacific Education Researcher*, 24(4), 1–5. http://doi.org/10.1007/s40299-014-0197-y.

Liszkowski, U., Carpenter, M., Henning, A., Striano, T., & Tomasello, M. (2004). Twelve-month-olds point to share attention and interest. *Developmental Science*, 7(3), 297–307. http://doi.org/10.1111/j.1467-7687.2004.00349.x.

Macedonia, M., & Klimesch, W. (2014). Long-term effects of gestures on memory for foreign language words trained in the classroom. *Mind*, 8(2), 74–88.

Macken, L., & Ginns, P. (2014). Pointing and tracing gestures may enhance anatomy and physiology learning. *Medical Teacher*, 36(7), 596–601. http://doi.org/10.3109/0142159X. 2014.899684.

Mavilidi, M. F., Okely, A. D., Chandler, P. A., Cliff, D. P., & Paas, F. (2015). Effects of integrated physical exercises and gestures on preschool children's foreign language voca-bulary learning. *Educational Psychology Review*, 27(3), 413–426. http://doi.org/10.1007/ s10648-015-9337-z.

Mayer, R. E. (2009). *Multimedia learning*. Cambridge University Press.

Mayer, R. E., & Moreno, R. (1998). A split-attention effect in multimedia learning: Evidence for dual processing systems in working memory. *Journal of Educational Psychology*, 90(2), 312–320. http://doi.org/10.1037/0022-0663.90.2.312.

Montessori, M. (1912/1964). *The Montessori method*. Cambridge, MA: Robert Bentley, Inc.

Mousavi, S. Y., Low, R., & Sweller, J. (1995). Reducing cognitive load by mixing auditory and visual presentation modes. *Journal of Educational Psychology*, 87(2), 319–334. http:// doi.org/10.1037/0022-0663.87.2.319.

Novack, M. A., Goldin-Meadow, S., & Woodward, A. L. (2015). Learning from gesture: How early does it happen? *Cognition*, 142(C), 138–147. http://doi.org/10.1016/j.cogni tion.2015.05.018.

Paas, F., & Sweller, J. (2012). An evolutionary upgrade of cognitive load theory: using the human motor system and collaboration to support the learning of complex cognitive tasks. *Educational Psychology Review*, 24(1), 27–45.

Pouw, W. T. J. L., Mavilidi, M.F., van Gog, T., & Paas, F. (2016). Gesturing during mental problem solving reduces eye movements, especially for individuals with lower visual working memory capacity. *Cognitive Processing*, 17(3), 1–9. http://doi.org/10.1007/ s10339-016-0757-6.

Sheu, F.R., & Chen, N. S. (2014). Taking a signal: A review of gesture-based computing research in education. *Computers & Education*, 78(c), 268–277. http://doi.org/10.1016/j. compedu.2014.06.008.

Smith, H. J., Higgins, S., Wall, K., & Miller, J. (2005). Interactive whiteboards: Boon or bandwagon? A critical review of the literature. *Journal of Computer Assisted Learning*, 21(2), 91–101. http://doi.org/10.1111/j.1365-2729.2005.00117.x.

Sweller, J., Ayres, P., & Kalyuga, S. (2011). *Cognitive load theory*. New York: Springer.

Tindall-Ford, S., Chandler, P., & Sweller, J. (1997). When two sensory modes are better than one. *Journal of Experimental Psychology: Applied*, 3(4), 257–287.

Wong, A., Marcus, N., Ayres, P., Smith, L., Cooper, G. A., Paas, F., & Sweller, J. (2009). Instructional animations can be superior to statics when learning human motor skills. *Computers in Human Behavior*, 25(2), 339–347. http://doi.org/10.1016/j.chb.2008.12.012.

12

EMBODIED COGNITION?

Effects of pointing and tracing gestures on learning performance, eye movement and cognitive load

Babette Park

JUSTUS-LIEBIG-UNIVERSITY GIESSEN, GERMANY; SAARLAND UNIVERSITY, GERMANY

Andreas Korbach

SAARLAND UNIVERSITY, GERMANY

Paul Ginns

THE UNIVERSITY OF SYDNEY, AUSTRALIA

Roland Brünken

SAARLAND UNIVERSITY, GERMANY

Empirical research on learning and instruction has historically considered the visual and auditory modalities (e.g. recent meta-analyses: Ginns, 2005) but relatively little scholarship in this area has considered the haptic, including kinesthetic and tactile, modalities (e.g. Pouw, Van Gog & Paas, 2014). The kinesthetic modality is considered when bodily activity or movement is involved in learning, e.g., tracing in the air in order to reflect on elements of geometry (Hu, Ginns & Bobis, 2015). The tactile modality is considered when there are interactions between the learning material and the learner's tactile sensations, e.g., tracing across paper-based lesson (e.g. Macken & Ginns, 2014) or when manipulating toy objects to simulate the actions described in a text in order to enhance the text comprehension (Glenberg, Gutierrez, Levin, Japuntich & Kaschak, 2004). With the latter two examples it seems also to be obvious that many haptic learning methods include both the kinesthetic as well as tactile modality. Pointing or tracing on the paper can also be seen as a form of gesturing due to hand movements and manipulating toy objects also includes bodily activity, therefore hinting to kinesthetic modality.

However, in the past few years, the so-called tracing effect has recently emerged as a very interesting effect; this effect refers to the learning benefits from pointing to and tracing on learning material. Macken and Ginns (2014), for example, show with their study that university-educated adults who pointed and traced at elements of a paper-based lesson achieved significantly higher performance on terminology and comprehension tests about the structure and function of the human heart compared to a study group, which was not allowed to use their hands. A further study by Hu et al. (2015) demonstrated tracing improves learning outcomes when incorporated into lessons built on mathematics worked examples on parallel lines. In their first experiment, children (11–12 year olds) who traced worked examples on the paper correctly solved more advanced test questions, solved them more quickly, made fewer errors, and rated those questions as less difficult than those who studied the worked examples by reading. In a follow-up experiment with similarly aged students, Hu et al. (2015) tested a hypothesised performance gradient (i.e., a sequence order of students' performance across the three experimental conditions – no tracing, tracing in the air, and tracing on the paper), predicting an ordinal correlation between the number of working memory modalities activated (modalities: visual only vs. visual + kinesthetic vs. visual + kinesthetic + tactile) and learning outcomes. Performance gradient hypotheses were supported for acquisition phase problem solving and error rate, test phase basic question test performance, and advanced question test performance, time to solution, and ratings of test question difficulty.

Together, such results indicate not only the suitability of different haptic methods for teaching and learning with kindergarten children, e.g., letter-learning by tracing on sandpaper or methods of phoneme identification (Bara, Gentaz, & Colé, 2007) or geometrical shape recognition (e.g. Kalenine, Pinnet & Gentaz, 2010) recommended by the Montessori Approach (e.g. Montessori, 1912, 1914, 1969), but also in times of the touchscreen-era it is highly relevant for multimedia learning. However, these studies with school students and university-educated adults were realised with paper and pencil materials and need to be replicated by further studies that introduce modern media like for example, a touchscreen-learning situation, as studied by Agostinho, Tindall-Ford, Ginns, Howard, Leahy and Paas (2015). Current contexts of learning and instruction with modern media, which offer new functions with touchpads or screens, highlight the tracing method under consideration of further learning content and different age groups. The present chapter therefore summarises different theoretical perspectives on the effect of pointing and tracing and provides an outlook on how to proceed with research on variation of haptic methods including guidelines for integrating up-to-date measures of learning performance, eye movements and cognitive load.

Three different theoretical perspectives on the effect of pointing and tracing

Two of the most relevant models of empirical research on learning and instruction, the Cognitive Theory of Multimedia Learning (CTML, e.g. Mayer, 2009) as well as cognitive load theory (e.g. Sweller, Ayres, & Kalyuga, 2011) have initiated the development of numerous instructional methods. The positive effects of these methods are based upon considerations of the theoretically assumed human cognitive architecture and/or advantageous influence on cognitive load. Different modalities have been focused upon when comparing, for example, learning from pure visual material (e.g. text-picture information) with audiovisual material (e.g. narration-picture information). Other modalities have rarely been considered, even though a variation of CTML, e.g. the Cognitive-Affective Theory on Learning with Media (Moreno, 2006; Moreno & Mayer, 2007) hint to other modalities. In this model, not only visual and auditory information but also tactile, olfactory and gustatory information is mentioned as incoming information in the sensory memory. All of this discriminable sensory information can potentially be manipulated within instruction, and should therefore be differentiated at least in the sensory memory of working memory models. The following assumed cognitive processing in working memory, filtered by attention and selection processes, leads to the construction of mental models, which may not necessarily be assigned to the mentioned different modalities anymore. At this stage of processing, authors of working memory models differentiate between verbal and non-verbal or pictorial mental models and cross-modality processing is recognised (e.g., Mayer, 2009; Moreno, 2006; Paivio, 1986). At this point, several questions arise: Does additional tactile information induce an intensified construction of mental models because of the additional and to be processed tactile information? Or do tactile processes simply provoke a more focused direction of attention? And what is the nature of cognitive load when using tactile learning methods? These three questions will be discussed within the framework of the following three perspectives on the effect of pointing and tracing from research on haptics, attention and cognitive load. These three perspectives moreover represent three different views on recent discussions about embodied cognition (see for example: Barsalou, 2008; Pouw et al., 2014).

Pointing and tracing from the perspective of research on haptics

Empirical research on haptic working memory processing falls far short of research on visual and auditory channels (for an overview see Kaas, Stoekel & Goebel, 2008). However, there is an increasing consideration of possible intersensory facilitation of visual processing by movement. For instance, in Baddeley's (2012) recent version of his working memory model the haptic sensory information, which includes kinesthetic and tactile input, are mentioned as a possible influencing factor on processing in the visuo-spatial sketchpad (one of the sub-systems of working memory in his model, contrasting another sub-system: the phonological loop). Other authors have discussed the phenomenon that the inclusion of tactile and kinesthetic modalities has an effect on cognitive processing with the haptic channel assumption. The application of the tactile or kinesthetic modality is assumed to induce the activation and use of the haptic channel in working memory (Alibali & Nathan, 2012; Glenberg, Witt & Metcalf, 2013; Kaas, Stoeckel, & Goebel, 2008). This explanation could also serve as the basis for reasoning why several tactile

instructional methods like the pointing and tracing method lead to learning benefits. However, questions about the format of the haptic channel raise other questions: Does such an additional channel provide additional working memory
capacity, or simply more efficient use of available capacity? Recent insights contradict the separate haptic channel assumption, as information perception is associated with cross-modal selection and organisation processes because visual and
tactile information perception do not seem to be independent (Eck, Kaas &
Goebel, 2013). This insight from research on the interaction between haptic and
visual information processing hints to the assumption that the structure of working
memory including its different buffers is not the relevant aspect for information
processing but rather the characteristic of the information itself is the relevant
aspect. Here we start to switch from a perspective of research on haptics to a perspective of research on attention, as attention-guidance in learning processes is not
very dependent on the format but rather on the quality of incoming information,
which will be explained in the next section.

Pointing and tracing from the perspective of research on attention

When discussing learning processes and information processing with a focus on
attention, there is one working memory model that is distinctive in comparison to
the numerous buffer models (e.g. Atkinson & Shiffrin, 1968; Baddeley, 2012). The
buffer models explain our cognitive architecture by structured buffers (e.g. sensory
register, working memory and long-term memory) and the information that has to
pass through for processing. The Embedded-Processes Model of Working Memory
from Cowan (1999, 2000, 2005) is not based on the description of these structures,
but on the argument that the characteristics of to-be processed information is the
only relevant aspect in information processing. Therefore, working memory capacity is not limited by the structure of buffers, but only by the fleetingness of
information due to memory decay and interference with subsequent stimuli. In this
model, only the focus of attention with a fixed capacity limit in chunks (information units) is crucial. This framework therefore considers all modalities, including
the kinesthetic and tactile modality, because the central structure of this model is
conscious information, which can be represented over all modalities. This is why
the focus of attention could also provide the relevant explanation approach for the
effectiveness of haptic instruction methods. Based on this model, it is assumed that
the tracing method induces an attention-guiding process, which explains its positive effect on learning outcomes. From this point of view, there are higher order
cognitive processes, especially the focus of attention, that contribute to and guide
the learning process. Pointing and tracing gestures could therefore foster the guidance and focus of attention (Hu et al., 2015), serving as a primitive but effective
attention-guiding prompt. This function of pointing can already be observed in
interactions with toddlers around the age of 12 months, when attention and
interest is guided by themselves or their interacting partners (Liszkowski, Brown,
Callaghan, Takada, & de Vos, 2012). Recent studies on the interaction of visual

attention and hand positions provide supporting evidence that pointing gestures can be used as attention-guiding prompts. The positioning of hands near an object changes the visual attention and perception in the direction of the object in the way that the object will stand out of the background or environment (Cosman & Vecera, 2010). Thus, the object in question will be investigated and inspected for a longer time and in a more detailed way (Reed, Grubb & Steele, 2006). In order to investigate visual attention in instructional design research, it is necessary to draw on valid and reliable indicators, which have been already applied in parts in empirical research on learning and instruction. A series of appropriate and recently discussed indicators of eye-movement behavior are summarised below.

Pointing and tracing from the perspective of research on cognitive load

A further possible theoretical explanation for positive learning effects of haptic instructional methods is based on cognitive load theory (e.g. Sweller et al., 2011). Research on cognitive load aims at formulating practical implications for the instructional design of learning materials and activities. These implications are derived from empirical studies on the relation between information presentation and the characteristics of our human cognitive system (Kirschner, 2002; Paas, Renkl & Sweller, 2003; Plass, Moreno & Brünken, 2010; Sweller et al., 2011). In order to specify the interaction between external information presentation and internal information processing, cognitive load theory has been conceptualised on the basis of three general assumptions. Cognitive load theory assumes that (1) different learning issues can be distinguished by complexity of the learning task, (2) human working memory, the cognitive subsystem for processing current information, is limited in its capacity for processing (Baddeley, 1986; Miyake & Shah, 1999), and (3) learned content is stored in a capacity-unlimited long-term memory by using meaningful structured complex mental representations, in the form of schemata (Rumelhart & Ortony, 1976; Schank & Abelson, 1977). The description of additional, more specific assumptions of cognitive load theory exists already in numerous publications and the following one is out of a paper on cognitive and affective processes in multimedia learning by Park, Flowerday, and Brünken (2015). Cognitive load theory (Kirschner, 2002; Plass et al., 2010; Sweller et al., 2011) assumes, after the three general assumptions mentioned above and further more recent assumptions integrating an evolution theoretical perspective (see for example Sweller, 2010), that knowledge acquisition depends on the efficiency of the use of available (limited) cognitive resources. The extent of cognitive load is thereafter determined by three components (Sweller, van Merriënboer & Paas, 1998).

First, intrinsic cognitive load (ICL) is related to the complexity of the learning content in terms of number of elements and the interactivity between those elements. Thus, intrinsic load depends on the number of elements and the relationships between them that must be simultaneously processed in working memory to learn the material being taught. The larger the number of elements of the to-be-learned material and the higher the interactivity of those elements, the higher the intrinsic load of the material. Second, extraneous cognitive load (ECL) is caused by the cognitive demands imposed by instructional design that is not conducive to learning. The better the learning material is presented, considering the cognitive architecture and empirically proved instructional design principles, the lower the extraneous cognitive load. Instructional material which does not specifically support learning and/or distracts from learning (e.g., search behavior which is not part of the learning goal) should therefore be avoided. Finally, germane cognitive load (GCL) is the load that results from engaging in learning activities that effectively and efficiently foster schema acquisition. Germane cognitive load is thereafter also elicited by instructional material that facilitates or is beneficial for effective and efficient learning processes and therefore beneficial for the learning outcome.

Whereas extraneous sources of load hinder learning, intrinsic sources of load reflect the complexity of the given learning task in relation to the learner's level of expertise, and germane sources of load promote learning by helping students engage in the process of schema formation and automation. This triarchic model of cognitive load theory (for a summary see also Moreno & Park, 2010) has been updated by recent discussions on cognitive load theory (Choi, van Merriënboer & Paas, 2014; Kalyuga, 2011). Fundamental changes of the model concern the load type's intrinsic and germane load. Both types are now defined as overall intrinsic. This has been revised due to the strong relation between the theoretical constructs of intrinsic and germane load. In addition, the difficulty in defining and measuring the individual contributions of both load types for the overall cognitive load led to the decision to consider germane load as germane resource, which reflects the magnitude of working memory capacity that is associated with learning. The differentiation between intrinsic and extraneous cognitive load nevertheless remains, so that the following explanations on how haptic instruction methods affect learning are associated with the increase of intrinsic cognitive load or the reduction of extraneous cognitive load.

The first explanation of the pointing and tracing effect from the perspective of cognitive load theory holds that the haptic method induces intensified information processing that should be reflected by an increased cognitive activity in the learning phase. This positive activation should result in enhanced schema construction and thereafter a significantly higher learning performance of students' learning with pointing and tracing in contrast to learners of a control group. Moreover, a significant difference should be apparent in intrinsic cognitive load ratings that are associated with a learning-enhancing cognitive load during the learning phase due to a facilitated and more detailed inspection of learning material (Abrams, Davoli, Du, Knapp, & Paull, 2008). Evidence for this intrinsic cognitive load explanation has not yet been provided. The second explanation of the pointing and tracing effect from the cognitive load perspective reflects the necessary searching and assigning processes of different information (e.g., picture and text information) during the learning process, which can be facilitated by pointing to and tracing the relevant areas of the learning material and thereby reducing extraneous cognitive load (Hu et al., 2015). For this hypothesis, again, no empirical confirmation has been provided. However, a first hint of possible cognitive load effects of pointing and tracing was found in the study by Hu et al. (2015) showing that learners who used the haptic method rated the intrinsic cognitive load, measured by difficulty of learning test questions, to be significantly lower in the test phase when information has to be retrieved in contrast to a control group. In sum, further studies have to be carried out to test these cognitive load assumptions as an explanation for the pointing and tracing effect in learning.

How to integrate the three perspectives in future research on pointing and tracing

In order to investigate the pointing and tracing method under reconsideration of all the mentioned perspectives above, three indicators should be measured in an appropriate way: learning performance, eye-tracking and cognitive load measures. These three aspects in combination allow us to inspect the induced modified cognitive processing in a more detailed way and are outlined separately in the next sections.

Measuring learning performance in a distinctive way

Learning performance could be measured by using different subscales, which should not only include the inspection of different processing levels as operationalised by pure recall or retention tasks versus comprehension and transfer tasks (Mayer, 2009). The analysis of learning performance could specifically profit from the differentiation of knowledge that reflects the structure of the learning content in contrast to knowledge, which explicitly refers to procedures or processes within the learning material at hand (Park, Münzer, Seufert & Brünken, 2016). For instance, it would be interesting not only to investigate if learners know about the structure of the human heart, but also if they are able to explain the function and processes that are going on that also includes blood flow directions and ideas of consequences in this heart system in case of diverse malfunctions. This is probably the key to find specific effects of haptic methods, which should especially foster knowledge about processes or functions and not only about the structure of to be learned systems. More specifically, due to the different perspectives from above, using haptic methods should elicit cognitive processing that integrates kinesthetic and/or tactile modality. Therefore, this should specifically foster the integration of mentally represented models which include information on processes, movements and/or tactile characteristics relevant for complex learning goals such as knowing specific procedures in to be learned complex systems. Thus, haptic methods should not only foster knowledge about the structure of complex systems, but also and specifically about the processes within the systems. And for both types of knowledge, structure or process knowledge, it is possible to ask recall, comprehension or transfer questions.

Measuring visual attention while learning by eye-tracking

For measuring visual attention while learning, different valid and reliable indicators are required, which have already been used within empirical research on learning and instruction. A series of eye-tracking indicators could be appropriate in order to specify the learning processes directly within the learning phase. Recently discussed indicators of eye-movement behavior can provide information about the focus of visual attention (Haider & Frensch, 1999; Jarodzka, Scheiter, Gerjets & van Gog, 2010; Laeng, Ørbo, Holmlund & Miozzo, 2011). The main assumption that basically allows interpreting eye-movement behavior as an indicator for visual attention is already expressed by the eye-mind-hypothesis developed by Just and Carpenter (1976, 1980, 1993). Mayer (2010) goes one step further by assuming that everything that verifiably is in the visual focus of the learner can be seen as processed information and therefore serves as an indicator for cognitive activity. Often-used indicators for the degree of cognitive processes are fixations as well as the number and duration of fixations amongst others (Boucheix & Lowe, 2010; Canham & Hegarty, 2010; Meyer, Rasch & Schnotz, 2010). Fixations can provide detailed information about visual information processing and hint a the current allocation of attention. Finally, in combination with measures of learning performance, these eye-tracking indicators can be used as information on the focus of mental effort and cognitive activity (Folker, Ritter & Sichelschmidt, 2005; Mayer, 2010; Pomplun et al., 2001). For example, studies on fostering instructional methods in multimedia learning show that the total fixation time on picture information increases over the time of a lesson, which is an indicator of learning-relevant cognitive processes, and is related to search-and-match activities (mapping) of the different representations in multimedia learning (Korbach, Brünken & Park, 2016; Mayer 2010; Park, Knörzer, Plass, & Brünken, 2015; Park, Korbach, & Brünken, 2015; Rayner, Li, Williams, Cave, & Well, 2007; Reichle, Rayner, & Pollatsek, 2003). Additionally, the number of transitions between corresponding picture- and text-information is seen in many of these studies as an indicator for integrative cognitive processing and engagement in schema construction The authors assume that a high number of transitions reflect high cognitive engagement for integrating verbal and pictorial information (Schmidt-Weigand, Kohnert, & Glowalla, 2010). Additionally, visual switches between related information on so-called areas of interest (AOIs), which can be determined before learning, are used as indicators for mental integration processes. These visual switches can represent processes of searching and matching the related information of different locations in the learning material (Holsanova, Holmberg, & Holmqvist 2009; Schmidt-Weigand et al., 2010).

Across all these eye-movement indicators, there is a recurring question of whether anything that is in our visual focus is required to be processed. In other words, not everything that is in the visual focus will be processed automatically (Holmqvist et al., 2011). This is why it is necessary to combine measures of learning performance with the eye-tracking data. Only in this way is it possible to get clear results of the positive relation between different eye-tracking process variables during learning and the learning output in order to draw the appropriate conclusions concerning the relation between the visual focus and mental processing of learning information.

Measuring cognitive load by current methods

There are many possibilities on how to measure cognitive load. A detailed summary is beyond the scope of the present chapter. However, we recommend using the following measures and reading the relevant summaries on how to operationalise subjective rating scales like the one created by Leppink and colleagues (Leppink, Paas, Van Gog, Van der Vleuten, & Van Merriënboer, 2014) or objective methods like one of the numerous dual-task methods summarised in Park and Brünken (2018) ranging from modality-specific (e.g. Marcus, Cooper, & Sweller, 1996) to overall (e.g. Chandler & Sweller, 1996) and continuous (e.g. Park, & Brünken, 2015) cognitive load measures. Other interesting options are summarised in Brünken, Seufert, and Paas (2010) as well as experimentally compared in recent studies of Korbach, Brünken, and Park (2017, 2018).

Conclusion

As the underlying functions of pointing and tracing are still unclear, future research should seek to explain the underlying mechanisms of the tracing effect. Moreover, there are a range of open questions, such as how much activity is necessary for fostering the learning process, or if too much activity can reverse to distraction. These further steps are also relevant for research on other effects of gestures and movement in learning. While there is clear initial evidence that pointing and tracing gestures enhance learning, there is still much to be learnt about the underlying mechanisms and boundary conditions for the effectiveness of this instructional design. Future studies should consider different learner characteristics like prior knowledge or other relevant factors (e.g., spatial ability) in order to move beyond the basic tracing effect established with novice learners. Such research will support more precise educational guidance to educators and instructional designers regarding pointing and tracing when learning.

References

Abrams, R., Davoli, C., Du, F., Knapp, W.III, & Paull, D. (2008). Altered vision near the hands. *Cognition*, 107, 1035–1047.

Agostinho, S., Tindall-Ford, S., Ginns, P., Howard, S. J., Leahy, W., & Paas, F. (2015). Giving learning a helping hand: Finger tracing of temperature graphs on an iPad. *Educational Psychology Review*, 27, 427–443.

Alibali, M. & Nathan, M. (2012). Embodiment in mathematics teaching and learning: Evidence from learners' and teachers' gestures. *Journal of Learning Science*, 21, 247–286.

Atkinson, R. C., & Shiffrin, R. M. (1968). Human memory: A proposed system and its control processes. In K. W. Spence, & J. T. Spence (Eds.), *The psychology of learning and motivation* (Volume 2). New York: Academic Press.

Baddeley, A. D. (1986). *Working memory*. Oxford: Oxford University Press.

Baddeley, A. D. (2012). Working memory: Theories, models, and controversies. *The Annual Review of Psychology*, 63, 1–29. doi:10.1146/annurev-psych-120710–100422.

Bara, F., Gentaz, E., & Colé, P. (2007). Haptics in learning to read with children from low socio economic status families. *British Journal of Developmental Psychology*, 25, 643–663. doi:10.1348/026151007X186643.

Barsalou, L. W. (2008). Grounded cognition. *Annual Review of Psychology*, 59, 617–645.

Boucheix, J. M., & Lowe, R. K. (2010). An eye tracking comparison of external pointing cues and internal continuous cues in learning with complex animations. *Learning and Instruction, 20*, 123–135. doi:10.1016/j.learninstruc.2009.02.015.

Brünken, R., Seufert, T., & Paas, F. (2010). Measuring cognitive load. In J. L. Plass, R. Moreno, & R. Brünken (Eds), *Cognitive load theory* (pp. 181–202). Cambridge: University Press.

Canham, M., & Hegarty, H. (2010). Effects of knowledge on display design on comprehension of complex graphics. *Learning and Instruction, 20*, 155–166. doi:10.1016/j.learninstruc.2009.02.014.

Chandler, P., & Sweller, J. (1996). Cognitive load while learning to use a computer program. *Applied Cognitive Psychology*, 10, 151–170.

Choi, H., van Merriënboer, J. J. G., & Paas, F. (2014). Effects of the physical environment on cognitive load and learning. Towards a new model of cognitive load. *Educational Psychology Review*, 26, 225–244. doi:10.1007/s10648–10014–9262–9266.

Cosman, J., & Vecera, S., (2010). Attention affects visual perceptual processing near the hand. *Psychological Science*, 21, 1254–1258.

Cowan, N. (1999). An embedded-processes model of working memory. In A. Miyake & P. Shah (Eds), *Models of working memory* (pp. 62–101). Cambridge, UK: Cambridge University Press.

Cowan, N. (2000). The magical number 4 in short-term memory: A reconsideration of mental storage capacity. *Behavioral and Brain Sciences*, 24, 87–185.

Cowan, N. (2005). *Working memory capacity*. Hove, UK: Psychology Press.

Eck, J., Kaas, A. L., & Goebel, R. (2013). Crossmodal interactions of haptic and visual texture information in early sensory cortex. *Neuroimage, 75*, 123–135. doi:10.1016/j.neuroimage.2013.02.075.

Folker, S., Ritter, H., & Sichelschmidt, L. (2005). Processing and integrating multimodal material. The influence of color-coding. In B. G. Bara, L. Barsalou & M. Bucciarelli (Eds.), *Proceedings of the 17th Annual Conference of the Cognitive Science Society CogSci 2005*, S. 690–695.

Ginns, P. (2005). Meta-analysis of the modality effect. *Learning and Instruction*, 15, 313–331.

Glenberg, A. M., Gutierrez, T., Levin, J. R., Japuntich, S., & Kaschak, M. P. (2004). Activity and imagined activity can enhance young children's reading comprehension. *Journal of Educational Psychology*, 96, 424–436.

Glenberg, A. M., Witt, J. K., & Metcalfe, J. (2013). From the revolution to embodiment: 25 years of cognitive psychology. *Perspectives on Psychological Science*, 8, 573–585.

Haider, H., & Frensch, P. (1999). Eye movement during skill acquisition: More evidence for the information-reduction hypothesis. *Journal of Experimental Psychology: Learning, Memory and Cognition*, 25, 172–190.

Holmqvist, K., Nyström, M., Andersson, R., Dewhurst, R., Jarodzka, H., & van de Weijer, J. (2011). *Eye tracking – A comprehensive guide to methods and measures*. New York: Oxford University Press.

Holsanova, J., Holmberg, N., & Holmqvist, K. (2009). Reading information graphics: The role of spatial contiguity and dual attentional guidance. *Applied Cognitive Psychology*, 23, 1215–1226.

Hu, F., Ginns, P., & Bobis, J. (2015). Getting the point: Tracing worked examples enhances learning. *Learning and Instruction*, 35, 85–93.

Jarodzka, H., Scheiter, K., Gerjets, P., & van Gog, T. (2010). In the eyes of the beholder: How experts and novices interpret dynamic stimuli. *Learning and Instruction*, 20, 146–154.

Just, M. A., & Carpenter, P. A. (1976). Eye fixations and cognitive processes. *Cognitive Psychology*, 8, 441–480.

Just, M. A., & Carpenter, P. A. (1980). A theory of reading: From eye fixations to comprehension. *Psychological Review*, 87, 329.

Just, M. A., & Carpenter, P. A. (1993). The intensity dimension of thought: Pupillometric indices of sentence processing. *Canadian Journal of Experimental Psychology*, 47, 310–329.

Kaas, A. L., Stoeckel, M. C., & Goebel, R. (2008). The neural base of haptic working memory. In M. Grunwald (Ed.), *Human haptic perception: Basics and applications* (pp. 113–129). Basel: Birkhäuser.

Kalenine, S., Pinet, L., & Gentaz, E. (2011). The visual and visuo-haptic exploration of geometrical shapes increases their recognition in preschoolers. *International Journal of Behavioral Development*, 35, 18–26.

Kalyuga, S. (2011). Cognitive load theory: How many types of load does it really need? *Educational Psychology Review*, 23, 1–19.

Kirschner, P. (2002). Cognitive load theory [special issue]. *Learning and Instruction*, 12.

Korbach, A., Brünken, R., & Park, B. (2016). Learner characteristics and information processing in multimedia learning: A moderated mediation of the seductive details effect. *Learning and Individual Differences*, 51, 59–68.

Korbach, A., Brünken, R., & Park, B. (2017). Measurement of cognitive load in multimedia learning: A comparison of different objective measures. *Instructional Science*, 45, 515–536.

Korbach, A., Brünken, R., & Park, B. (2018). Differentiating different types of cognitive load: A comparison of different measures. *Educational Psychology Review*, 30, 503–529. doi:10.1007/s10648-017-9404-8.

Laeng, B., Ørbo, M., Holmlund, T., & Miozzo, M. (2011). Pupillary stroop effects. *Cognitive Processing*, 12, 13–21.

Leppink, J., Paas, F., van Gog, T., van der Vleuten, C. P. M., & van Merriënboer, J. J. G. (2014). Effects of pairs of problems and examples on task performance and different types of cognitive load. *Learning and Instruction*, 30, 32–42.

Liszkowski, U., Brown, P., Callaghan, T., Takada, A., & de Vos, C. (2012). A prelinguistic gestural universal of human communication. *Cognitive Science*, 36, 698–713. doi:10.1111/j.1551-6709.2011.01228.x.

Macken, L., & Ginns, P. (2014). Pointing and tracing gestures may enhance anatomy and physiology learning. *Medical Teacher*, 36, 596–601.

Marcus, N., Cooper, M., & Sweller, J. (1996). Understanding instructions. *Journal of Educational Psychology*, 88, 49–63.

Mayer, R. E. (2009). *Multimedia learning*. Cambridge: University Press.

Mayer, R. E. (2010). Unique contributions of eye-tracking research to the study of learning with graphics. *Learning and Instruction*, 20, 167–171.

Meyer, K., Rasch, T., & Schnotz, W. (2010). Effects of animation's speed of presentation on perceptual processing and learning. *Learning and Instruction*, 20, 136–145.

Miyake, A., & Shah, P. (1999). *Models of working memory: Mechanisms of active maintenance and executive control*. New York, NY US: Cambridge University Press.

Montessori, M. (1969). *Die Entdeckung des Kindes*, ed. with Introduction by P. Oswald, & G. Schulz-Benesch. Freiburg: Herder Verlag.

Montessori, M. (1912). *The Montessori method*. London: Heineman.

Montessori, M. (1914). *Dr. Montessori's own handbook*. London: William Heinemann.

Moreno, R. (2006). When worked examples don't work: Is cognitive load theory at an impasse? *Learning and Instruction*, 16, 170–181.

Moreno, R. & Mayer, R. (2007). Interactive multimodal learning environments, special issue on interactive learning environments: Contemporary issues and trends. *Educational Psychology Review*, 19, 309–326.

Moreno, R., & Park, B. (2010). Cognitive load theory: Historical development and relation to other theories. In J. Plass, R. Moreno, & R. Brünken (Eds.), *Cognitive load theory* (pp. 9–28). New York: Cambridge University Press.

Paas, F., Renkl, A., & Sweller, J. (2003). Cognitive load theory and instructional design: Recent developments. *Educational Psychologist*, 38, 1–4.

Paivio, A. (1986) *Mental representation: A dual coding approach*. Oxford: Oxford University Press.

Park, B., & Brünken, R. (2015). The rhythm method: A new method for measuring cognitive load – an experimental dual-task study. *Applied Cognitive Psychology*, 29, 232–243. doi:10.1002/acp.3100.

Park, B., & Brünken, R. (2018). Secondary task as a measure of cognitive load. In R. Zheng (Ed.), *Cognitive load measurement and application: A theoretical framework for meaningful research and practice* (pp. 75–92). New York: Routledge.

Park, B., Flowerday, T., & Brünken, R. (2015). Cognitive and affective effects of seductive details in multimedia learning. *Computers in Human Behavior*, 44, 267–278.

Park, B., Knörzer, L., Plass, J. L., & Brünken, R. (2015). Emotional design and positive emotions in multimedia learning: An eye tracking study on the use of anthropomorphisms. *Computers & Education*, 86, 30–42.

Park, B., Korbach, A., & Brünken, R. (2015). Do learner characteristics moderate the seductive-details-effect? A cognitive-load-study using eye-tracking. *Journal of Educational Technology & Society*, 18, 24–36.

Park, B., Münzer, S., Seufert, T., & Brünken, R. (2016). The role of spatial ability when fostering mental animation in multimedia learning: An ATI-study. *Computers in Human Behavior*, 64, 497–506.

Plass, J., Moreno, R., & Brünken, R. (Eds.) (2010). *Cognitive load theory*. New York: Cambridge University Press.

Pomplun, M., Sichelschmidt, L., Wagner, K., Clermont, T., Rickheit, G., & Ritter, H. (2001). Comparative visual search: A difference that makes a difference. *Cognitive Science*, 25, 3–36. doi:10.1016/S0364-0213(00)00037-9.

Pouw, W. L., van Gog, T., & Paas, F. (2014). An embedded and embodied cognition review of instructional manipulatives. *Educational Psychology Review*, 26, 51–72. doi:10.1007/s10648-014-9255-5.

Rayner, K., Li, X., Williams, C. C., Cave, K. R., & Well, A. D. (2007). Eye movements during information processing tasks: Individual differences and cultural effects. *Vision Research*, 47, 2714–2726.

Reed, C. L., Grubb, J. D., & Steele, C. (2006). Hands up: Attentional prioritization of space near the hand. *Journal of Experimental Psychology: Human Perception and Performance*, 32, 166–177. doi:10.1037/0096-1523.32.1.166.

Reichle, E. D., Rayner, K., & Pollatsek, A. (2003). The E-Z Reader model of eye-movement control in reading: Comparisons to other models. *Behavioral and Brain Sciences*, 26, 445–526.

Rumelhart, D. E., & Ortony, A. (1976). The representation of knowledge in memory. In R. C. Anderson, R. J. Spiro, & W. E. Montague (Eds.), *Semantic factors in cognition*. Hillsdale, NJ: Erlbaum.

Schank, R. C., & Abelson, R. (1977). *Scripts, plans, goals and understanding*. Hillsdale, NJ: Erlbaum.

Schmidt-Weigand, F., Kohnert, A., & Glowalla, U. (2010). A closer look at split visual attention in system- and self-paced instruction in multimedia learning. *Learning and Instruction*, 20, 100–110.

Sweller, J. (2010). Cognitive load theory: Recent theoretical advances. In J. Plass, R. Moreno, & R. Brünken (Eds.), *Cognitive load theory* (pp. 29–47). New York: Cambridge University Press.

Sweller, J., Ayres, P., & Kalyuga, S. (2011). *Cognitive load theory*. New York: Springer.

Sweller, J., van Merriënboer, J. J. G., & Paas, F. G. W. C. (1998). Cognitive architecture and instructional design. *Educational Psychology Review*, 10, 251–296.

PART 4

New effects and new conditions required for old effects

13

SELF-MANAGEMENT OF COGNITIVE LOAD

Potential and challenges

Faisal Mirza

SCHOOL OF EDUCATION/EARLY START, UNIVERSITY OF WOLLONGONG, WOLLONGONG, AUSTRALIA

Shirley Agostinho

SCHOOL OF EDUCATION/EARLY START, UNIVERSITY OF WOLLONGONG, WOLLONGONG, AUSTRALIA

Sharon Tindall-Ford

SCHOOL OF EDUCATION/EARLY START, UNIVERSITY OF WOLLONGONG, WOLLONGONG, AUSTRALIA

Fred Paas

DEPARTMENT OF PSYCHOLOGY, EDUCATION, AND CHILD STUDIES, ERASMUS UNIVERSITY ROTTERDAM, ROTTERDAM, THE NETHERLANDS; SCHOOL OF EDUCATION/EARLY START, UNIVERSITY OF WOLLONGONG, WOLLONGONG, AUSTRALIA

Paul Chandler

SCHOOL OF EDUCATION/EARLY START, UNIVERSITY OF WOLLONGONG, WOLLONGONG, AUSTRALIA

Cognitive load theory research has primarily focussed on how teachers or instructional designers can apply cognitive load theory principles to design optimal instructional materials to support student learning. This can be considered as teacher-managed cognitive load. However, learners do not always access materials that are designed according to cognitive load theory principles (Ayres & Paas, 2012; Agostinho, Tindall-Ford, & Roodenrys, 2013). It is thus important for students to understand cognitive load theory design principles and to be able to apply these principles themselves when exposed to instructional materials that are non-cognitive load theory compliant (Agostinho, Tindall-Ford, & Bokosmaty, 2014; Agostinho et al., 2013; Roodenrys, Agostinho, Roodenrys, & Chandler, 2012). A new line of cognitive load theory research has evolved that examines how learners can self-manage their own cognitive load. Learners are taught how to apply cognitive load theory principles when exposed to instructional materials that are non-cognitive load theory compliant (e.g., Agostinho et al., 2013; Gordon, Tindall-Ford,

Agostinho, & Paas, 2016; Roodenrys et al., 2012; Sithole, Chandler, Abeysekera, & Paas, 2017; Tindall-Ford, Agostinho, Bokosmaty, Paas, & Chandler, 2015). Most of the studies that have examined the self-management of cognitive load have been conducted with the split-attention effect (e.g., Agostinho et al., 2013; Gordon et al., 2016; Roodenrys et al., 2012; Sithole et al., 2017; Tindall-Ford et al., 2015). A recent study extended this research by exploring another cognitive load theory effect; the redundancy effect.

The next section summarises the research conducted on the self-management of the split-attention effect and the educational potential of this self-management effect. The chapter then presents a recent study that investigated the self-management of the redundancy effect. Some practical educational guidelines are offered based on the empirical findings to date and how the self-management effect can be further explored.

Self-management of the split attention effect

Split-attention occurs when mutually related sources of information (e.g., diagram and text), are physically separated, requiring mental integration by the learner. When related sources of information are displayed apart from each other, additional mental effort in working memory is required to mentally integrate the separate sources of information. To integrate separated related sources of information, learners adopt search and match processes, resulting in additional cognitive load. The additional load is caused purely by the instructional format, placing a demand on working memory which does not support learning. This additional cognitive load has been defined as extraneous cognitive load (Clark, Nguyen, & Sweller, 2006; Sweller, van Merriënboer, & Paas, 1998).

Self-management of the split-attention effect involves learners firstly recognising when split-attention is evident in instructional materials, and then applying strategies to match or link related sources of information. This may involve the learners drawing circles and arrows on paper-based materials or moving text in digitally based materials to reorganise the information. Essentially the aim for the learner is to adapt the diagram to reduce the amount of searching and matching to mentally integrate textual information with diagrammatic information to reduce extraneous cognitive load on working memory (Agostinho et al., 2014).

The first research study on self-management of cognitive load was conducted by Roodenrys et al. (2012). Using paper-based instructional materials the researchers tested postgraduate university students' ability to integrate text with diagrams containing evident split-attention, as an alternative to instructor designed instructions. There were three instructional conditions: split-attention material, integrated material, and split-attention material with guidance that explains how split-attention can be self-managed. The guidance to self-manage split attention required the learners to link related diagram and text through drawing circles and arrows (see Roodenrys et al., 2012, pp.880–881). The results from two of the experiments showed that the self-management condition significantly outperformed the split-attention condition

on both near and far transfer items. In all three experiments there was no significant difference in mental effort across the three groups, suggesting that learners'
mental effort across the three conditions was similar. The study provided evidence
that it is possible to teach learners how to manage split attention to improve their
learning. The research showed that those learners who self-managed split-attention
materials by integrating related information, successfully transferred this skill to split
source instructional materials in a different content domain. Overall the results
showed the potential of teaching learners to self-manage split-attention materials.

Following Roodenrys et al.'s (2012) study, self-management of the split-attention effect has been examined in a number of research studies with learners in
different content domains (Agostinho et al., 2013; Tindall-Ford et al., 2015).
Gordon et al. (2016) investigated self-management of split-attention with primary
school students using paper-based science instructional material. While the results
of these studies provided evidence for the feasability for self-management of split-
attention, evidence for self-management reducing learners' cognitive load was not
supported.

A recent study on self-management of cognitive load conducted by Sithole et al.
(2017) was the first study to report significant effects for both performance and
cognitive load measures. The study explored self-management of split-attention
using accounting paper-based material with undergraduate students. Similar to
previous self-management of cognitive load research discussed above, participants
were presented three conditions: split-attention format, integrated format, and self-
management format which included guidance. Similar to Roodenrys et al.'s (2012)
study, the guidance asked participants to draw circles around the textual information and draw arrows linking the information to its corresponding place on the
diagram; highlight, underline or circle key words; and place ordering numbers on
the diagram and text. Results from the first experiment showed that the self-
management condition performed significantly better and had lower mental effort
ratings than the other two conditions. Additionally, Experiment 2 tested the
transferability of the self-management technique taught in Experiment 1. The results
of Experiment 2 showed when provided with new learning material, the self-
management condition obtained significantly higher test scores in all performance
measures; recall, near and far transfer and reported significantly lower levels of
cognitive load than the split-attention condition. This study provided further
evidence of the transferability of self-management of spilt attention.

The studies discussed above (i.e., Roodenrys et al., 2012; Agostinho et al., 2013;
Tindall-Ford et al., 2015; Gordon et al., 2016; Sithole et al., 2017) provide evidence
of the potential for learners to self-manage split-attention. Importantly evidence
was provided to suggest that the skills for manipulating instructional materials by
learners themselves may be transferable to different learning contexts (Sithole, et al.
2017). A question to consider, then, is: could this emergent self-management effect
be applied to another cognitive load theory effect?

The redundancy effect is a cognitive load theory effect that is based on
providing learning instructions where unnecessary (redundant) information is

removed. The following discussion summarises a recent study in the self-management of cognitive load where instructional materials included redundant information. The study examined if teaching learners to remove unnecessary information improves learning outcomes and reduces the cognitive load experienced by learners.

Self-management of the redundancy effect

The redundancy effect requires instructional designers to omit information that is not necessary for learning to occur (Chandler & Sweller, 1991; Jamet & Le Bohec, 2007; Moussa-Inaty, Ayres & Sweller, 2012). Research on the redundancy effect (e.g., Chandler & Sweller, 1991, 1996; Jamet & Le Bohec, 2007; Mayer, Heiser, & Lonn, 2001; Moussa-Inaty et al., 2012) has shown that presenting redundant instructional material may cause working memory (WM) resources to be unnecessarily overloaded. This generates an extraneous cognitive load that can impede learning by directing WM resources away from learning, that is schema construction. Research has shown that learning is enhanced when redundant information is removed from instructional material, as this can reduce extraneous cognitive load, freeing WM resources that can be directed to activities germane to learning (Sweller, Ayres, & Kalyuga, 2011).

The study adopted a similar research design to Gordon et al. (2016) using science instructions on the water cycle appropriate for primary school students. Three experiments were conducted with three different cohorts of primary school students. The studies investigated whether primary school students could self-manage the redundancy effect on instructional material with evident redundancy when they were provided guidance on how to remove redundant information. There were three instructional conditions: redundancy condition; redundancy-free condition; and redundancy with guidance condition. The instructional materials were designed to contain redundant information by repeating information provided in the diagram as textual information. The instructions presented a diagram of the water cycle and seven pairs of text boxes integrated within the diagram. The first text box presented information necessary for understanding the water cycle, the second text box, situated below the first, simply repeated what the diagram provided visually, such as direction of arrows and step number, rendering the information redundant. Figure 13.1 presents an example of one pair of the text boxes that were integrated within the watercycle diagram.

To self-manage redundant information learners were taught to carry out the following tasks: 1) look at the picture and read all the text boxes in the order presented; 2) read all the text boxes again and in the same time remove the text boxes that were not useful to understand the water cycle; and 3) look at the picture and only read the text boxes that were left on the diagram.

Results from the three experiments showed statistically significant findings for mental effort across the three experiments and for instructional efficiency in

When clouds become too big from the water droplets, the water falls back to the earth. This process is called **precipitation**.

This is the sixth step of the water cycle. It is shown by the large cloud, which has many water droplets falling back to the

FIGURE 13.1 An example of one pair of the text boxes that were overlayed on the diagram of the water cycle

Experiment 1. There were no statistical significant results from Experiment 2 and 3, however the redundancy with guidance condition outperformed (not at a statistically significant level) both the redundancy and redundancy-free conditions on far-transfer performance test items. Additionally, the means and effect sizes for the redundancy with guidance condition were similar to the redundancy-free condition in each of the three experiments for recall, and near transfer, suggesting that teaching learners to remove redundant information provides similar benefits as instructor managed materials. The results suggest there are benefits in teaching primary school students how to self-manage the redundancy effect. However what was realised from the research is that self-management of redundancy is not as "straight-forward" as the self-management of split-attention. Redundant information can be evident in instructional materials in different ways; for example, it can take the form of exact replication of information, partial repetition of information or, in the case of this study, elaboration on information evident in the diagram as textual information.

Based on the experimental results and new understandings on the nuance of the redundancy effect, it was considered important to investigate how the redundancy effect was evident in the instructional materials used in previous cognitive load theory redundancy effect research. By understanding the key characteristics in the way redundancy was applied in previous cognitive load theory studies, it was anticipated that this may provide further insights into the current experiment's results. The following section explains how this review of the research literature was conducted and findings from the review.

Review of literature to examine how the redundancy effect is evident in instructional materials

We reviewed the literature on redundancy effect research by conducting a search using the SCOPUS database using the key words "redundancy" and "cognitive load" for the period between 1990 and 2017, and reviewing the studies reported in Sweller et al. (2011). This book included a chapter on the redundancy effect (Chapter 11) where 16 studies are discussed. These studies are considered seminal redundancy effect research and thus all were included. The SCOPUS search resulted in 58 research articles (excluding research reviews and book chapters). To identify "seminal" from this SCOPUS search a criteria of greater than 100 citations was applied. This resulted in 18 articles to be examined in detail. The two articles added to the 16 studies reported in Sweller et al. (2011) were Leahy, Chandler, and Sweller (2003) and Yeung, Jin and Sweller (1998).

As the redundancy effect has often been investigated with the split-attention effect in the literature (e.g., Kalyuga, Chandler, & Sweller, 1999; Pociask & Morrison, 2008), each of the 18 articles were closely examined to identify experiments that solely focused on the redundancy effect. A total of 33 experiments were identified. Each experiment was examined in depth to determine the following:

1. How redundancy was evident in the instructional materials, e.g., whether text and diagrams or diagrams, text and audio were used;
2. Learning purpose, i.e., conceptual (teaching a concept) or procedural (teaching how something is performed);
3. Type of participant cohort (e.g., secondary school students) and prior knowledge;
4. How the materials were presented, e.g., holistic or segmented presentation. For example, the presentation of the materials was considered holistic if all the to-be-learned information was presented on one whole page, while it was considered segmented if the information was presented in multiple pages;
5. Why there was redundancy, i.e., the nature of the redundancy (e.g., written text duplicating to-be learned information provided by self-explanatory diagrams); and
6. The interdependency of information sources, i.e., whether a source of information is totally repeating the information (total repetition), partially repeating the information (partial repetition) or providing elaboration on the information (a form of elaboration).

The 18 articles that discuss the 33 experiments that focused on the redundancy effect, are identified in the reference list by an asterisk*. There are two themes which surfaced from this literature review as characterising the instructional materials. The first theme was *interdependency of information sources*. That is, whether more or less explicit sources of redundant information were used. For example, Chandler and Sweller (1991, Experiment 2) examined the redundancy effect using paper-based material containing written text and a diagram on electrical circuits. The textual information repeated the same information provided in the self-explanatory diagram, thus it is an explicit source of redundancy. The study by Mayer et al. (2001, Experiment 1) is an example of a less explicit form of redundancy. The material used was text and audio plus animated diagrams. The text was concurrently presented with the audio text and provided either a summary or full duplication of the audio. The condition where the written text provided partial repetition of the information is an example of a less explicit source of redundancy.

The second theme characterising instructional materials was the *complexity of the instructional materials* in terms of how the materials were presented to the participants. That is, whether a holistic or segmented presentation was used. For example, the study by Chandler and Sweller (1991, Experiment 2) discussed above presented all the to-be-learned information to the participants on one page (i.e., one whole chunk). Thus the presentation of the material was considered holistic. An example of an experiment where the presentation of the material was segmented is the study by Mayer et al. (2001, Experiment 1). The material was presented in multiple slides presented on a computer screen (i.e., multiple small chunks), thus was considered as presented in segments (i.e., segmented).

Sweller et al. (2011, p. 152) identified the following conditions for applicability of the redundancy effect: 1) sources of information must be understood independently; 2) learning materials must be high in element interactivity; 3) for the multimedia redundancy effect, audio and written text must be lengthy, complex and presented concurrently; and 4) use of learners who are novice to the information presented. The first theme identified from this literature review, i.e., *interdependency of information sources*, provides further insight on condition 1 stated above because it was found that both explicit sources and less explicit forms of redundancy (i.e., either partial repetition or a form of elaboration) can produce the redundancy effect. The second theme, i.e., *complexity of the instructional materials* in terms of how the materials were presented, serves as an additional condition to those identified by Sweller et al. (2011) because the way in which the materials are presented (e.g., holistic or segmented presentation) influences the level or complexity of redundancy evident.

Each study is plotted based on an analysis where the study "sits", firstly in terms of the explicitness of the redundant information (x axis), ranging from total repetition (full redundancy) to partial repetition (partial redundancy and/or elaboration). Secondly, the complexity/element interactivity of how the information is presented (y axis), ranging from information presented in a segmented format to information presented holistically. For example, the experiments that used instructional materials with total repetition of the to-be-learned information, presented in a segmented format are visually represented in the bottom left quadrant (e.g., Diao et al., 2007, Experiment 1).

Figure 13.2 shows that most (79%) of the experiments examined fall in the two bottom quadrants whereby the instructional materials are characterised as explicit redundancy, i.e., full repetition of the to-be-learned information (e.g., Cerpa,

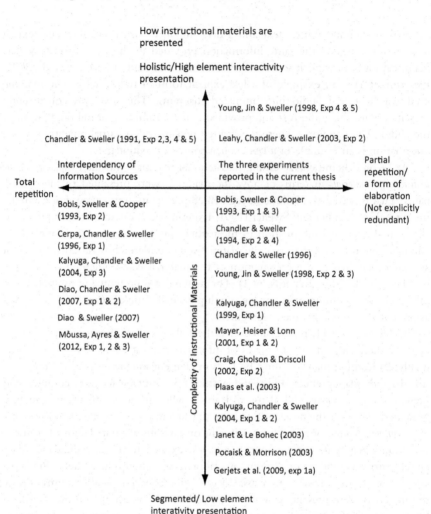

FIGURE 13.2 The 33 experiments were plotted across two axes
i) the horizontal x axis represents the degree of interdependency of information sources;
ii) the vertical y axis represents the degree of the complexity of the presentation of instructional material.

Chandler, & Sweller, 1996, Experiment 1) or less explicit redundancy, i.e., either partial repetition or a form of elaboration on the to-be-learned information (e.g., Plass, Chun, Mayer, & Leutner, 2003) but the instructional materials were presented in a segmented, low element interactivity format. Fewer experiments were plotted in the two top quadrants. The experiments in the top left quadrant (12%) are characterised by using instructional materials that used explicit redundant information, yet the materials were presented in a high element interactivity, holistic format (e.g., Chandler & Sweller, 1991, Experiment 3). Similarly, the experiments in the top right quadrant (9%) used instructional materials that had less explicit redundancy and the instructional materials were presented in a holistic, high element interactivity format (e.g., Leahy et al., 2003, Experiment 2).

Importantly, what this literature review has found is that the self-management of redundancy study reported in this chapter was characterised as a form of less explicit source of redundant information. In other words, it was not an obvious form of redundant information such as repetition of the same text. In addition, the instructional material was presented in a holistic, high element interactivity format. What can be inferred is that the form of redundancy applied in the self-management of redundancy study was a more nuanced form of redundancy, that is, a more complex form of redundancy. Finally, we infer that the additional text (which was added to serve as redundant information for purposes of the experiment) may in fact serve to elaborate on the information provided in the diagram by offering guidance to students on where to look in the diagram.

Thus a conclusion drawn from this study is the textual information may not have been redundant for the students, thus explaining the limited statistical significance found. This highlights a challenge in teaching learners on how to self-manage redundancy as the redundancy effect can take various forms. For future research on the self-management of redundancy, studies should try to focus first on examining more explicit and "extreme" types of redundancy, before examining more nuanced forms of redundancy, such as the one used in this study.

Practical implications for educators

From the research discussed in this chapter, some advice can be offered to learners for self-managing instructional materials during learning. With regard to paper-based split-attention materials using text and diagram, learners can be taught to circle text information and draw arrows from the circled information to the relevant parts of a diagram. With regard to computer-based split-attention materials, learners should be enabled to move text information closer to the relevant parts of a diagram. Whether it is paper based or computer based materials, we posit that learners should be explicitly taught the reasons why integrating text with diagram supports learning. We suggest that this may support the transfer of self-management skills to other instructional materials. With regard to self-managing redundant learning materials, as the current study has shown, what constitutes the redundancy effect is more complex and nuanced than the split-attention effect. Thus, self-managing the redundancy effect is more complex than self-managing split-attention and different forms of redundancy may lend themselves better towards self-management. So in conclusion, further research is required before definitive practical implications can be drawn.

Conclusion

This chapter has discussed an emergent new cognitive load theory effect whereby learners can apply cognitive load theory principles themselves to manage their own cognitive load – the self-management effect. The majority of research conducted in this new line of research has focused on self-managing the split-attention effect and the findings have shown the potential and feasibility of learners self-managing split-attention. The redundancy effect was introduced as another cognitive load effect that could potentially be self-managed by students. The results of a first experimental study into this topic, as well as the results of a systematic analysis of the variety of ways redundancy effects can be evident, made clear that self-management of redundancy is more challenging than the self-management of split-attention. Clearly, more research into self-management in the context of the redundancy effect and other cognitive load effects is needed.

References

(Note: References marked with "★" were included in the redundancy literature review.)

Agostinho, S., Tindall-Ford, S., & Bokosmaty, S. (2014). Adaptive diagrams: A Research agenda to explore how learners can manipulate online diagrams to self-manage cognitive load. *Handbook of human centric visualization* (pp. 529–550). Springer.

Agostinho, S., Tindall-Ford, S., & Roodenrys, K. (2013). Adaptive diagrams: Handing control over to the learner to manage split-attention online. *Computers & Education, 64*, 52–62. doi:10.1016/j.compedu.2013.01.007.

Ayres, P., & Paas, F. (2012). Cognitive load theory: New directions and challenges. *Applied Cognitive Psychology, 26*(6), 827–832. doi:10.1002/acp.2882.

★Bobis, J., Sweller, J., & Cooper, M. (1993). Cognitive load effects in a primary-school geometry task. *Learning and Instruction, 3*(1), 1–21. doi:10.1016/s0959-4752(09)80002-9.

★Cerpa, N., Chandler, P., & Sweller, J. (1996). Some conditions under which integrated computer-based training software can facilitate learning. *Journal of Educational Computing Research, 15*(4), 345–367.

★Chandler, P., & Sweller, J. (1991). Cognitive load theory and the format of instruction. *Cognition and Instruction, 8*(4), 293–332. doi:10.1207/s1532690xci0804_2.

★Chandler, P., & Sweller, J. (1996). Cognitive load while learning to use a computer program. *Applied Cognitive Psychology, 10*(2), 151–170.

Clark, R. C., Nguyen, F., & Sweller, J. (2006). *Efficiency in learning: Evidence-based guidelines to manage cognitive load.* Chichester: John Wiley.

★Craig, S. D., Gholson, B., & Driscoll, D. M. (2002). Animated pedagogical agents in multimedia educational environments: Effects of agent properties, picture features and redundancy. *Journal of Educational Psychology, 94*(2), 428.

★Diao, Y., Chandler, P., & Sweller, J. (2007). The effect of written text on comprehension of spoken English as a foreign language. *The American Journal of Psychology*, 237–261.

★Diao, Y., & Sweller, J. (2007). Redundancy in foreign language reading comprehension instruction: Concurrent written and spoken presentations. *Learning and Instruction, 17*(1), 78–88. doi:10.1016/j.learninstruc.2006.11.007.

★Gerjets, P., Scheiter, K., Opfermann, M., Hesse, F. W., & Eysink, T. H. S. (2009). Learning with hypermedia: The influence of representational formats and different levels of learner control on performance and learning behavior. *Computers in Human Behavior, 25* (2), 360–370. doi:10.1016/j.chb.2008.12.015.

Gordon, C., Tindall-Ford, S., Agostinho, S., & Paas, F. (2016). Learning from instructor-managed and self-managed split-attention materials. *Applied Cognitive Psychology, 30*(1), 1–9.

★Jamet, E., & Le Bohec, O. (2007). The effect of redundant text in multimedia instruction. *Contemporary Educational Psychology*, 32(4), 588–598. doi:10.1016/j.cedpsych.2006.07.001.

★Kalyuga, S., Chandler, P., & Sweller, J. (1999). Managing split-attention and redundancy in multimedia instruction. *Applied Cognitive Psychology*, 13(4), 351–371. doi:10.1002/(sici) 1099-0720(199908)13:4-351:aid-acp589-3.0.co;2-6.

★Kalyuga, S., Chandler, P., & Sweller, J. (2004). When redundant on-screen text in multimedia technical instruction can interfere with learning. *Human Factors*, 46(3), 567–581. doi:10.1518/hfes.46.3.567.3795.

★Leahy, W., Chandler, P., & Sweller, J. (2003). When auditory presentations should and should not be a component of multimedia instruction. *Applied Cognitive Psychology*, 17(4), 401–418. doi:10.1002/acp.877.

★Mayer, R. E., Heiser, J., & Lonn, S. (2001). Cognitive constraints on multimedia learning: When presenting more material results in less understanding. *Journal of Educational Psychology*, 93(1), 187.

Mirza, F. Y. (2018). *Investigating how primary school students can self-manage cognitive load when presented with redundant information*, Doctor of Philosophy thesis, School of Education, University of Wollongong, Australia.

★Moussa-Inaty, J., Ayres, P., & Sweller, J. (2012). Improving listening skills in English as a Foreign Language by reading rather than listening: A cognitive load perspective. *Applied Cognitive Psychology*, 26(3), 391–402. doi:10.1002/acp.1840.

★Plass, J. L., Chun, D. M., Mayer, R. E., & Leutner, D. (2003). Cognitive load in reading a foreign language text with multimedia aids and the influence of verbal and spatial abilities. *Computers in Human Behavior*, 19(2), 221–243. doi:10.1016/S0747-5632(02)00015–00018.

★Pociask, F. D., & Morrison, G. R. (2008). Controlling split attention and redundancy in physical therapy instruction. *Educational Technology Research and Development*, 56(4), 379–399.

Roodenrys, K., Agostinho, S., Roodenrys, S., & Chandler, P. (2012). Managing one's own cognitive load when evidence of split attention is present. *Applied Cognitive Psychology*, 26 (6), 878–886. doi:10.1002/acp.2889.

Sithole, S. T. M., Chandler, P., Abeysekera, I., & Paas, F. (2017). Benefits of guided self-management of attention on learning accounting. *Journal of Educational Psychology*, 109(2), 220–232. doi:10.1037/edu0000127.

Sweller, J., Ayres, P. L., & Kalyuga, S. (2011). *Cognitive load theory*. New York: Springer.

★Sweller, J., & Chandler, P. (1994). Why some material is difficult to learn. *Cognition and Instruction*, 12(3), 185–233.

Sweller, J., van Merriënboer, J. J. G., & Paas, F. G. W. C. (1998). Cognitive architecture and instructional design. *Educational Psychology Review*, 10(3), 251–296. doi:10.1023/ a:1022193728205.

Tindall-Ford, S., Agostinho, S., Bokosmaty, S., Paas, F., & Chandler, P. (2015). Computer-based learning of geometry from integrated and split-attention worked examples: The power of self-management. *Journal of Educational Technology & Society*, 18(4), 89–99.

★Yeung, A. S., Jin, P., & Sweller, J. (1998). Cognitive load and learner expertise: Split-attention and redundancy effects in reading with explanatory notes. *Contemporary Educational Psychology*, 23(1), 1–21.

14

EFFECTS OF INFORMED USE

A proposed extension of the self-management effect

Alexander Eitel, Lisa Bender and Alexander Renkl

UNIVERSITY OF FREIBURG, GERMANY

Introducing a new topic in mathematics or physics courses is usually associated with high demands on students' working memory capacity. Hence, instructors (e.g. textbook designers or teachers in school) should be careful not to induce additional demands on students' working memory that are, in principle, avoidable. There are many recommendations derived from cognitive load theory on how to design instruction to keep the (unnecessary) demands as low as possible. For instance, by removing irrelevant information from instruction, or by presenting information from multiple representations in an integrated (rather than in a separate) manner to reduce unnecessary search processes (e.g., Sweller, Ayres, & Kalyuga, 2011). Although it is certainly helpful to optimise instructional design, more can be done to optimise learning. Even an optimal instructional design (from the viewpoint of the instructor) may not be used in an optimal way by students. This can be due to the manner in which students' process instruction not just being determined by the design, but also by their prior knowledge as well as their beliefs, heuristics, and strategies on how to (best) learn with the provided materials (e.g., Bjork, Dunlosky, & Kornell, 2013; Boekaerts, 2017). These beliefs may lead to a discrepancy between the students' actual processing and how they should process instruction according to the instructional designer. The quality of learning thus depends on both the instructional design and how it is used by students.

Of course, how students process instruction is (partially) driven by the design. In this chapter we argue that students can profit from insights into the vices and virtues of the given instructional design so that they can optimise their cognitive processing. We provide two illustrative studies showing that informing students about the roles of the different representations within instructional materials moderates the effectiveness of the instructional design.

Cognitive load theory and the self-management effect

Knowledge that is typically taught in schools, such as how to calculate probabilities in a mathematics lesson requires deliberate and conscious cognitive effort. To a large extent, such conscious cognitive processing is carried out in working memory – a memory subsystem that is heavily limited in terms of its capacity (Atkinson & Shiffrin, 1968; Baddeley, 1992). Current working memory models suggest that only three to five meaningful elements can be held in working memory (Cowan, 2010). If the elements interact with each other in complex ways, working memory can probably process even fewer elements simultaneously (Paas & Sweller, 2014).

Hence, learning about a complex topic that requires processing of multiple interacting elements, such as deciding how to calculate probabilities based on a problem description (e.g. Figure 14.3a), places a heavy load on a student's limited working memory capacity. In terms of cognitive load theory (Paas, Renkl, & Sweller, 2003; Sweller et al., 2011), students experience a high *intrinsic* cognitive load (ICL) due to the complex nature of the learning task. In such a situation, any additional load on the cognitive system should be kept to a minimum, otherwise students might be hindered in processing the essential elements of the information presented and their interactions. Specifically, additional load that is due to a suboptimal design of the instruction (extraneous cognitive load; ECL) should be avoided. A number of design recommendations can be derived from cognitive load theory on how to reduce ECL (e.g., Sweller et al., 2011). In this chapter, we will especially refer to two of them.

First, higher ECL due to the processing of information that is irrelevant and/or redundant for achieving the instructional goal should be avoided (e.g., Kalyuga & Sweller, 2014). For instance, instructional materials are often enriched with interesting but hardly relevant details. Such details might make the page look more appealing, but do not relate to the main ideas to be learnt (cf. Figure 14.1, information on top of learning pages). The recommendation is thus to exclude such details from the instruction to prevent increased ECL due to unnecessary processing (Mayer & Moreno, 2003). Second, higher ECL due to the need to search for corresponding elements between information sources (e.g. text, diagram, equations) should be avoided by presenting text and diagrams in an integrated manner and/or by adding visual signals to the different representations to highlight corresponding elements (cf. Figure 14.3a, multiplication sign with same color both in graph and equation). Such instructional techniques have been found to prevent unnecessary cognitive load and hence foster learning outcomes (e.g., Ginns, 2006; Renkl & Scheiter, 2017; Richter, Scheiter, & Eitel, 2016; Scheiter & Eitel, 2015).

These recommendations typically address the design of the instructional materials with the assumption that the way materials are presented affords how they are processed. The argument being that the design of the instruction determines the students' processing, and hence, the cognitive load associated with it. For example, the student is bound to experience high ECL and demonstrate decreased levels of performance when redundant or irrelevant information (e.g. in the form of interesting but irrelevant details) is presented. The instructor decides upon the students' cognitive load, which is considered to be exclusively instructor-managed. We argue in this chapter that this is a too one-sided view of cognitive load. Cognitive load is, at least in part, self-determined or "self-managed", as also the self-management effect assumes (e.g., Mirza, Agostinho, Tindall-Ford, Paas, & Chandler, Chapter 13; Gordon, Tindall-Ford, Agostinho, & Paas, 2016; Roodenrys, Agostinho, Roodenrys, & Chandler, 2012).

Specifically, the self-management effect refers to the finding that students show better learning outcomes and reduced ECL when they are instructed on how to modify a suboptimal instructional design by themselves. In typical experiments, students performed better when they were instructed on how to physically integrate text pieces into diagrams – either by pasting paper-cuts in the diagrams or by drag-and-drop in a digital learning environment (Gordon et al., 2016; Roodenrys et al., 2012). In doing so, students reduced split attention; they improved the instructional design in terms of cognitive load by themselves, which was in turn beneficial to performance. Self-management research posits that the theoretical focus should be moved away from a completely instructor-managed cognitive load. The self-management of cognitive load theory, thus, refers to the idea that learners apply (previously taught) load-reducing techniques themselves (Roodenrys et al., 2012). Hence an alternative to instructor managed cognitive load is students being taught cognitive load theory design principles, which they can apply on their own, and thus, improve the instructional design themselves. This might in turn reduce cognitive load and foster learning outcomes.

Extending the self-management effect

Within this chapter, we argue that the amount of cognitive load is not just determined by the instructional design that is, in turn, completely instructor-managed. Rather, under certain conditions students are able to reduce cognitive load on their own (cf. self-management effect; Roodenrys et al., 2012). In contrast to the previous conceptualisation of the self-management effect, we argue and present empirical research for the idea that much less guidance for learners is needed so that they can reduce cognitive load by themselves. We thus emphasise the role of the "self" within the self-management effect.

Specifically, as we understand the previous literature, self-management refers (only) to the fact that students themselves, and not the instructor, improve the instructional design along the guidelines derived from cognitive load theory (e.g., Gordon et al., 2016; Roodenrys et al., 2012). Students are explicitly taught on how to manually improve an instructional design in terms of reducing ECL. After improving the instructional design by themselves, students learn with a good design that induces low ECL and therefore fosters learning outcomes. ECL may thus still be considered a direct function of the instructional design: before learners improved the instruction, it induced high ECL; after adapting it, it induced lower ECL and was beneficial for learning.

By contrast, we argue that ECL is not just a function of the design, but rather, that this relation is moderated by student characteristics. A suboptimal instructional design, for instance, because of irrelevant information, does not necessarily lead to higher ECL. It is up to the students' processing behavior whether the presence of irrelevant information increases ECL. The student may decide *not* to process redundant or unnecessary information, even if it is presented within an instruction. In consequence, irrelevant information may not increase ECL, because even if the design is suboptimal, it may not be processed in a suboptimal fashion. This idea aligns with the concept of a self-regulated learner who decides on his or her own about when and which information to process (cf. Bjork et al., 2013; Boekarts, 2017). Students *self*-manage their cognitive load by *self*-regulating their learning, for instance, by deciding not to process irrelevant information. This implies that students do not have to be specifically guided on how to physically improve the instructional design so that ECL is reduced. Rather, as the following illustrative studies will reveal, it is sufficient to inform students about the roles of different representations in instructional materials so that they get an idea about how to optimally deal with them in a self-regulated manner (Eitel, Bender, & Renkl, 2019; Schwonke, Berthold, & Renkl, 2009).

Illustrative study 1: Informed use of seductive details

This illustrative study of Eitel et al. (2019) deals with the effects of interesting but irrelevant details. Specifically, textbooks or e-learning materials are often enriched with nice and interesting details to potentially increase motivation by adding rewarding information, or to just make a page look more appealing (cf. Figure 14.1, information on top of learning pages). However, these details are often irrelevant with respect to understanding the main message of the instruction. In terms of cognitive load theory, processing of these details thus requires students to coordinate irrelevant with essential information, which increases ECL and potentially decreases performance (e.g., Kalyuga & Sweller, 2014). And indeed, the empirical research confirms this assumption as adding such details to instruction has been proven to increase ECL and decrease performance (e.g. Park, Moreno, Seufert, & Brünken, 2011; Rey, 2012; Sanchez & Wiley, 2006).

Specifically, in previous research – in part using eye-tracking – these details were found to *seduce* students, and thus, to draw their attention away from the learning contents at the expense of processing pertinent information (Park, Korbach, & Brünken, 2015; Rey, 2014). Such details were thus aptly termed *seductive details*. Hence, from an instructor's point of view, students process instructional materials with seductive details in a suboptimal fashion as they unnecessarily invest time and effort trying to memorise and/or to integrate irrelevant seductive details information with essential information from the instruction.

We argue, however, that this is only true when students are *not* informed about the role of the seductive details, as it was typically the case in prior research (see Rey, 2012, for a review). Students process irrelevant seductive details only to a substantial degree when they erroneously believe this information might be relevant; for example when they believe they should also learn seductive details to be well prepared for a subsequent test. Hence, a higher ECL is not just a function of whether irrelevant information in the form of seductive details are present in the instruction, but rather, it is due to a student's suboptimal processing of them; that is, if the student processes seductive details in order to learn them instead of processing them as if they were irrelevant. In other words, a higher ECL and poor performance are only to be expected when seductive details are present and when students are *not* informed about their irrelevance. Informing students about the irrelevance of seductive details should reduce ECL and foster performance.

We tested these hypotheses in a recent experiment (Eitel et al., 2019), in which students (*N*=85) learned either without seductive details (control condition) or

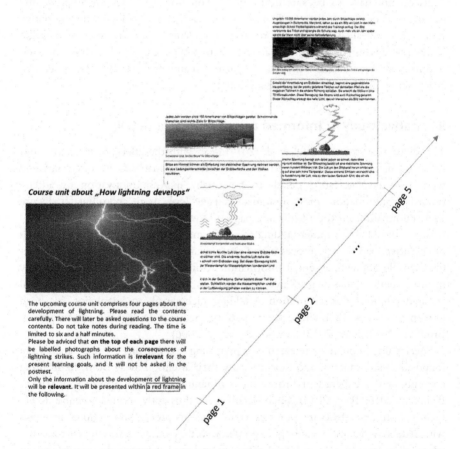

FIGURE 14.1 Experimental procedure in the study of Eitel et al. (2019), in particular in the condition in which students were informed about the irrelevance of seductive details. In this condition, the second part of the instruction on page 1 was added (compared to the uninformed seductive details condition)

with seductive details, in the latter case either without or with additional information about the irrelevance of seductive details (cf. Figure 14.1). Materials were adapted from Harp and Mayer (1998). The instruction was about the formation of lightning. Seductive details were associated but irrelevant with respect to the topic of lightning formation; that is, they comprised photographs with small stories about the consequences of lightning strikes which were presented on top of each page. Directly after learning, students were asked to indicate their cognitive load (questionnaire items adapted from Klepsch, Schmitz, & Seufert, 2017). After indicating their cognitive load, students were asked to work on post-test problems targeting recall and transfer.

As hypothesised, results revealed that the detrimental effects of seductive details on ECL and performance were found only when students were not informed about their irrelevance. ECL was higher in the "uninformed" than in both the "informed" seductive details and the control condition. Performance was lower in the "uninformed" than in both the "informed" seductive details and the control condition (see Figure 14.2).

In addition, results revealed that better performance in the informed compared to the uninformed seductive details condition were significantly mediated by ECL. Informing students about the irrelevance of the seductive details reduced extraneous cognitive load that, in turn, fostered post-test performance.

To conclude, being informed about seductive details can mitigate their negative effects on learning outcomes. The mere presence of seductive details is not detrimental. It is the suboptimal processing associated with them that hampers learning when students are *not* informed about the details' role (i.e., that they are irrelevant). Hence, we do not entirely agree with the recommendation based on previous research, namely that seductive details ought to be generally excluded from instructions to not risk performance detriments due to a cognitive overload (Mayer & Moreno, 2003). Following this recommendation, we believe that potential beneficial effects of seductive details on positive affect and motivation might be

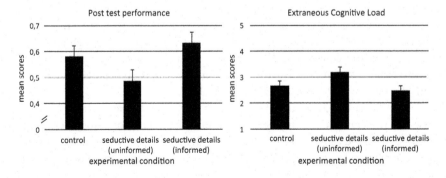

FIGURE 14.2 Results for post-test performance (left panel) and extraneous cognitive load (right panel) as a function of experimental condition in the study of Eitel et al. (2019)

overlooked (Magner, Schwonke, Aleven, Popescu, & Renkl, 2014; Magner, Glogger, & Renkl, 2016; Lenzner, Schnotz, & Müller, 2013; Wang & Adesope, 2016).

Illustrative study 2: Informed use of multiple representations

This illustrative study of Schwonke et al. (2009) deals with the effects of integrating multiple representations. Theoretically, there are strong benefits associated with displaying pertinent information by not just one, but multiple representations (e.g., Mayer, 2014; Schnotz, 2014). Multiple representations can complement each other to make processing of pertinent information more efficient (Larkin & Simon, 1987). Multiple representations can also help students construct deeper understanding of an instructional message because integrating the different representations can expose the underlying structure of the problem or domain represented (construction function; Ainsworth, 2006). For example, integrating information from text and equations in a worked example on probability theory requires abstracting from superficial features of the two representations; information can only be meaningfully integrated on the level of what it means in mathematical terms (cf. Figure 14.2). Hence, such abstraction may foster deeper understanding of the underlying mathematical principle. However, students often struggle with integration of multiple representations so that the benefits from displaying multiple representations sometimes do not occur (Lindner, Eitel, Barenthien, & Köller, 2018; Renkl & Scheiter, 2017; Scheiter & Eitel, 2015). Students rely on just one representation and somehow ignore the others (e.g. Eitel, 2016; Folker, Ritter, & Sichelschmidt, 2006), or they try but fail to integrate representations on a conceptual level, which would be required for deeper understanding (Schnotz, 2014).

Using a diagram may alleviate this problem in probability learning. It may function as a translational aid between the text on the problem situation and the formalised equation, thereby fostering integration and deeper understanding. For instance, as can be seen in Figure 14.3a, it may be easier to make stepwise referential connections between the text, the branches of the tree diagram, and the fraction denominators in the equation than directly between the doughnut story in the text and the equation. Hence, students should be able to construct deeper understanding when they integrate information between the different representations with the help of the diagram as a translational aid.

Schwonke et al. (2009) revealed in a first experiment, that students are hardly aware of the construction function of multiple representations. Moreover, as eye-tracking data indicated, students hardly used the diagram as a translational aid between text and equation. They failed to do so, even though color codes were added to the different representations (i.e., corresponding elements highlighted in the same color) that supported integration (e.g., Berthold & Renkl, 2009). In other words, even though it was well designed instruction, students' processing was not optimal. This sub-optimal processing might be attributed to missing knowledge or false beliefs about the functions of multiple representations. Using the diagram as an integration aid between text and equation requires knowing about the fact that diagrams can fulfil this function.

In a second experiment, Schwonke et al. (2009) randomly assigned participants to two conditions. Prior to learning with worked examples about probability theory, students either received the usual instruction (*uninformed*; cf. Figure 14.3a) or they were additionally told that "there are two solutions procedures—tree diagram and arithmetic equation—and that the tree diagram should be used to gain an understanding on how the arithmetic equation is related to the problem formulation." For this purpose, the metaphor of a bridge was used, that is, the tree diagrams "build" a bridge between the problem texts and the equations (*informed*; cf. Figure 14.3b).

Results showed that informing students about the diagram's functions had a substantial positive effect on learning outcomes compared to not informing them ($r = .47$). In addition, informing students (with high prior knowledge) increased visual attention on the diagrams; the higher visual attention on the diagrams was in turn related to better learning outcomes. Results, thus, suggest that students made use of being informed about the functions of multiple representations. To conclude, well-designed, multi-representational instruction may only be processed optimally when students are additionally informed about the roles that the different representations may play.

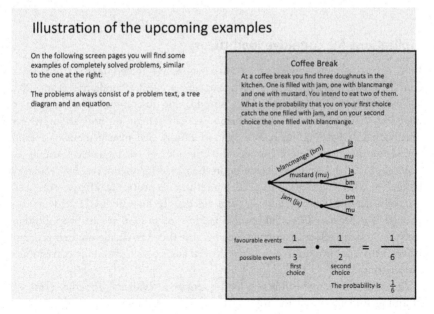

FIGURE 14.3A Advance organiser in the uninformed condition. A worked example on probability learning was presented to students

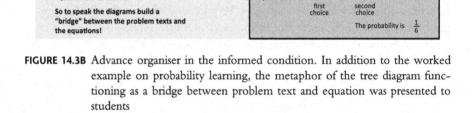

FIGURE 14.3B Advance organiser in the informed condition. In addition to the worked example on probability learning, the metaphor of the tree diagram functioning as a bridge between problem text and equation was presented to students

Implications for cognitive load theory

Based on the findings reviewed in this chapter, we recommend to broaden the scope of cognitive load theory self-management effect (Roodenrys et al., 2012). Self-management of cognitive load should not just mean that students can reduce ECL "on their own" when being explicitly taught on how to improve the instructional design (e.g., to reduce split-attention). Self-management of cognitive load should be more closely connected to the idea of self-regulated learning (e.g., Bjork et al., 2013). Students decide upon their load for themselves by deciding for themselves what information to process and how to process it. Hence, even a sub-optimally designed instruction may not necessarily increase ECL; it depends on whether it is processed in a suboptimal fashion, or not (cf. results from illustrative study 1). Students self-manage their load because they can decide on their processing behavior that, in turn, leads to the experienced cognitive load and the corresponding learning outcomes.

The two illustrative studies provide tentative evidence for the claim that informing students about the roles of the different representations affects whether the instructional design is effective, or not. They address two typical instructional situations that involve learning with interesting but i rrelevant details, and learning with multiple representations. In the first illustrative study, students did not fall prey to a "poorly" designed instruction involving seductive details when they were informed about the irrelevance of these details. In the second illustrative study, students used a well-designed multi-representational instruction only to its full potential when they were informed about the roles of the multiple representations. In both studies, students' actual processing deviated from the processing behavior intended by the instructional design when students were not informed about how to use it.

Nevertheless, further research is needed to map out the boundary conditions of these effects. For instance, providing instruction about what is irrelevant information that should be ignored is often a double-edged sword. Such instruction may unintentionally highlight the irrelevant information and may make it even more difficult for students to ignore such information. In the study of Eitel et al. (2019), this problem did not occur, because the relevant – and not the irrelevant – information was highlighted by means of a red frame (cf. Figure 14.1). Hence, beneficial effects of informed use may depend on how information about the irrelevance is operationalised.

Educational implications

The present results may be promising for educational practice as they suggest that potential negative effects of sub-optimally designed instructions can be alleviated by informing students about it. Besides from physically manipulating the design (as in previous research on the self-management effect; Gordon et al., 2016; Roodenrys, 2012), even implicit educational interventions in the sense of informing about the functions of representations can reduce ECL, and thus, foster learning outcomes. Such interventions may be of particular relevance for educational practice since often the design of, for example, textbooks used in schools cannot be altered, so that managing one's own load by changing the design is impossible. By contrast, an informed-use of representations is an easy-to-implement intervention that may help students in their self-regulated learning efforts.

References

Ainsworth, S. (2006). DeFT: A conceptual framework for considering learning with multiple representations. *Learning and Instruction*, 16, 183–198.

Atkinson, R. C., & Shiffrin, R. M. (1968). Human memory: A proposed system and its control processes. In K. W. Spence, & J. T. Spence (Eds.), *The psychology of learning and motivation* (Vol. 2, pp. 89–195). New York: Academic Press.

Baddeley, A. (1992). Working memory. *Science*, 255, 556–559.

Berthold, K., & Renkl, A. (2009). Instructional aids to support a conceptual understanding of multiple representations. *Journal of Educational Psychology*, 101, 70–87.

Bjork, R. A., Dunlosky, J., & Kornell, N. (2013). Self-regulated learning: Beliefs, techniques, and illusions. *Annual Review of Psychology*, 64, 417–444.

Boekaerts, M. (2017). Cognitive load and self-regulation: Attempts to build a bridge. *Learning and Instruction*, 51, 90–97.

Cowan, N. (2010). The magical mystery four: How is working memory capacity limited, and why? *Current Directions in Psychological Science*, 19, 51–57.

Eitel, A. (2016). How repeated studying and testing affects multimedia learning: Evidence for adaptation to task demands. *Learning and Instruction*, 41, 70–84.

Eitel, A., Bender, L., & Renkl, A. (2019). Are seductive details seductive only when you think they are relevant? An experimental test of the moderating role of perceived relevance. *Applied Cognitive Psychology*, 33, 20–30.

Folker, S., Ritter, H., & Sichelschmidt, L. (2005). Processing and integrating multimodal material: The influence of color-coding. In B. G. Bara, L. Barsalou, & M. Bucciarelli (Eds.), *Proceedings of the 27th annual conference of the cognitive science society* (pp. 690–695). Mahwah, NJ: Erlbaum.

Ginns, P. (2006). Integrating information: A meta-analysis of the spatial contiguity and temporal contiguity effects. *Learning and Instruction*, 16, 511–525.

Gordon, C., Tindall-Ford, S., Agostinho, S., & Paas, F. (2016). Learning from instructor-managed and self-managed split-attention materials. *Applied Cognitive Psychology*, 30, 1–9.

Harp, S. F., & Mayer, R. E. (1998). How seductive details do their damage: A theory of cognitive interest in science learning. *Journal of Educational Psychology*, 90, 414–434.

Kalyuga, S., & Sweller, J. (2014). The redundancy principle in multimedia learning. In R. E. Mayer (Ed.), *The Cambridge handbook of multimedia learning*. 2nd edition (pp. 247–262). Cambridge: Cambridge University Press.

Klepsch, M., Schmitz, F., & Seufert, T. (2017). Development and validation of two instruments measuring intrinsic, extraneous, and germane cognitive load. *Frontiers in Psychology*, 8.

Larkin, J. H., & Simon, H. A. (1987). Why a diagram is (sometimes) worth ten thousand words. *Cognitive Science*, 11, 65–100.

Lenzner, A., Schnotz, W., & Müller, A. (2013). The role of decorative pictures in learning. *Instructional Science*, 41, 811–831.

Lindner, M. A., Eitel, A., Barenthien, J., & Köller, O. (2018). An integrative study on learning and testing with multimedia: Effects on students' performance and metacognition. *Learning and Instruction*. doi:10.1016/j.learninstruc.2018.01.002.

Magner, U. I. E., Glogger, I., & Renkl, A. (2016). Which features make illustrations in multimedia learning interesting? *Educational Psychology*, 36, 1596–1613.

Magner, U. I. E., Schwonke, R., Aleven, V., Popescu, O., & Renkl, A. (2014). Triggering situational interest by decorative illustrations both fosters and hinders learning in computer-based learning environments. *Learning and Instruction*, 29, 141–152.

Mayer, R. E. (2014). *The Cambridge handbook of multimedia learning*. 2nd edition. Cambridge: Cambridge University Press.

Mayer, R. E., & Moreno, R. (2003). Nine ways to reduce cognitive load in multimedia learning. *Educational Psychologist*, 38, 43–52.

Paas, F., Renkl, A., & Sweller, J. (2003). Cognitive load theory and instructional design: Recent developments. *Educational Psychologist*, 38, 1–4.

Paas, F., & Sweller, J. (2014). Implications of cognitive load theory for multimedia learning. In R. E. Mayer (Ed.), *The Cambridge handbook of multimedia learning*. 2nd edition (pp. 27–44). Cambridge: Cambridge University Press.

Park, B., Korbach, A., & Brünken, R. (2015). Do learner characteristics moderate the seductive-details-effect? A cognitive-load-study using eye-tracking. *Journal of Educational Technology & Society*, 18, 24–36.

Park, B., Moreno, R., Seufert, T., & Brünken, R. (2011). Does cognitive load moderate the seductive details effect? A multimedia study. *Computers in Human Behavior*, 27, 5–10.

Renkl, A., & Scheiter, K. (2017). Studying visual displays: How to instructionally support learning. *Educational Psychology Review*, 29, 599–621.

Rey, G. D. (2012). A review of research and a meta-analysis of the seductive detail effect. *Educational Research Review*, 7, 216–237.

Rey, G. D. (2014). Seductive details and attention distraction – an eye tracker experiment. *Computers in Human Behavior*, 32, 133–144.

Richter, J., Scheiter, K., & Eitel, A. (2016). Signaling text-picture relations in multimedia learning: A comprehensive meta-analysis. *Educational Research Review*, 17, 19–36.

Roodenrys, K., Agostinho, S., Roodenrys, S., & Chandler, P. (2012). Managing one's own cognitive load when evidence of split attention is present. *Applied Cognitive Psychology*, 26, 878–886.

Sanchez, C. A., & Wiley, J. (2006). An examination of the seductive details effect in terms of working memory capacity. *Memory and Cognition*, 34, 344–355.

Scheiter, K., & Eitel, A. (2015). Signals foster multimedia learning by supporting integration of highlighted text and diagram elements. *Learning and Instruction*, 36, 11–26.

Schnotz, W. (2014). Integrated model of text and picture comprehension. In R. E. Mayer (Ed.), *The Cambridge handbook of multimedia learning*. 2nd edition (pp. 72–104). Cambridge: Cambridge University Press.

Schwonke, R.Berthold, K., & Renkl, A. (2009). How multiple external representations are used and how they can be made more useful. *Applied Cognitive Psychology*, 23, 1227–1243.

Sweller, J., Ayres, P., & Kalyuga, S. (2011). *Cognitive load theory*. New York: Springer.

Wang, Z., & Adesope, O. (2016). Exploring the effects of seductive details with the 4-phase model of interest. *Learning and Motivation*, 55, 65–77.

15

FACTORS THAT IMPACT ON THE EFFECTIVENESS OF INSTRUCTIONAL ANIMATIONS

Paul Ayres

SCHOOL OF EDUCATION, UNIVERSITY OF NEW SOUTH WALES, SYDNEY, AUSTRALIA

Juan C. Castro-Alonso

CENTER FOR ADVANCED RESEARCH IN EDUCATION (CIAE), UNIVERSIDAD DE CHILE, SANTIAGO, CHILE

Mona Wong

FACULTY OF EDUCATION, THE UNIVERSITY OF HONG KONG, HONG KONG, HONG KONG

Nadine Marcus

SCHOOL OF COMPUTER SCIENCE & ENGINEERING, UNIVERSITY OF NEW SOUTH WALES, SYDNEY, AUSTRALIA

Fred Paas

DEPARTMENT OF PSYCHOLOGY, EDUCATION, AND CHILD STUDIES, ERASMUS UNIVERSITY ROTTERDAM, ROTTERDAM, THE NETHERLANDS; SCHOOL OF EDUCATION/EARLY START, UNIVERSITY OF WOLLONGONG, WOLLONGONG, AUSTRALIA

This chapter examines a number of significant issues associated with the design of instructional animations. The term *animation* used here refers to visualisations composed of a number of static pictures that are shown in rapid sequence. This broad definition includes many different types of instructional materials, such as sequential presentations, simulations, videos, and other types of dynamic visualisations.

Despite the immense promise of animations to enhance learning, proof of their effectiveness has lagged behind many educators' enthusiasm for using them. We argue that the research has not only failed to find convincing evidence in support of the wide-scale use of instructional animations, but also the research itself has in many instances, failed to consider or control for significant moderating factors. This chapter discusses these factors and their implications for designing effective instructional animations. We begin our discussion by examining the research into studies that have compared animations with static presentations. This comparison has been an important methodology in deciding whether moving pictures provide any learning advantage compared to static pictures.

Animations versus static pictures research

Although many studies have shown that dynamic visualisations are an advantage over statics, the overall evidence is far from conclusive (see Tversky, Morrison, & Betrancourt, 2002). There are studies that show: (a) animation superior to statics (e.g., Stebner, Kühl, Höffler, Wirth, & Ayres, 2017; Yarden & Yarden, 2010), (b) static pictures superior to animations (e.g., Koroghlanian & Klein, 2004), and (c) neither format superior to the other (e.g., Kühl, Scheiter, Gerjets, & Gemballa, 2011).

One example that demonstrates the mixed outcomes of this type of research can be found in the meta-analysis of Berney and Bétrancourt (2016). Overall, the meta-analysis showed an overall advantage of animation over statics. However, closer examination of the data reveals that in their 140 pair-wise comparisons, 59% of the studies failed to show significant differences between either type of visualisations, 10% showed static dominance, and only 31% favoured animations.

These research findings suggest somewhat mixed results making it difficult to conclude that animations are the best form of presentation format for all conditions. Complicating the issue even further is that the research base has been often tainted by the inclusion of design biases, which are discussed next.

Design biases in animation research

Examinations of the design details used in studies comparing statics to animations have shown that they have often failed to consider a number of moderating variables (Tversky et al., 2002). For example, there are biased comparisons that have not controlled for variables such as *appeal, variety, media, size*, and *interaction* (see Castro-Alonso, Ayres, & Paas, 2016). A typical example of appeal bias is observed in comparisons that do not match the degree of colour included in both visualisations, and, for example, compare coloured animation to black and white statics (e.g., Yang, Andre, Greenbowe, & Tibell, 2003). As colour influences memorisation and multimedia learning (e.g., Matthews, Benjamin, & Osborne, 2007), a failure to control for this variable will influence learning outcomes. The variety bias is observed when one of the compared formats presents more visual elements than the other, for example, the static pictures include signalling arrows, which are lacking in the animated design (e.g., Lewalter, 2003). Any extra quantity of visual elements can generate advantageous *cueing* or *signalling* effects (e.g., Xie et al., 2017) or unfavourable *redundancy* effects (see Kalyuga & Sweller, 2014). The media bias is observed when the comparison is not made in the same medium, such as paper static images compared to computer animations (e.g., Marbach-Ad, Rotbain, & Stavy, 2008). Variations in media can lead to different learning effects (e.g., Salomon, 1984). An example of size bias is produced when a larger animation is compared to the smaller images of statics (e.g., Ng, Kalyuga, & Sweller, 2013), most likely hindering the effectiveness of the static pictures. Last, the interaction bias includes comparisons where the animated visualisation includes interactive buttons, for example to pause or fast forward the content, whereas these features are not included in the static format (e.g., Watson, Butterfield, Curran, & Craig, 2010). As the inclusion of interaction can help multimedia learning (e.g., Evans & Gibbons, 2007), such comparisons are biased in favour of the animated format. Hence, studies that investigate animation-static comparisons should ensure that such moderating variables are controlled for. Furthermore, there are a number of learners' individual characteristics that may also influence these studies, such as spatial ability, gender, and prior knowledge.

Impact of individual characteristics

Spatial ability

Spatial ability is considered an important skill in extracting and understanding visual information when learning from animations and static pictures (see, Hegarty, Kriz, & Cate, 2003; Hegarty, Montello, Richardson, Ishikawa, & Lovelace, 2006; Hegarty & Sims, 1994; Hegarty & Waller, 2005; Narayanan & Hegarty, 2002). The meta-analysis of Höffler (2010) found a correlation between spatial ability and learning from instructional animations, showing that the effectiveness of animations can be influenced by the spatial ability of learners. Similarly, research has also found that spatial ability is highly correlated with mental animation (see Hegarty et al., 2003; Hegarty et al., 2006). When static pictures are used to display dynamic processes, the learner must mentally animate the processes in order to understand the motion depicted (Hegarty et al., 2003). In other words, motion must be inferred, and therefore learners with low spatial ability may find it difficult to make these inferences. On the contrary, there is evidence showing that learners with low spatial ability may be advantaged by learning from animations rather than statics in comparison to learners with high spatial ability (Höffler, 2010). This finding suggests that because learners with low spatial ability find it difficult to mentally animate static pictures, animations reduce the amount of mental animation that needs to be made and therefore provide an advantage. In contrast, learners with high spatial ability have fewer problems with mentally animating statics, and therefore show fewer pronounced differences in learning from statics and animation.

Another issue associated with spatial ability is that there have been a number of ambiguous definitions and different psychometric tests used to obtain a general measure of spatial ability (for details, see Wong, Castro-Alonso, Ayres, & Paas, 2018). As also outlined by Castro-Alonso, Ayres, Wong, and Paas (Chapter 8, this book), if spatial ability is measured, often there is a disparity between the actual test used and the content to-be-learned, for example, a paper folding task may have little in common with learning science concepts.

It can be concluded that if spatial ability is an important skill in learning from animations (and statics), then it is important to measure it using the appropriate tests.

Gender effects

Spatial ability research generally suggests that females have a lower spatial ability (in particular, mental rotation ability) than males (e.g. Halpern, 2011; Maeda & Yoon, 2013).There is also evidence that instructional animations can support females more than males (e.g., Falvo & Suits, 2009; Sánchez & Wiley, 2010; Wong, Castro-Alonso, Ayres, & Paas, 2015). Consequently, it has been argued that any advantage for females from instructional animations is due to their lower spatial ability (e.g. Sánchez & Wiley, 2010; Yezierski & Birk, 2006), as animations generally benefit learners with low spatial ability (Höffler, 2010) rather than static pictures.

Similar to the treatment of spatial ability, gender is often not reported leading to potential biases with treatment sampling. More females in one group may produce a different result to more males. There is a lack of rigorous investigation linking the effectiveness of animations with gender and spatial ability measures, despite research showing that gender may have a significant impact on the effectiveness of instructional animations (see Wong et al., 2018).

Prior knowledge

A major finding of cognitive load theory is that expertise can influence the effec-tiveness of learning strategies (Kalyuga, Ayres, Chandler, & Sweller, 2003). Strate-gies that are helpful for novices may be detrimental to those with greater knowledge. Animated environments are no exception in demonstrating this expertise reversal effect. A study by Spanjers, Wouters, van Gog, and van Mer-riënboer (2011), demonstrated an effect using a segmentation strategy. One method of improving the effectiveness of animations is to segment the presentation into smaller parcels of information. However, Spanjers et al. (2011) found that the segmentation strategy was only effective for learners with low domain-specific knowledge compared to learners with greater knowledge. Arguably, learners with more prior-knowledge are able to deal with more information at a time, due to expertise information chunking advantages (see Sweller, Ayres & Kalyuga, 2011). Furthermore, Kalyuga (2008) also showed that greater domain-specific knowledge could reduce the negative effects of transient information, which is discussed next.

The transient information effect

As described above there are number of factors that have influenced the research into animation-static studies. By not controlling for these factors the research base has been tainted to some degree, and it is difficult to form a conclusion that ani-mations are superior. In addition, there are theoretical grounds suggesting that statics may be superior to animations. Animations, when used as instructional resources share a common feature: they convey transient visual information. This transiency feature is present in animations but not in their constituent static pictures. Ayres and Paas (2007) observed that because animations are dynamic consisting of a series of frames, which roll from one to another, visual information often disappears from sight. If information from previous frames is needed to understand later frames, the learner has to remember previous information and mentally integrate it with newly presented information. This processing requires additional working memory resources and from a cognitive load theory perspective has negative effects on learning. In contrast, static presentations are more permanent, generating less transient information, which allows more working memory processes to be allotted to learning.

The transient information effect occurs when non-transient information leads to higher learning than the same information presented in a transient form (Castro-Alonso, Ayres, Wong, & Paas, 2018). This effect has been demonstrated in animation studies involving mechanical systems (Mayer, Hegarty, Mayer, & Campbell, 2005) and symbol memorisation tasks (Castro-Alonso, Ayres, & Paas, 2014) where statics have been found to be superior to animations. The effect has also been found with spoken narration, which is a more fundamental form of transient information (see Singh, Marcus, & Ayres, 2017; Wong, Leahy, Marcus & Sweller, 2012).

Animations and learning human movement skills

Considerations of transient information suggest that animations may not create the optimum learning environment, although levels of transiency are an important factor in deciding the extent to which they inhibit learning (Leahy & Sweller, 2011). Nevertheless, there is some clear evidence that animations are conducive for promoting learning for a particular class of tasks. The meta-analysis of Höffler and Leutner (2007) identified a number of conditions under which animations were more effective than equivalent statics. In particular, the largest effect size was found when the animations featured procedural-motor knowledge. Our own research has since supported this conclusion, and has shown that when learning cognitive tasks involving human motor skills, animations are an advantage. For example, we have found that animations are superior to statics in learning to tie knots (Marcus, Cleary, Wong, & Ayres, 2013), build Lego shapes (Castro-Alonso, Ayres, & Paas, 2015a), and make origami shapes (Ayres, Marcus, Chan, & Qian, 2009; Wong et al., 2009). Other researchers have also found similar advantages, for example when learning surgical skills (Masters, Lo, Maxwell, & Patil, 2008).

The prediction that transient information reduces the impact of animations and the findings that animations are very helpful for learning human movement tasks creates an obvious dichotomy: How can both be true? Paas and Sweller (2012) suggest that humans have evolved to learn human movement skills more easily than other types of skills (see also van Gog, Paas, Marcus, Ayres, &

Sweller, 2009). Based on the work of Geary (2008) it can be argued that human movement is a form of biologically primary knowledge that requires little conscious processing of information. As a result, when learning about human movement from an animation, working memory may be less affected by transient information. In other words, learning about human movement might be a special case, where humans have evolutionary advantages that are not afforded to other types of learning topics.

Methods to improve the effectiveness of animations

Multimedia principles

Badly designed animations reduce their potential significantly, regardless of any inherent difficulties associated with them. Features like how and when text is applied is critical. The meta-analysis of Berney and Bétrancourt (2016) found significant advantages when spoken explanatory text was added to animations. This finding is consistent with the modality effect where spoken text and pictures generate higher learning outcomes than written text and pictures (Low & Sweller, 2014). Adding text to pictorial information creates a multimedia learning environment (see Mayer, 2014), where there are a number of guiding principles that should be followed based on cognitive load theory (Ayres, 2015). For example, these principles include: a) synchronising the spoken text with the relevant pictures to avoid split-attention effects (Ayres & Sweller, 2014); b) ensuring that the spoken text and pictures do not convey the same information leading to redundancy (Kalyuga & Sweller, 2014); and c) avoiding lengthy spoken text that can cause the transient information effect (Leahy & Sweller, 2011).

Compensatory strategies

Using best-practice multimedia principles in the design of instructional animations ensures that many potential negative effects can be avoided. However, they do not guarantee that animated transitory effects will be reduced. To deal with transitory information a number of compensatory strategies have been employed. Animations can be paused either through learner control or system control (Mayer & Chandler, 2001), or segmented into smaller sections (Spanjers et al., 2011; Wong et al., 2012). Both interventions (pausing or segmenting) deal with the transient information by reducing the amount of information that the learner must cope with at a given time. That reduction can ameliorate the negative effects of transience when using animated instructional presentations. Whereas these compensatory strategies are helpful, they also have some disadvantages. Segmentation can make it more difficult to integrate knowledge across segments (see Singh et al., 2017) and learner interactivity can be a burden for novice learners who do not have the expertise to know when to stop and start animations at key points in the presentations (Hasler, Kersten, & Sweller, 2007).

Using general learning strategies

Much of the research into instructional visual representations has tended to focus on ways to improve the presentation formats, by for example, adding text. There has been less emphasis on combining multimedia formats with other learning strategies. Two notable exceptions have been the use of worked examples (see Renkl, 2014) and self-explanations (see Wylie & Chi, 2014), where favourable results have been found when these strategies have been used in multimedia settings. In contrast, little research of this type has been conducted with animations, especially in regard to the transitory information issue. However, one promising new research direction has been to examine the impact of gesturing used in conjunction with animations. Gesturing, which is described next, can be considered a general learning strategy as it can be applied in many learning environments. We finish this section by suggesting how a second general learning strategy, collaboration, can also be used in tandem with instructional animations.

Gesturing

Gesturing has been shown to enhance learning, either in the case of learners who express information in gesture (Cook, Mitchell, & Goldin-Meadow, 2008), or learners who observe instructors expressing information by gesture (Cook & Tannenhaus, 2009). Studies have found gesturing advantages across a number of learning disciplines such as science (Agostinho et al., 2015; Castro-Alonso, Ayres, & Paas, 2015b), and second language acquisition (Lajevardi, Narang, Marcus, & Ayres, 2017; Mavilidi, Okely, Chandler, Cliff, & Paas, 2015). These findings support the embodied cognition view (see Barsalou, 2008; Glenberg, 1997) that observing making movements (i.e. gestures) leads to richer encoding and therefore richer cognitive representations, that allow students to perform faster and more accurately on tasks. Direct evidence that gesturing can lower cognitive load, was found by Ping and Goldin-Meadow (2010) with mathematics tasks.

The evidence suggests that gesturing can improve learning and reduce cognitive load, which is often referred to as cognitive offloading, where the use of physical actions generate cognitive savings (Risko & Gilbert, 2016). From the perspective of learning from animations, there are potential benefits for including gesturing in animation environments where cognitive load may be high due to transient effects. By reducing cognitive load gesturing is automatically/ effortlessly integrated into cognitive schemata, thereby enriching the schemata (embodied cognition), and at the same time helping to reduce cognitive load generated by the instructional format. As some evidence exists that gesturing can be combined effectively with viewing videos as an example of animations (e.g. Lajevardi et al., 2017), gesturing may alleviate the difficulties posed by the transient information of animations.

Collaboration

Collaborative learning is widely used and has significant academic, social and psychological benefits (see Johnson, Johnson, & Smith, 1998). Explanations for this advantage are usually grounded in social constructivist theory or social independence theory (Johnson & Johnson, 1994; Schreiber & Valle, 2013); however, some fresh insights can be gained by considerations of cognitive load theory. From this theoretical perspective collaborative learning uses the borrowing and re-organising principle (see Paas and Sweller, 2012). Learners, with a gap in their knowledge can fill that gap from knowledge provided by other members of the group (borrowed) if such group members have that knowledge (Khawaja, Chen, & Marcus, 2012). A second advantage of collaboration is that it can help share working memory load by having different members of a group contribute knowledge particular to them but not otherwise available to other members of the group. F. Kirschner, Paas, & P. A. Kirschner (2009) have suggested that collaboration generates an expanded processing capacity with reduced collective cognitive load compared to individuals. Instead of one working memory dealing with the load, several working memories work together and share the load (i.e., collective working memory effect, F. Kirschner, Paas, & P. A. Kirschner & Janssen, 2011). Further findings from collaborative memory research suggest that individuals learn from listening to others recall information (Blumen & Rajaram, 2008) and are able to rehearse known information recalled by others (Rajaram & Periera-Pasarin, 2010).

As far as we know little research has been conducted into using collaboration to learn more effectively from animations, as most research focuses on using animation to support collaboration. Computer-based facilities are used to enhance collaboration in what is often referred to as computer-supported collaborative learning (Zhang, Ayres, & Chan, 2011). Significantly, the advantages detailed above, where individuals can gain and rehearse information from others, especially key information that was missed, can alleviate the difficulties associated with transient information. Further being part of a group with an enhanced collective working memory can be expected to enhance the capabilities of learning from animations.

In summary, adding gesturing and collaboration to animations provide the capacity to not only deal with transient information, but they are also powerful learning strategies themselves. These two strategies are expected to enhance animations. Future research could also identify other general strategies that have similar positive effects, such as imagination or visualisation techniques (see Cooper, Tindall-Ford, Chandler, & Sweller, 2001).

Conclusions

This chapter has outlined a number of factors that have impacted on the research into instructional animations. Whereas many research findings indicate that animations can be more effective than equivalent static pictures, there are examples where there is no difference, or in some cases static pictures generate higher learning outcomes. As some of the studies have included design biases, we believe that the findings of the literature base must be treated with some caution. Variables that have an impact on instructional presentations such as appeal, variety, media, size, and interaction, have not been consistently controlled for. Furthermore, three individual characteristics of learners (spatial ability, gender, and prior knowledge) have been shown to influence the effectiveness of dynamic representations, yet many studies have not considered these factors. Therefore, important interactions between them, as well as with the learning materials, have been missed. Learning topics have also been found to be an important factor. Mounting evidence suggests that animations seem to be particularly more suited to learning cognitive tasks containing human motor skills rather than other types of knowledge and skills. However, because of the noted issues associated with the research base, this conclusion is far from being established as a fact.

A major impediment to learning from animations is the transient nature of the information presented. Such information can tax working memory resources and reduce learning. To prevent this situation a number of compensatory strategies are available such as learner interactivity and segmentation. In addition, because of the multimedia nature of animations, there are a number of multimedia principles that can be followed to ensure best-practice animations. There is also the potential to use more general learning strategies such as gesturing and collaboration, to ease the cognitive load and facilitate learning further.

Implications for education

A number of implications can be identified from the research outlined in this chapter, relevant to teachers, instructional designers, and researchers. *Teachers* have to be careful in choosing their animations. Consistent with most teaching and learning paradigms an appropriate match has to be found between the learner and the learning content. Animations, as previously noted, generate some unique conditions. In some cases, an animation may not be the best choice, and static pictures should be chosen. Regardless, animations (and static pictures), should be chosen that have been developed with sound multimedia principles in place. In cases where transient animations must be used because of Government and School policies or other external factors, gesturing and collaboration strategies could be considered. Failure to adapt to such animations could decrease the chances of learning.

An important issue for *instructional designers* is to understand that animations that contain highly transitory information can reduce their effectiveness. Hence, where possible, animations should be constructed that prevent this type of extraneous cognitive load. If unavoidable, options must be available to provide learner-interactivity and/or segmentation facilities. Other intrinsic methods to reduce transitory effects should be considered, as well as following multimedia principles in order to construct high quality animations.

Regarding *researchers*, considerable research is required in future to fully understand the conditions under which animations are most helpful. There is also the scope to investigate the combination of animations with other general learning strategies such as gesturing and general collaboration. It is essential that such research is free of design biases and includes the many factors that can influence the effectiveness of learning from animations.

Of interest to all stakeholders is that it may be important to determine students' spatial ability and prior knowledge and adapt the animations to this. It is important for all to realise that animations are just a sequences of statics. The speed at which the sequence is shown could be slowed down to make the information less transient for low spatial ability and/or low prior knowledge students, and speed up for high spatial ability and/or high prior knowledge students. In addition, students could be given control of the pacing to self-manage their cognitive load. Further research is required to provide specific guidelines between the relationship between spatial ability, prior knowledge and learning from animations.

References

Agostinho, S., Tindall-Ford, S., Ginns, P., Howard, S. J., Leahy, W., & Paas, F. (2015). Giving learning a helping hand: Finger tracing of temperature graphs on an iPad. *Educational Psychology Review*, 27, 427–443. doi:10.1007/s10648–10015–9315–9315.

Ayres, P. (2015). State-of-the-Art research into multimedia learning: A commentary on Mayer's handbook of multimedia learning. *Applied Cognitive Psychology*, doi:10.1002/acp.3142.

Ayres, P., Marcus, N., Chan, C., & Qian, N. (2009). Learning hand manipulative tasks: When instructional animations are superior to equivalent static representations. *Computers in Human Behavior*, 25, 348–353.

Ayres, P., & Paas, F. (2007). Can the cognitive load approach make instructional animations more effective? *Applied Cognitive Psychology*, 21, 811–820.

Ayres, P., & Sweller, J. (2014). The split-attention principle in multimedia learning. In R. E. Mayer (Ed.), *The Cambridge handbook of multimedia learning* (2nd ed., pp. 206–226). New York, N.Y.: Cambridge University Press.

Barsalou, L. W. (2008). Grounded cognition. *Annual Review of Psychology*, 59, 617–645.

Berney, S., & Bétrancourt, M. (2016). Does animation enhance learning? A meta-analysis. *Computers & Education*, 101, 150–167. doi:10.1016/j.compedu.2016.06.005.

Blumen, H. M., & Rajaram, S. (2008). Influence of re-exposure and retrieval disruption during group collaboration on later individual recall. *Memory*, 16, 231–244.

Castro-Alonso, J. C., Ayres, P., & Paas, F. (2014). Learning from observing hands in static and animated versions of non-manipulative tasks. *Learning and Instruction*, 34, 11–21. doi:10.1016/j.learninstruc.2014.07.005.

Castro-Alonso, J. C., Ayres, P., & Paas, F. (2015a). Animations showing Lego manipulative tasks: Three potential moderators of effectiveness. *Computers & Education*, 85, 1–13.

Castro-Alonso, J. C., Ayres, P., & Paas, F. (2015b). The potential of embodied cognition to improve STEAM dynamic visualizations. In X. Ge, D. Ifenthaler, & J. M. Spector (Eds.), *Full STEAM ahead: Emerging technologies for STEAM*. New York, NY: Springer.

Castro-Alonso, J. C., Ayres, P., & Paas, F. (2016). Comparing apples and oranges? A critical look at research on learning from statics versus animations. *Computers & Education, 102*, 234–243. doi:10.1016/j.compedu.2016.09.004.

Castro-Alonso, J. C., Ayres, P., Wong, M., & Paas, F. (2018). Learning symbols from permanent and transient visual presentations: Don't overplay the hand. *Computers & Education*, 116, 1–13. doi:10.1016/j.compedu.2017.08.011.

Castro-Alonso, J. C., Ayres, P., Wong, M., & Paas, F. (In press). Visuospatial tests and multimedia learning: The importance of employing relevant instruments. In J. Sweller, S. Tindall-Ford, & S. Agostinho (Eds.), *Advances in cognitive load theory: Rethinking teaching*. Australia: Routledge.

Cook, S. W., Mitchell, Z., & Goldin-Meadow, S. (2008). Gesturing makes learning last. *Cognition*, 106, 1047–1058.

Cook, S. W., & Tannenhaus, M. K. (2009). Embodied communication: Speakers' gestures affect listeners' actions. *Cognition*, 113, 98–104.

Cooper, G., Tindall-Ford, S., Chandler, P., & Sweller, J. (2001). Learning by imagining. *Journal of Experimental Psychology: Applied*, 7(1), 68–82.

Evans, C., & Gibbons, N. J. (2007). The interactivity effect in multimedia learning. *Computers & Education*, 49(4), 1147–1160. doi:10.1016/j.compedu.2006.01.008.

Falvo, D. A., & Suits, J. P. (2009). Gender and spatial ability and the use of specific labels and diagrammatic arrows in a micro-level Chemistry animation. *Journal of Educational Computing Research*, 41(1), 83–102. doi:10.2190/EC.41.1.d.

Geary, D. (2008). An evolutionarily informed education science. *Educational Psychologist*, 43, 179–195.

Glenberg, A. M. (1997). What memory is for. *The Behavioral and Brain Sciences*, 20, 1–55.

Halpern, D. F. (2011). *Sex differences in cognitive abilities* (4th ed.). New York: Psychology Press.

Hasler, B. S., Kersten, B., & Sweller, J. (2007). Learner control, cognitive load and instructional animation. *Applied Cognitive Psychology*, 21, 713–729.

Hegarty, M., Kriz, S., & Cate, C. (2003). The roles of mental animations and external animations in understanding mechanical systems. *Cognitive and Instruction*, 21(4), 325–360. doi:10.1207/s1532690xci2104_1.

Hegarty, M., Montello, D. R., Richardson, A. E., Ishikawa, T., & Lovelace, K. (2006). Spatial abilities at different scales: Individual differences in aptitude-test performance and spatial-layout learning. *Intelligence*, 34(2), 151–176. doi:10.1016/j.intell.2005.09.005.

Hegarty, M., & Sims, V. K. (1994). Individual differences in mental animation during mechanical reasoning. *Memory & Cognition*, 22(4), 411–430. doi:10.3758/BF03200867.

Hegarty, M., & Waller, D. (2005). Individual difference in spatial abilities. In P. Shah & M. Akira (Eds.), *The Cambridge handbook of visuospatial thinking*. New York, NY: Cambridge University Press.

Höffler, T. N. (2010). Spatial ability: Its influence on learning with visualizations—a meta-analytic review. *Educational Psychology Review*, 22(3), 245–269. doi:10.1007/s10648-010-9126-7.

Höffler, T. N., & Leutner, D. (2007). Instructional animation versus static pictures: A meta-analysis. *Learning and Instruction*, 17, 722–738.

Johnson, D. W., & Johnson, R. T. (1994). *Learning together and alone: Cooperative, competitive and individualistic learning*. Needham Height, MA: Allyn and Bacon.

Johnson, D. W., Johnson, R. T., & Smith, K. A. (1998). Cooperative learning returns to college: What evidence is there that it works? *Change: The Magazine of Higher Learning*, 30, 26–35.

Kalyuga, S. (2008). Relative effectiveness of animated and static diagrams: An effect of learner prior knowledge. *Computers in Human Behavior*, 24, 852–861.

Kalyuga, S., Ayres, P., Chandler, P., & Sweller, J. (2003). The expertise reversal effect. *Educational Psychologist*, 38, 23–31.

Kalyuga, S., & Sweller, J. (2014). The redundancy principle in multimedia learning. In R. E. Mayer (Ed.), *The Cambridge handbook of multimedia learning* (2nd ed., pp. 247–262). New York, N.Y.: Cambridge University Press.

Khawaja, A., Chen, F., & Marcus, N. (2012). Analysis of collaborative communication for linguistic cues of cognitive load. *Human Factors: The Journal of the Human Factors and Ergonomics Society –Special Section: Methods for the Analysis of Communication*, 54(4), 518–529.

Kirschner, F., Paas, F., & Kirschner, P. A. (2009). A cognitive load approach to collaborative learning: United brains for complex tasks. *Educational Psychology Review*, 21, 31–42.

Kirschner, F., Paas, F., Kirschner, P. A., & Janssen, J. (2011). Differential effects of problem-solving demands on individual and collaborative learning outcomes. *Learning and Instruction*, 21, 587–599.

Koroghlanian, C., & Klein, J. D. (2004). The effect of audio and animation in multimedia instruction. *Journal of Educational Multimedia and Hypermedia*, 13(1), 23–46.

Kühl, T., Scheiter, K., Gerjets, P., & Gemballa, S. (2011). Can differences in learning strategies explain the benefits of learning from static and dynamic visualizations? *Computers & Education, 56*(1), 176–187. doi:10.1016/j.compedu.2010.08.008.

Leahy, W., & Sweller, J. (2011). Cognitive load theory, modality of presentation and the transient information effect. *Applied Cognitive Psychology*, 25, 943–951.

Lajevardi, N., Narang, N. S., Marcus, N., & Ayres, P. (2017). Can mimicking gestures facilitate learning from instructional animations and static graphics? *Computers & Education*, 110, 64–76. http://dx.doi.org/10.1016/j.compedu.2017.03.010.

Lewalter, D. (2003). Cognitive strategies for learning from static and dynamic visuals. *Learning and Instruction, 13*(2), 177–189. doi:10.1016/s0959-4752(02)00019-1.

Low, R., & Sweller, J. (2014). The modality principle in multimedia learning. In R. E. Mayer (Ed.), *The Cambridge handbook of multimedia learning* (2nd ed., pp. 227–246). New York, N.Y.: Cambridge University Press.

Maeda, Y., & Yoon, S. (2013). Are gender differences in spatial ability real or an artifact? Evaluation of measurement invariance on the revised PSVT:R. *Journal of Psychoeducational Assessment*, 34(4), 397–403. doi:10.1177/0734282915609843.

Marcus, N., Cleary, B., Wong, A., & Ayres, P. (2013). Should hand actions be observed when learning hand motor skills from instructional animations? *Computers in Human Behavior*, 29, 2172–2178.

Marbach-Ad, G., Rotbain, Y., & Stavy, R. (2008). Using computer animation and illustration activities to improve high school students' achievement in molecular genetics. *Journal of Research in Science Teaching*, 45(3), 273–292. doi:10.1002/tea.20222.

Masters, R. S., Lo, C. Y., Maxwell, J. P., & Patil, N. G. (2008). Implicit motor learning in surgery: Implications for multi-tasking. *Surgery*, 143(1), 140–145. doi:doi:10.1016/j.surg.2007.06.018.

Matthews, W. J., Benjamin, C., & Osborne, C. (2007). Memory for moving and static images. *Psychonomic Bulletin & Review*, 14(5), 989–993. doi:10.3758/bf03194133.

Mavilidi, M., Okely, A. D., Chandler, P., Cliff, D. P., & Paas, F. (2015). Effects of integrated physical exercises and gestures on preschool children's foreign language vocabulary learning. *Educational Psychology Review*, 27, 413–426.

Mayer, R. (2014). *The Cambridge handbook of multimedia learning* (2nd ed.). New York, N.Y.: Cambridge University Press.

Mayer, R. E., & Chandler, P. A. (2001). When learning is just a click away. Does simple user interaction foster deeper understanding of multimedia messages? *Journal of Educational Psychology*, 93 (2), 390–397.

Mayer, R. E., Hegarty, M., Mayer, S., & Campbell, J. (2005). When static media promote active learning: Annotated illustrations versus narrated animations in multimedia instruction. *Journal of Experimental Psychology: Applied*, 11, 256–265.

Narayanan, N. H., & Hegarty, M. (2002). Multimedia design for communication of dynamic information. *International Journal of Human-Computer Studies*, 57, 279–315. doi:10.1006/ijhc.2002.1019.

Ng, H. K., Kalyuga, S., & Sweller, J. (2013). Reducing transience during animation: A cognitive load perspective. *Educational Psychology*, 33(7), 755–772. doi:10.1080/01443410.2013.785050.

Paas, F., & Sweller, J. (2012). An evolutionary upgrade of cognitive load theory: Using the human motor system and collaboration to support the learning of complex cognitive tasks. *Educational Psychology Review*, 24(1), 27–45. doi:10.1007/s10648-011-9179-2.

Ping, R., & Goldin-Meadow, S. (2010). Gesturing saves cognitive resources when talking about non-present objects. *Cognitive Science*, 34, 602–619.

Rajaram, S., & Pereira-Pasarin, L. P. (2010). Collaborative memory: Cognitive research and theory. *Perspectives on Psychological Science*, 5, 649–663.

Renkl, A. (2014). The worked examples principle in multimedia learning. In R. E. Mayer (Ed.), *The Cambridge handbook of multimedia learning* (2nd ed., pp. 391–412). New York, N.Y.: Cambridge University Press.

Risko, E. F. & Gilbert, S.J. (2016). Cognitive offloading. *Trends in Cognitive Science*, 20, 676–688.

Salomon, G. (1984). Television is "easy" and print is "tough": The differential investment of mental effort in learning as a function of perceptions and attributions. *Journal of Educational Psychology*, 76(4), 647–658.

Sánchez, C. A., & Wiley, J. (2010). Sex differences in science learning: Closing the gap through animations. *Learning and Individual Differences*, 20, 271–275. doi:10.1016/j.lindif.2010.01.003.

Schreiber, L. M., & Valle, B. E. (2013). Social constructivist teaching strategies in the small group classroom. *Small Group Research*, 44(4), 395–411. doi:10.1177/1046496413488422.

Singh, A.-M., Marcus, N., & Ayres, P. (2017). Strategies to reduce the negative effects of spoken explanatory text on integrated tasks. *Instructional Science*, 45(2), 239–261. doi:10.1007/s11251-016-9400-2.

Spanjers, I. A., Wouters, P., van Gog, T., & van Merriënboer, J. J. (2011). An expertise reversal effect of segmentation in learning from animated worked-out examples. *Computers in Human Behavior*, 27, 46–52.

Stebner, F., Kühl, T., Höffler, T. N., Wirth, J., & Ayres, P. (2017). The role of process information in narrations while learning with animations and static pictures. *Computers & Education*, 104, 34–48. doi:10.1016/j.compedu.2016.11.001.

Sweller, J., Ayres, P., & Kalyuga, S. (2011). *Cognitive load theory*. New York: Springer.

Tversky, B., Morrison, J. B., & Betrancourt, M. (2002). Animation: Can it facilitate? *International Journal of Human-Computer Studies*, 57, 247–262.

van Gog, T., Paas, F., Marcus, N., Ayres, P., & Sweller, J. (2009). The mirror neuron system and observational learning: Implications for the effectiveness of dynamic visualizations. *Educational Psychology Review*, 21, 21–30. doi:10.1007/s10648-008-9094-3.

Watson, G., Butterfield, J., Curran, R., & Craig, C. (2010). Do dynamic work instructions provide an advantage over static instructions in a small scale assembly task? *Learning and Instruction*, 20(1), 84–93. doi:10.1016/j.learninstruc.2009.05.001.

Wong, A., Marcus, N., Ayres, P., Smith, L., Cooper, G. A., & Paas, F. (2009). Instructional animations can be superior to statics when learning human motor skills. *Computers in Human Behavior*, 25, 339–347.

Wong, M., Castro-Alonso, J. C., Ayres, P., & Paas, F. (2015). Gender effects when learning manipulative tasks from instructional animations and static presentations. *Educational Technology & Society*, 18(4), 37–52.

Wong, M., Castro-Alonso, J. C., Ayres, P., & Paas, F. (2018). Investigating gender and spatial measurements in instructional animation research. *Computers in Human Behavior*. doi:10.1016/j.chb.2018.02.017.

Wong, A., Leahy, W., Marcus, N., & Sweller, J. (2012). Cognitive load theory, the transient information effect and e-learning. *Learning and Instruction, 22*(6), 449–457. doi:10.1016/j. learninstruc.2012.05.004.

Wylie, R., & Chi, M. T. H. (2014). The self-explanation principle in multimedia learning. In R. E. Mayer (Ed.), *The Cambridge handbook of multimedia learning* (2nd ed., pp. 413–432). New York, N.Y.: Cambridge University Press.

Xie, H., Wang, F., Hao, Y., Chen, J., An, J., Wang, Y., & Liu, H. (2017). The more total cognitive load is reduced by cues, the better retention and transfer of multimedia learning: A meta-analysis and two meta-regression analyses. *PLoS ONE, 12*(8), e0183884. doi:10.1371/journal.pone.0183884.

Yang, E.-M., Andre, T., Greenbowe, T. J., & Tibell, L. (2003). Spatial ability and the impact of visualization/animation on learning electrochemistry. *International Journal of Science Education, 25*(3), 329–349. doi:10.1080/09500690210126784.

Yarden, H., & Yarden, A. (2010). Learning using dynamic and static visualizations: Students' comprehension, prior knowledge and conceptual status of a biotechnological method. *Research in Science Education, 40*(3), 375–402. doi:10.1007/s11165-009-9126-0.

Yezierski, E. J., & Birk, J. P. (2006). Misconceptions about the particulate nature of matter: Using animations to close the gender gap. *Journal of Chemical Education, 83*(6). doi:10.1021/ed083p954.

Zhang, L., Ayres, P., & Chan, K. (2011). Examining different types of collaborative learning in a complex computer-based environment: A cognitive load approach. *Computers in Human Behavior, 27*, 94–98. doi:10.1016/j.chb.2010.03.038.

16

THE EFFECTS OF SELF-REGULATION TRAINING ON SELF-REGULATED LEARNING COMPETENCIES AND COGNITIVE LOAD

Does socioeconomic status matter?

Ferdinand Stebner

RUHR UNIVERSITY BOCHUM, UNIVERSITÄTSSTRAßE 150, 44801 BOCHUM, GERMANY

Corinna Schuster

RUHR UNIVERSITY BOCHUM, UNIVERSITÄTSSTRAßE 150, 44801 BOCHUM, GERMANY

Theresa Dicke

AUSTRALIAN CATHOLIC UNIVERSITY, 33 BERRY STREET, NORTH SYDNEY NSW 2060, AUSTRALIA

Yves Karlen

UNIVERSITY OF APPLIED SCIENCES AND ARTS NORTHWESTERN SWITZERLAND FHNW, SCHOOL OF EDUCATION, BAHNHOFSTRAßE 6, 5210 WINDISCH, SWITZERLAND

Joachim Wirth

RUHR UNIVERSITY BOCHUM, UNIVERSITÄTSSTRAßE 150, 44801 BOCHUM, GERMANY

Detlev Leutner

UNIVERSITY DUISBURG-ESSEN, UNIVERSITÄTSSTRAßE 2, 45141 ESSEN, GERMANY

Students who are able to self-regulate their learning effectively are more likely to achieve specific learning goals, therefore it is worthwhile for educational systems to promote students' self-regulated learning (SRL) competencies (Artelt, Baumert, McElvany, & Peschar, 2003). Research has increasingly dealt with the promotion of SRL, resulting in a large number of intervention studies showing that SRL can be promoted in an effective way (Dignath & Büttner, 2008). Nevertheless, using cognitive learning strategies and controlling their use by using metacognitive strategies, as we understand SRL (Schreiber, 1998), is highly demanding for students' working memory. This might be especially the case for students with poor learning prerequisites, resulting, e.g., from low socioeconomic status (SES). It has been suggested that students with low SES lack SRL competencies because of, for instance, qualitatively low parental help when planning, organising and reflecting learning actions at home (Levine, 1993; Pino-Pasternak, Whitebread, & Tolmie, 2010). Therefore, when it comes to SRL training, these students with lower SES might be cognitively overloaded, at least more loaded than students with higher SES. However, research examining the effects of determinants such as SES on the effectiveness of SRL trainings is scarce. Furthermore, the number of SRL studies taking cognitive load theory (Sweller, 1988) into account is even smaller – although it seems to be a fruitful connection (de Bruin & van Merriënboer, 2017). In this chapter we present a study examining the effects of students' SES on the effectiveness of SRL training taking students' cognitive load into account.

Self-regulated learning competencies

SRL is an inherently constructive and self-directed process (Winne, 1995), in which learners monitor, regulate and control their cognition, their motivation and their behavior in relation to their own learning goals and contextual conditions (Pintrich, 2000). Accordingly, SRL refers to a series of reciprocally related cognitive processes that operate together on different components of the information processing system that makes the use of different strategies highly relevant (Boekaerts, 1999). In her SRL model, Schreiber (1998) combines metacognitive strategies, such as planning, monitoring, and reacting (Bandura, 1986), with cognitive strategies, such as using text-highlighting when learning from text or conducting experiments when learning in science classes (Klauer, 1985). In this combination, the goal of metacognitive strategies is to ensure a high step-by-step quality of the application of the specific cognitive strategy when, for instance, highlighting texts or conducting experiments. Whereas some metacognitive processes might run automatically with only limited load on working memory, connecting metacognitive strategies with cognitive strategies might be cognitively demanding and therefore need practice.

Training self-regulated learning

Meta-analyses (e.g., Dignath & Büttner, 2008) show that SRL can generally be promoted. This is also true for training programs that were based on Schreiber's SRL model (Schreiber, 1998). Leutner, Barthel, and Schreiber (2001) combined in their training the promotion of metacognitive strategies with a cognitive strategy intended to motivate oneself for learning an unpopular topic. In terms of strategy knowledge and learning performance, the group of students receiving training on both metacognitive and cognitive strategies outperformed the group receiving training on the cognitive strategy only as well as the control group without any. In three experiments, Leopold and Leutner (2015) showed that the metacognitive self-regulation component of their training enhanced students' performance on science text comprehension whereby the pure training of only cognitive strategies did not work. Stebner, Schmeck, Marschner, Leutner, and Wirth (2015) combined metacognitive strategies with a cognitive experimentation strategy in science learning. Students either received training (1) on metacognitive and cognitive strategies, (2) on cognitive strategies only, or (3) had no specific training. Results revealed an advantage of group 1 over groups 2 and 3 in terms of strategy knowledge and learning outcome after 15 weeks of training.

These previous studies were partly conducted in laboratory settings outside the classroom, with researchers conducting the training. Following Dignath and Büttner (2008), there is empirical evidence that whether teachers or researcher apply the training could have an effect on students' learning. Furthermore, it might be crucial to support SRL in the classroom in order to help students to transfer, for instance, metacognitive strategies to other strategies. Leopold, den Elzen-Rump, and Leutner (2006) implemented SRL training on text-highlighting in regular science classes. Where teachers followed the required procedure, students outperformed the control group in terms of processing and learning success on follow up measures.

To summarise, there are studies showing that the training of metacognitive strategies in combination with cognitive strategies can be helpful for promoting students' SRL competencies. However, field studies are rare, showing small (and delayed) effects, possibly resulting from the high cognitive load that students perceive during learning. Depletion of students' limited working memory may occur following extensive mental effort due to the combination of metacognitive and cognitive strategies resulting in decreased performance (Chen, Castro Alonso, Paas, & Sweller, 2018). Delayed training effects may then occur when students recovered from the before mentioned depletion. Therefore, it seems worthwhile to take cognitive load theory into account when promoting SRL competencies.

Cognitive load in research on self-regulated learning

In order to autonomously plan, execute, and evaluate learning processes, learners' decisions during SRL are related to metacognitive demands (Wirth & Leutner, 2008). Compared to externally regulated learning (e.g., regulated by a teacher), these metacognitive demands are additional demands imposing additional cognitive load on the learner (Seufert, 2018; Sweller, 1988; but see also Sweller & Paas, 2017, for critical statements). According to Paas and van Merriënboer (1994), cognitive load can be defined as a multidimensional construct reflecting the concepts of mental load, mental effort, and performance (Paas, Tuovinen, Tabbers, & van Gerven, 2003). Mental load originates from the interaction between task and learner and may be interpreted as task difficulty. Mental effort is the capacity that a learner uses to handle the demands imposed by a task. Performance is the learner's achievement (for more details see Paas et al., 2003). Briefly, cognitive load can be affected by both, (external) task and (internal) learner characteristics. Intervention studies on SRL trainings, however, focus on effects of external task characteristics on training effectiveness (see, e.g., Dignath & Büttner, 2008). Internal learner characteristics, as suggested by cognitive load theory research (Seufert, 2018), have been largely neglected in SRL trainings research so far.

Role of learner characteristics

There is research showing that individual factors such as school grades (Pintrich & de Groot, 1990), cognitive abilities (Veenman, Prins, & Elshout, 2002), and gender (Maag Merki, Ramseier, & Karlen, 2013) might explain interindividual differences in students' SRL competencies. Students with better grades, higher cognitive abilities and girls are often assumed to be more effective self-regulated learners. However, another crucial concept is students' socioeconomic status (SES). As in most learning areas, SRL should profit from role models and intensive practice (Bandura, 1986; Sweller, van Merriënboer, & Paas, 1998). Therefore, students who have limited role models at home (due, for example, to parents' academic education) may practice less and finally struggle when helpful learning routines should be automated (Artelt et al., 2003). SES is a fundamental determinant of human functioning across the life span, including development, well-being, and physical and mental health (American Psychological Association, 2007). There is empirical evidence that the acquisition of SRL is affected by SES (Artelt et al., 2003). Karlen, Maag Merki, & Ramseier (2014), for instance, were able to show that $10^{th}/11^{th}$ graders differed in SRL competencies according to their level of SES: students with higher SES showed higher metacognitive strategy knowledge than students with lower SES. Furthermore, SES affected the promotion of metacognitive strategy knowledge across one school term in terms of a Matthew effect (Renkl, 1996). The Matthew effect is when students with high SES showed higher gains in metacognitive strategy knowledge than students with low SES. Other studies showed that families with high SES support their children with higher cognitive demands as well as interacting with their children more, which has positive effects on the promotion of the childrens' SRL competencies (Pino-Pasternak et al., 2010).

Research question and hypotheses

Firstly, we expected the training to be effective (Hypothesis 1): students of the experimental group (EG) with SRL training should outperform students of the control group (CG) without SRL training in terms of SRL competencies, that is, applying metacognitive and cognitive strategies to a new (fictional) learning task (Hypothesis 1a). In contrast to prior studies, we also measured cognitive load when students described how they would apply metacognitive and cognitive strategies to a new (fictional) learning task and we expected the EG to differ from the CG in terms of decreased perceived difficulty (Hypothesis 1b) and decreased mental effort (Hypothesis 1c).

Individual factors such as students' SES might be a crucial determinant of SRL competencies and cognitive load. We would expect students with a higher SES to be more systematic in using metacognitive and cognitive strategies in order to learn more successfully and perceive less cognitive load. Reasons for that would be, for instance, more prior practice at home due to the help of parents with a relatively high academic education (Karlen et al., 2014).

Secondly, we expected the training to be more beneficial for students with high SES in comparison to students with low SES (Matthew effect; Hypothesis 2) in terms of SRL competencies (Hypothesis 2a). Furthermore, this Matthew effect was also expected in terms of students' perceived difficulty (Hypothesis 2b), and mental effort (Hypothesis 2c) when students had to describe how they would apply metacognitive and cognitive strategies to a new (fictional) learning task.

Method

Study design and participants

The present study was part of the German full-day school development project "Ganz In".[1] In this project, 29 schools were scientifically supported to change from half-day to full-day schools. The project contained several sub-projects that aimed at minimising social disadvantage. One sub-project was called "self-regulated learning". In previous studies of this SRL sub-project, a newly developed training in SRL competencies was evaluated several times (experimentally and quasi-experimentally) to examine its effects on students' learning (Stebner et al., 2015). In this study, the SRL training was conducted by teachers, who joined a two-day teacher training program beforehand. On the first day, the teachers were motivated to take part in this project, and learned the theoretical background of SRL. On the second day, they went through the learning material and learned how to adapt their own learning material in order to promote SRL. The goal was to integrate SRL training into regular class lessons.

The students of the EG were trained by these teachers on SRL. The SRL training lasted over 15 weeks (half a school term) with 90 minutes training each week. First, students learned how to regulate their learning motivation and their emotions, how to set goals properly, and why SRL is worthwhile. Then, students learned how to connect metacognitive with cognitive strategies when conducting student experiments in their science classes. In the training lessons, students had to read science texts about topics like meteorites or thermal insulation in order to deduce a research question that was subsequently examined experimentally. Students conducted those experiments increasingly on their own from week to week. For reading as well as for experimentation, students used an algorithm that combined metacognitive and cognitive strategies (e.g., for experimentation: set goals, derive hypothesis, conduct experiment, conclude, monitor, and react) as presented in Schreiber's (1998) model of SRL (see p. 00).

In the current study, 865 German fifth grade students (age $M = 10.51$; $SD = .63$; 50% female) from 34 classes took part. The students attended the secondary school for half a year before SRL was taught specifically in the second half school term. The school classes were either randomly assigned to the EG ($n_{EG} = 424$ students) receiving the training, or to the CG ($n_{CG} = 441$ students) receiving no training but regular school lessons at the same time. All schools were higher secondary; "Gymnasium". We calculated the intraclass correlation coefficients ($.09 < ICCs < .18$). The nested structure had a small effect on our analyses, however, it did not change the pattern of results. Therefore, due to space restrictions and to minimise the complexity of the results, we present the results without multilevel analyses.

Measures

We measured students' SRL competencies and cognitive load as dependent variables, as well as SES, cognitive abilities and school grades as covariates and potential moderator variables. Furthermore, we asked students to answer a few demographic questions. All measures (except demographic data) were applied twice, before the training had started (pre) as well as directly after the training had finished (post).

SRL competencies. The multi-strategy test (MST; Stebner et al., 2015) is an open-answer format in which students are asked to describe how they would conduct an experiment in order to answer a certain research question (time 10 minutes). That is, students have to describe how they would apply metacognitive and cognitive strategies to a new (fictional) learning task. The test was coded by two raters looking for metacognitive and cognitive strategies (Cohen's kappa mean $> .80$). Each strategy named by the students resulted in one point. We present the sum score. The manual to code the students' answers was built on all (trained) strategies that could have been mentioned, with the possible range from zero to 20. In previous studies, this test correlated significantly with learning outcome and further strategy knowledge tests. Due to time restrictions, we were unable to implement more measures aiming at measuring SRL competencies in this study.

Cognitive load. We measured cognitive load with subjective ratings of *perceived difficulty* asking how difficult it had been to fill in the MST (from 1 "very very easy" to 9 "very very difficult"; (Kalyuga, Chandler, & Sweller, 1999), and *mental effort* asking how much mental effort students had invested when filling in the MST (from 1 "very very low" to 9 "very very high"; Paas, 1992). Both items were in German and presented to the students directly after they had filled in the MST.

Socio economic status (SES). We measured students' SES with ten items asking for cultural and welfare goods (OECD, 2010) and with one item asking for the number of books the family had at home (OECD, 2010). We z-standardised both measures and aggregated the scores, in order get a more robust indicator of SES and to minimise the complexity of the results. Analysing both measures separately revealed the same results and conclusions.

Cognitive abilities, grades and demographic data. We measured students' cognitive abilities with the nonverbal subtest of the Cognitive Ability Test (CAT; Heller, Gaedike, & Weinhändler, 1985). Furthermore, we asked students for their average grade on their last school certificate. We also asked for some demographic data such as age, gender etc.

All scales showed acceptable to good reliability scores. As Kolmogorow-Sminov tests revealed that the assumption of normality was violated in some cases (e.g., SES), we will present Spearman's Rho as correlation coefficients. Regarding the hypotheses, using non-parametric analyses did not change the pattern of the main results analysed within the framework of the General Linear Model (Horton, 1978). Furthermore, as ANCOVAs are considered fairly robust against violations of normality (Glass, Peckham, & Sanders, 1972), we will present the results of the parametric analyses.

Results

Descriptive statistics and prior group differences

Descriptive statistics are shown in Table 16.1. A MANOVA revealed prior differences between EG and CG in terms of cognitive abilities, $p < .001$, $\eta_p^2 = .05$ (higher in CG) and school grades, $p < .05$, $\eta_p^2 = .01$ (better in CG). Therefore, we used these two variables as covariates when comparing EG and CG. For Hypothesis 1, the whole sample was used for statistical analyses. According to the research question, for Hypothesis 2, only the EG was used for statistical analyses.

Hypothesis 1 (Treatment Check)

We conducted ANCOVAS with repeated measures on MST scores (Hypothesis 1a), perceived difficulty (Hypothesis 1b), and mental effort (Hypothesis 1c) as dependent variables, cognitive abilities and school grades as covariates, and group (EG or CG) as the independent variable.

With respect to the MST score, the ANCOVA revealed no main effect for time, $F < 1$, but a significant main effect for group, $F(1, 541) = 90.848, p < .001, \eta_p^2 = .144$, indicating that the students of the EG scored significantly higher than the CG. In line with Hypothesis 1a, the ANCOVA revealed a significant interaction of time and group, $F(1, 541) = 21.098, p < .001, \eta_p^2 = .038$, indicating a higher gain in the MST score for students from the EG.

With respect to perceived difficulty, the ANCOVA revealed no main effect for time, $F < 1$, but a main effect for group, $F(1, 518) = 4.398, p = .036, \eta_p^2 = .008$ indicating that the students of the EG rated higher on perceived difficulty. In line with Hypothesis 1b, the results reveal a significant interaction of time and group, $F(1, 647) = 15.233, p < .001, \eta_p^2 = .023$, indicating a higher decrease in perceived difficulty for the EG than for CG.

TABLE 16.1 Means (and standard deviations) of covariates and dependent variables for EG and CG

	Covariates			
	CAT	Welfare goods (SES)	Books (SES)	School grades
EG	0.68 (0.29)	0,80 (0.18)	4.00 (1.06)	2.22 (0.51)
CG	0.80 (0.23)	0.81 (0.18)	3.99 (1.09)	2.11 (0.54)
MEAN	0.73 (0.28)	0.81 (0.18)	4.00 (1.07)	2.17 (0.53)
Possible range	0–1	0–1	1–5	1–6

	Dependent variables					
	MST pre	MST post	Difficulty pre	Difficulty post	Effort pre	Effort post
EG	2.45 (2.45)	4.04 (3.25)	3.91 (2.01)	2.87 (1.61)	3.69 (1.87)	3.16 (1.82)
	1.69 (2.07)	2.03 (2.59)	3.49 (1.93)	3.03 (1.73)	3.49 (1.76)	3.07 (1.80)
	2.14 (2.33)	3.21 (3.15)	3.70 (1.98)	2.95 (1.67)	3.59 (1.82)	3.12 (1.81)
Possible range	0–20*	0–20*	1–9	1–9	1–9	1–9

* The manual to code the students' answers was built on all strategies that could have been mentioned. Therefore, the possible range is large.

With respect to mental effort, the ANCOVA revealed no main effect for time, $F < 1$, and no main effect for group, $F < 1$. Contrary to Hypothesis 1c, the ANCOVA also revealed no significant interaction of time and group, $F < 1$, indicating the same decrease in mental effort for both EG and CG.

Hypothesis 2 (Matthew effect)

We conducted ANCOVAS with repeated measures for the MST scores (Hypothesis 2a), perceived difficulty (Hypothesis 2b), and mental effort (Hypothesis 2c) as dependent variables, and SES as a covariate.

With respect to the MST score, the ANCOVA revealed a main effect of time, $F(1, 325) = 62.750$, $p < .001$, $\eta_p^2 = .162$, indicating an overall increase of the MST score. The ANCOVA revealed no main effect of SES, $F(1, 325) = 3.058$, $p = .081$, $\eta_p^2 = .009$, and, contrary to Hypothesis 2a, no significant interaction of time and SES, $F < 1$, indicating that there was no Matthew effect: students with high and low SES benefited the same way from the training.

With respect to perceived difficulty, the ANCOVA revealed a main effect of time, $F(1, 312) = 84,252$, $p < .001$, $\eta_p^2 = .213$, indicating an overall decrease of perceived difficulty. However, the ANCOVA revealed neither a main effect for SES, $F < 1$, nor a significant interaction of time and SES, $F < 1$. Contrary to Hypothesis 2b, there was no Matthew effect: the decrease in perceived difficulty was the same for students with high and low SES.

With respect to mental effort, the ANCOVA revealed a main effect of time, $F(1, 306) = 18.642$, $p < .001$, $\eta_p^2 = .057$, indicating an overall decrease in mental effort. The ANCOVA revealed, however, neither a main effect for SES, $F < 1$, nor a significant interaction, $F < 1$. Contrary to Hypothesis 2c, there was no Matthew effect: The decrease in mental effort was the same for students with high and low SES.

Additional analysis

With respect to MST, further analyses showed a main effect for school grades, $F(1, 545) = 8.454$, $p = .004$, $\eta_p^2 = .015$, indicating an overall advantage of students with better grades. Furthermore, there was a significant main effect for CAT, $F(1, 659) = 13.674$, $p < .001$, $\eta_p^2 = .020$, indicating an overall advantage of students with higher cognitive abilities. Gender was not related to the MST scores.

With respect to perceived difficulty, further analyses showed a main effect for grades, $F(1, 522) = 11.076$, $p = .001$, $\eta_p^2 = .021$, indicating that students with better grades reported less difficulty when filling in the MST. Furthermore, there was a significant interaction between time and CAT, $F(1, 632) = 4.302$, $p = .038$, $\eta_p^2 = .007$, indicating that the decrease in perceived difficulty was stronger for students with lower scores in the CAT (which represents a compensator effect).

With respect to mental effort, further analyses showed a main effect for grades, $F(1, 519) = 10.334$, $p = .001$, $\eta_p^2 = .020$, indicating that students with better grades invested less mental effort when filling in the MST.

Discussion and future directions

In this study, we measured SRL competencies by asking students to describe their behavior when conducting experiments. Due to the fact that we taught them to combine metacognitive with cognitive strategies while conducting experiments, when analysing their tests, we looked for the naming of those strategies. Perceived difficulty and mental effort, as indicators for cognitive load, however, were measured after completing the test. Therefore, it is the students' cognitive load during testing giving insights into how demanding it was to *describe* their behavior when conducting experiments. As in our previous studies and in line with Hypothesis 1, the promotion of SRL over half a school term is effective (cf. Stebner et al., 2015): Students from the EG outperformed students from the CG in terms of SRL competencies and perceived difficulty. In comparison to the CG, the EG acquired more SRL competencies and showed a stronger decrease in perceived difficulty during testing. Because there were no triggers prompting students to name metacognitive and cognitive strategies, the fact that students named them during free recall is important. Next to well-established multiple-choice measures (e.g., MSLQ; Pintrich, Smith, Garcia, & McKeachie, 1991) or high-tech measures (e.g., eye tracking; Azevedo et al., 2013), this open answer format seems to be a fruitful option to measure SRL competencies.

To measure SES in the present study, we used a scale of welfare and economic goods as well as an item asking for the number of books reflecting a family background with an emphasis on education. Students with a high SES might therefore have more opportunities to make meaningful learning experiences outside school (Karlen et al., 2014) and become more successful students (Hansen & Munk, 2012). However, in the present study, SES neither affected SRL competencies nor cognitive load, and it did not affect the effectiveness of the SRL training. Contrary to our assumptions, there was no Matthew effect: students with a high SES did not acquire more SRL competencies nor did they demonstrate a stronger decrease in cognitive load during testing. One possible explanation might be the students' age. SES might only be relevant after a longer period of schooling. Therefore, future studies should examine the promotion of SRL over a longer period of time. Furthermore, the way we measured SES might be an issue. In future studies, the breadth of SES by regarding further sub-components of SES (e.g., parents' income) could be taken into account. Another possible explanation for no Matthew effect might be the teacher role: Due to the fact that teachers generally lack knowledge about metacognition and spend only limited time directly teaching metacognitive strategies (Dignath & Büttner, 2018) it appears particularly meaningful to take the teacher role into account. Therefore, in the present study, teachers were trained so that SRL could be promoted in numerous school classes. However, related to the high external validity of this study, we do not know exactly what happened during the training phase. Nevertheless, observing teachers while promoting SRL would be interesting because there are studies showing that teachers do not always fulfil prior agreements during teaching (e.g., induced by missing pre-designed material; Werth et al., 2012). Furthermore, when examining the effects of SES, one could assume, that certain students (e.g., students with a lower SES) are supported more by teachers through additional guidance or differentiated lessons. This might then have a compensating effect on the role of SES when promoting SRL.

Although the results are quite consistent, measuring SRL competencies and cognitive load the way we did can only be a first step. In further studies, learning outcomes and especially far transfer should be considered in order to examine the effectiveness of SRL training (cf. Mokhlesgerami, Souvignier, Rühl, & Gold, 2007). Furthermore, cognitive load could be measured more often (e.g., also during the promotion; see Schmeck, Opfermann, van Gog, Paas, & Leutner, 2015) and with different scales (e.g., Leppink, Paas, van der Vleuten, van Gog, & van Merriënboer, 2013) in order to get further insights into the students' learning processes.

There are numerous studies showing that SRL can be promoted (Dignath & Büttner, 2008). However, Sweller and Paas (2017) hypothesised that SRL is a generic skill (Sweller, 2016) that has evolved over hundreds of years and therefore promoting these skills is nearly impossible. It could be compared with a professional runner who is able to run very quickly. The gift to run could be seen as an in-born generic skill, yet, training can still help to perfect his/her technique in order to become even faster. In this context, SRL might be an in-born generic skill, however, especially the connection between metacognitive and cognitive strategies could be practiced so as to improve the integration and application of these strategies in order to learn more successfully. To strengthen or falsify this generic skill hypothesis, we need controlled experiments examining the effects of SRL training on far transfer as a dependent variable. "Far transfer is required to ensure that differential test performance is due to differential acquisition of self-regulatory knowledge rather than differential domain-specific content" (Sweller & Paas, 2017, p. 88). Furthermore, we need data from follow up measurements due to the fact that working memory depletion and recovery might play a crucial role when learning complex skills (Chen et al., 2018).

In further analyses, we also looked for the role of other individual factors: Students' grades had an effect on SRL competencies as well as perceived difficulty and mental effort. Successful students were better in terms of SRL competencies, and they reported less difficulty and mental effort. These findings are in line with Karlen (2016), who showed that upper secondary school students with higher SRL competencies are more successful. Furthermore, students with higher cognitive abilities had higher SRL competencies and had a higher decrease of perceived difficulty during the training. This interaction could be interpreted as a compensator effect: Students with lower cognitive abilities started with a higher cognitive load but ended up on the same (low) level as students with high cognitive abilities. There were no significant effects of the students' gender. Previous studies found advantages to girls in terms of SRL competencies (Artelt, Beinick, Schlagmüller, & Schneider, 2009; Karlen et al., 2014).

Conclusions

The aim of the present study was to examine the role of SES in promoting SRL competencies. Based on existing literature (e.g., Artelt et al., 2003; Karlen et al., 2014), and in accord with the Matthew effect, it was hypothesised that 5th grade students with a high SES would benefit more from SRL training than students with a low SES. Firstly, the results show that the training which was used to promote SRL is effective: The experimental group, which was trained for half a school term, outperformed the control group in terms of a higher gain in SRL competencies and a stronger decrease of cognitive load. Secondly, the results show no Matthew effect as students with a high *and* low SES benefited equally from the training, in terms of both SRL competencies and cognitive load. We interpret the results as positive, although this finding was not in line with our hypothesis. A

Matthew effect would have increased social disadvantages due to a program that was actually established to give individual support in a pedagogical manner and to close the gap of social disadvantage.

From a practical perspective, the results are promising: teaching students already in the beginning of their secondary school career in SRL might be a fruitful way to prepare students for future life without disadvantaging students with low SES. The material used in the training program was rather similar to normal learning material with the difference that metacognitive processes were firstly trained and then regularly activated over the school term by adding metacognitive triggers (e.g., symbols, certain questions). Therefore, this training program is easily adaptable for daily school business.

To the best of our knowledge, this study was one of the first which examined the relation between SRL and SES from a cognitive load theory perspective. Based on the study's results, cognitive load theory made a fruitful contribution. Even if self-regulation is a generic skill, as Sweller and Paas (2017) state, we think that this should not automatically exclude cognitive load theory from SRL research.

Note

1 We thank Stiftung Mercator for the opportunity to conduct research on this topic. Furthermore, we thank the Center of Educational Studies for the support which enabled us to write this chapter together with international colleagues. Last but not least, we thank our student assistants for their support collecting the data.

References

American Psychological Association, Task Force on Socioeconomic Status. (2007). *Report of the APA Task Force on Socioeconomic Status*. Washington, DC: American Psychological Association.

Artelt, C., Baumert, J., McElvany, N., & Peschar, J. (2003). *Learners for life. Student approaches to learning. Results from PISA 2000*. Paris: OECD.

Artelt, C., Beinick, A., Schlagmüller, M., & Schneider, W. (2009). Diagnose von Strategiewissen beim Textverstehen [Diagnosing strategy knowledge in text comprehension]. *Zeitschrift für Entwicklungspsychologie und Pädagogische Psychologie, 41*, 96–103.

Azevedo, R., Harley, J., Trevors, G., Duffy, M., Feyzi-Behnagh, R., Bouchet, F., & Landis, R. (2013). Using trace data to examine the complex roles of cognitive, metacognitive, and emotional self-regulatory processes during learning with multi-agent systems. In R. Azevedo, & V. Aleven (Eds.), *International handbook of metacognition and learning technologies* (pp. 427–449). New York: Springer. doi:10.1007/978-1-4419-5546-3_28.

Bandura, A. (1986). *Social foundations of thought and action: A social cognitive theory*. Englewood Cliffs, NJ: Prentice-Hall.

Chen, O., Castro-Alonso, J. C., Paas, F. G., & Sweller, J. (2018). Extending cognitive load theory to incorporate working memory resource depletion: Evidence from the spacing effect. *Educational Psychology Review, 30*, 483–501.

de Bruin, A. B. H., & van Merriënboer, J. J. G. (2017). Bridging cognitive load and self-regulated learning research: A complementary approach to contemporary issues in educational research. *Learning and Instruction, 51*, 1–9.

Dignath, C., & Büttner, G. (2008). Components of fostering self-regulated learning among students. A meta-analysis on intervention studies at primary and secondary school level. *Metacognition Learning*, 3, 231–264.

Dignath, C., & Büttner, G. (2018). Teachers' direct and indirect promotion of self-regulated learning in primary and secondary school mathematics classes – insights from video-based classroom observations and teacher interviews. *Metacognition Learning*, doi:10.1007/s11409-11018-9181-x.

Glass, G. V., Peckham, P. D., & Sanders, J. R. (1972). Consequences of failure to meet assumptions underlying the fixed effects analyses of variance and covariance. *Review of Educational Research*, 42, 237–288.

Hansen, K. Y., & Munk, I. (2012). Exploring the measurement profiles of socioeconomic background indicators and their differences in reading achievement: A two-level latent class analysis. *IERI Monograph Series: Issues and Methodologies in Large-Scale Assessments*, 5, 49–77.

Heller, K., Gaedike, A. K., & Weinhändler, H. (1985). *Kognitiver Fähigkeitstest KFT (2. Verbesserte und erweitere Aufl.).* [Cognitive ability test CAT]. Weinheim: Beltz.

Horton, R. L. (1978). *The general linear model: Data analysis in the social and behavioral sciences.* London: McGraw-Hill.

Kalyuga, S., Chandler, P., & Sweller, J. (1999). Managing split-attention and redundancy in multimedia instruction. *Applied Cognitive Psychology*, 13, 351–371.

Karlen, Y. (2016). Differences in students' metacognitive strategy knowledge, motivation, and strategy use: A typology of self-regulated learners. *Journal of Educational Research, 109,* 253–265. doi:10.1080/00220671.2014.942895.

Karlen, Y., Maag Merki, K., & Ramseier, E. (2014). The effect of individual differences in the development of metacognitive strategy knowledge. *Instructional Science*, 42, 777–794. doi:10.1007/s11251-11014-9314-9319.

Klauer, K. J. (1985). Framework for a theory of teaching. *Teaching and Teacher Education*, 1, 5–17.

Leopold, C., & Leutner, D. (2015). Improving students' science text comprehension through metacognitive self-regulation when applying learning strategies. *Metacognition Learning*, 10, 313–346. doi:10.2007/s11409-11014-9130-9132.

Leopold, C., den Elzen-Rump, V., & Leutner, D. (2006). Selbstreguliertes Lernen aus Sachtexten [Self-regulated learning from science texts]. In M. Prenzel, & L. Allolio-Näcke (Eds.), *Selbstreguliertes Lernen aus Sachtexten* [Self-regulated learning from science texts], pp. 268–288. Münster: Waxmann.

Leppink, J., Paas, F. G., van der Vleuten, C. P. M., van Gog, T., & van Merriënboer, J. J. G. (2013). Development of an instrument for measuring different types of cognitive load. *Behavioral Research Methods*, 45, 1058–1072. doi:10.3758/s13428-13013-0334-0331.

Leutner, D., Barthel, A., & Schreiber, B. (2001). Studierende können lernen, sich selbst zu motivieren. Ein Trainingsexperiment [Students can learn to motivate themselves. A training experiment]. *Zeitschrift für Pädagogische Psychologie*, 21, 155–167.

Levine, H. (1993). Context and scaffolding in developmental studies of mother–child problem-solving dyads. In S. Chaiklin, & J. Lave (Eds.), *Understanding practice: perspectives on activity and context (Learning in doing: social, cognitive and computational perspectives)* (pp. 306–326). Cambridge: Cambridge University Press. doi:10.1017/CBO9780511625510.012.

Maag Merki, K., Ramseier, E., & Karlen, Y. (2013). Reliability and validity analyses of a newly developed test to assess learning strategy knowledge. *Journal of Cognitive Education and Psychology*, 12, 391–408.

Mokhlesgerami, J., Souvignier, E., Rühl, K., & Gold, A. (2007). Naher und weiter Transfer eines Unterrichtsprogramms zur Förderung der Lesekompetenz in der Sekundarstufe I.

[Proximal and distal transfer of a program aiming at fostering reading competence in secondary schools]. *Zeitschrift für Pädagogische Psychologie*, 21, 169–180.

OECD (2010). *PISA 2009 Ergebnisse: Potenziale nutzen und Chancengerechtigkeit sichern – Sozialer Hintergrund und Schülerleistungen* [PISA 2009 results: Benefit from potentials, and ensure educational justice – social background and students' achievement]. Paris: OECD.

Paas, F. G. (1992). Training strategies for attaining transfer of problem-solving skill in statistics: A cognitive-load approach. *Journal of Educational Psychology*, 84, 429–434.

Paas, F. G., Tuovinen, J. E., Tabbers, H. K., & van Gerven, P. W. (2003). Cognitive load measurement as a means to advance cognitive load theory. *Educational Psychologist*, 38, 63–71.

Paas, F. G., & van Merriënboer, J. J. G. (1994). Instructional control of cognitive load in the training of complex cognitive tasks. *Educational Psychology Review*, 6, 351–371.

Pino-Pasternak, D., Whitebread, D., & Tolmie, A. (2010). A multidimensional analysis of parent-child interactions during academic tasks and their relationships with children's self-regulated learning. *Cognition and Instruction*, 28, 219–272.

Pintrich, P. R. (2000). The role of goal orientation in self-regulated learning. In M. Boekaerts, P. R. Pintrich, & M. Zeidner (Eds.), *Handbook of self-regulation* (pp. 451–502). San Diego: Academic Press.

Pintrich, P. R., & de Groot, E. V. (1990). Motivational and self-regulated learning components of classroom academic performance. *Journal of Educational Psychology*, 82, 33–40.

Pintrich, P. R., Smith, D. A., Garcia, T., & McKeachie, W. J. (1991). *A manual for the use of the motivated strategies learning questionnaire (MSLQ)*. Ann Arbor, MI: University of Michigan, National Center for Research to Improve Postsecondary Teaching and Learning.

Renkl, A. (1996). Vorwissen und Schulleistung [Prior knowledge and school achievement]. In J. Möller, & O. Köller (Eds.), *Emotionen, Kognitionen und Schulleistung* (pp. 175–190). Weinheim: Beltz.

Schmeck, A., Opfermann, M., van Gog, T., Paas, F., & Leutner, D. (2015). Measuring cognitive load with subjective rating scales during problem solving: Differences between immediate and delayed ratings. *Instructional Science*, 43, 93–114.

Schreiber, B. (1998). *Selbstreguliertes Lernen. Entwicklung und Evaluation von Trainingsansätzen für Berufstätige* [Self-regulated learning. Development and evaluation of trainings for professionals]. Münster: Waxmann.

Seufert, T. (2018). The interplay between self-regulation in learning and cognitive load. *Educational Research Review*, 24, 116–129.

Stebner, F., Schmeck, A., Marschner, J., Leutner, D., & Wirth, J. (2015). Ein Training zur Förderung des selbstregulierten Lernens durch Experimentieren [A training on promoting self-regulated learning through experimentation]. In H. Wendt, & W. Bos (Eds.), *Auf dem Weg zum Ganztagsgymnasium. Erste Ergebnisse der wissenschaftlichen Begleitforschung zum Projekt „Ganz In – Mit Ganztag mehr Zukunft. Das neue Ganztagsgymnasium NRW"* (pp. 531–552). Münster: Waxmann.

Sweller, J. (1988). Cognitive load during problem solving: Effects on learning. *Cognitive Science*, 12, 257–285.

Sweller, J. (2016). Cognitive load theory, evolutionary educational psychology, and instructional design. In D. Geary, & D. Berch (Eds.), *Evolutionary perspectives on child development and education* (pp. 291–306). Switzerland: Springer.

Sweller, J., & Paas, F. G. (2017). Should self-regulated learning be integrated with cognitive load theory? A commentary. *Learning and Instruction*, 51, 85–89.

Sweller, J., van Merriënboer, J. J. G., & Paas, F. G. (1998). Cognitive architecture and instructional design. *Educational Psychology Review*, 10, 251–296.

Veenman, M. V. J., Prins, F. J., & Elshout, J. J. (2002). Initial inductive learning in a complex computer simulated environment: The role of metacognitive skills and intellectual ability. *Computers in Human Behavior, 18*, 327–341.

Werth, S., Wagner, W., Origin, S., Trautwein, U., Friedrich, A., Keller, S., Ihringer, A., & Schmitz, B. (2012). Förderung des selbstregulierten Lernens durch die Lehrkräftefortbildung „Lernen mit Plan": Effekte auf fokale Trainingsinhalte und die allgemeine Unterrichtsqualität [Fostering self-regulated learning through teacher training "Lernen mit Plan": Effects on focal training contents and general quality of lessons"]. *Zeitschrift für Pädagogische Psychologie, 26*, 291–305.

Winne, P. H. (1995). Inherent details in self-regulated learning. *Educational Psychologist, 30*, 173–187.

Wirth, J., & Leutner, D. (2008). Self-regulated learning as a competence. Implications of theoretical models for assessment methods. *Zeitschrift für Psychologie, 216*, 102–110.

17

WHAT SHOULD STUDENTS DO FIRST WHEN LEARNING HOW TO SOLVE A PHYSICS PROBLEM

Try to solve it themselves or study a worked example?

Slava Kalyuga

SCHOOL OF EDUCATION, UNIVERSITY OF NEW SOUTH WALES, SYDNEY, AUSTRALIA

Chih-Yi Hsu

THE NATIONAL TOU-LIU SENIOR HIGH SCHOOL, TAIWAN

If novice learners start trying to solve an unfamiliar problem on their own, their search for solution paths may generate high levels of mental effort that could be detrimental to learning from the perspective of cognitive load theory (Sweller, Ayres, & Kalyuga, 2011). According to this theory, instruction with comprehensive explicit instructional guidance such as examples with fully worked-out solutions is effective for novice learners without sufficient prior knowledge in a specific task domain (Sweller & Cooper, 1985; Van Gog, Paas, & van Merriënboer, 2008).

In contrast, the instructional theories of invention activity for future learning (Schwartz, Chase, Oppezzo, & Chin, 2011) and productive failure (Kapur, 2012; Kapur & Bielaczyc, 2012) assert that having novices encounter difficulties and challenge before receiving formal explicit instruction (e.g., using exploratory activities or problem solving attempts) may improve learners' performance, especially in the long term and on transfer tasks. It is claimed that these approaches may result in deeper conceptual understanding leading to better transfer performance (Glogger-Frey, Fleischer, Grüny, Kappich, & Renkl, 2015; Kapur & Bielaczyc, 2012; Loibl & Rummel, 2014a).

The present study investigated the effectiveness of the alternative (problem-first and worked example-first) approaches by comparing the learning outcomes from four instructional conditions in which students were initially engaged in problem-solving-related activities with different levels of explicit guidance. This initial learning stage was followed by a common explicit instruction as the second learning stage. The different levels of instructional guidance during the initial stage ranged from entirely independent problem solving (no guidance) to problem solving with partial, principle-based guidance and also with reflection on the learners' own solution attempts, and to entirely worked-out solution steps (comprehensive guidance).

The next theoretical section briefly reviews the worked example effect in cognitive load theory and the problem-first approach represented by productive failure theory. The experiment that follows compares the effectiveness of different instructional approaches, with the subsequent discussion of the results from the perspective of the recently suggested integrative theoretical framework (Kalyuga & Singh, 2016).

Theoretical Background

Worked example effect in cognitive load theory

Extensively using the study of worked examples instead of actual problem-solving activities is one of the instructional methods strongly supported by cognitive load theory, in particular for novice learners in the initial stages of cognitive skill acquisition. Worked examples provide information about all solution moves for a problem from the initial step to the final answer. Positive effects of worked examples on schema construction for novice learners have been proved by many empirical studies (Atkinson, Derry, Renkl, & Wortham, 2000; Kalyuga, Chandler, Tuovinen, & Sweller, 2001; Sweller & Cooper, 1985; Van Gog et al., 2008). From a cognitive load perspective, it would be detrimental to learning if novices start learning by problem solving (Kalyuga et al., 2001; Paas & Van Merriënboer, 1994). Because the demand on working memory when searching for solution paths (e.g., by using means-ends analysis) will increase, novices may not be able to pay sufficient attention to the critical information relevant to learning. Therefore, instructing by problem solving may engender an extraneous cognitive load for novices and inhibit their learning. Although worked examples can reduce unnecessary working memory load for novice learners, pure worked examples (i.e., examples with solution paths only) could be less effective compared to the ones with specific additions such as instructional explanations which can enhance conceptual understanding (Hsu, Kalyuga, & Sweller, 2015). Wittwer and Renkl (2010) conducted a meta-analysis of 21 studies related to the worked examples with instructional explanations and concluded that such examples could enhance the acquisition of conceptual knowledge. They suggested that instructional explanations should focus on appropriate contents such as domain concepts and principles (Wittwer & Renkl, 2008). Ross and Kilbane (1997) also suggested the use of embedded concrete principles in a worked example. Such principles were therefore employed in the worked examples used in the experimental study reported further in this chapter.

Initial problem solving in productive failure and invention activity approaches

In contrast to a cognitive load perspective, the instructional approaches of invention activity for future learning (Schwartz & Bransford, 1998; Schwartz et al., 2011;

Schwartz & Martin, 2004) and productive failure (Kapur, 2008, 2011, 2012; Kapur & Bielaczyc, 2012; Kapur & Rummel, 2012) favour having novice learners encounter challenges before receiving explicit instruction (we refer to these approaches as problem-first approaches, in contrast to the worked-example-first approach). For example, the students who participated in problem solving activities (even though most of them failed to obtain a successful solution) followed by delayed explicit instruction outperformed those in the explicit instruction condition comprising worked examples or a lecture.

On a close inspection, methodological issues can be found in some productive failure studies, such as uneven experimental manipulations between groups. For example, in the productive failure group, the lecture in the delayed instructional phase involved teacher-led activity in which students were instructed by comparing and contrasting the solutions generated during the preceding phase; however, this activity was not implemented in the lecture of the explicit instruction group (see Kapur, 2010, 2011, 2012; Kapur & Bielaczyc, 2012; and Westermann & Rummel, 2012 for a review). Therefore, it was sometimes difficult to determine exactly which variable was actually responsible for the results.

An important but not yet fully resolved issue in the problem-first approaches is the levels of support provided to learners during the initial problem-solving phase. According to a number of studies, it could be essential for the effectiveness of these approaches. For example, Arnold, Kremer, and Mayer (2014) found that an immediate support such as procedural knowledge and understanding instruction in a team-work inquiry task was necessary. In addition, providing contrasting cases may focus learners' attention on differences related to the deep structure of the problem (e.g. Schwartz & Martin 2004; Schwartz et al., 2011). Loibl and Rummel (2014a, 2014b) also indicated the importance of using contrasting cases as a form of instructional guidance during the initial problem-solving phase. Holmes, Day, Park, Bonn, and Roll (2014) demonstrated the effects of metacognitive activity on invention learning. The findings showed that the group with metacognitive orientation and reflection prompts as another form of guidance during the initial problem-solving phase outperformed the group without such prompts in the conceptual test for first-year university students learning graphical representation of data. However, there was no difference between the groups in the procedural test. Generally, metacognitive activities such as reflection on learning processes and evaluating learning outcomes may improve the transfer of acquired concepts (Schraw, Crippen, & Hartley, 2006). The possibility of effects resulting from metacognitive activities of reflection and evaluation during the initial problem-solving phase on the performance in concept-related tests could not be excluded and it was also investigated in the current experiment.

To compare the relative effectiveness of the above two approaches (i.e., problem-first vs. worked example-first), the first (generation) phase of the productive failure/invention learning approach was experimentally manipulated by changing the levels of guidance from fully unguided problem solving to fully guided worked example. The second (explicit instruction) phase was the same for all the compared conditions, since the need for this phase is not questioned by any of the compared approaches. Two research questions were investigated:

1. Which instructional strategy (letting learners solve the problem first or presenting them with a worked-out solution) would result in better learning outcomes in terms of delayed post-test performance and mental effort?
2. Would a problem-first approach benefit from additional instructional guidance provided to learners and/or their post-hoc reflection on problem-solving activities?

Within the problem-first approach, different levels of instructional guidance were incorporated into the first phase of instruction. In addition to problem solving only and problem solving with principle guidance conditions, the reported experiment also involved an initial problem-solving condition with principle guidance and a reflection activity that might complement the effects caused by the guidance.

Thus, there were four different levels of guidance in the initial phase: unguided problem solving only, problem solving with principle guidance, problem solving with principle guidance and reflection, and worked example with principle guidance conditions. In all groups, the initial phase was followed by robust, delayed direct instruction as the second learning phase. Partially guided (by principle information and reflection prompts) or unguided attempts at finding problem solutions were implemented in accordance with the frameworks of productive failure and invention activities. The comprehensive guidance provided by a worked example was in correspondence with cognitive load theory. The effectiveness of these instructional conditions was measured by the learner ability to transfer the acquired knowledge to a relatively new problem-solving situation in a delayed post-test (one week later). Students' levels of experienced cognitive load were also evaluated.

Method

Participants

Sixty Year 10 students (age $M = 16.00$ years, $SD = 0.53$; 27 males and 33 females) from a Taiwanese high school were randomly assigned to one of the aforementioned four experimental conditions with 12 participants in the worked example group and 16 participants in each of the other three groups (the original pool consisted of 64 students equally distributed between the conditions, however four students in the worked example condition cancelled their participation just before the instructional session due to a school meeting that they had to attend). With a Type I error of .05 and a Type II error of .20, the effect size was .44 for such sample size (calculated with Gpower 3.1: Faul, Erdfelder, Buchner, & Lang, 2009). This effect size was acceptable for a quantitative study since it was above the larger effect size (.40) (Huck, 2008). In order to evaluate the level of prior physics knowledge for these groups, the performance in a physics mid-semester examination was analysed prior to the experiment. The results indicated no significant differences in the performance between the groups, $F(3, 56) = .15$, $MSE = 69.16$, $p = .93$.

Experimental Design

The learning topic was about a collision between two objects, which would normally be taught in the physics curriculum of the second semester for Year 11 students. Accordingly, the participants were regarded as novice students in this learning area because of insufficient prior knowledge and experience in solving the relevant problems. The learning materials involved two parts corresponding to the two phases of the learning session.

During the first phase, the four groups used different types of learning materials based on the experimental manipulations but the problems used in these learning materials were identical and concerned with a collision in which two objects separated after colliding. This problem could be solved using two physics principles, the law of conservation of linear momentum and the law of conservation of mechanical energy. In the problem-solving only condition, the participants were presented with a problem and asked to try their best to solve it. In both the problem-solving with principle guidance condition and the problem-solving with principle guidance and reflection condition, the materials included the same problem statement but it was also supplemented with guidance indicating the two physics principles to be used. Moreover, the latter condition additionally involved a follow-up activity requesting the participants to reflect and write down their difficulties encountered during problem solving. In the worked example condition, the learning material included worked-out solutions of the same problem, and this worked example was also embedded with principle guidance.

The learning materials for the second phase of the learning session were the same for all the experimental groups. It comprised an introduction of the two physics principles followed by two pairs of worked example-problem practice combinations. Example-problem pairs were used in this study, as a problem-solving task following a study of a worked example might offer novice learners a chance to reinforce the knowledge acquired from the worked example. In the introduction of the physics principles, the textual descriptions included the definitions of the principles, the conditions of their applicability and the mathematical equations. In each pair of worked example-problem practice, the problem cover stories were similar but the provided and unknown (to be calculated) quantities were different. The first example-problem pair concerned the situation in which two objects collided and then separated; while the second pair was concerned with the situation in which two objects collided and then combined with each other. All problems could be solved by the two described physics principles. The physics principles required to solve the problem were presented as practical instances before the worked-out solutions.

Delayed post-test

This test was conducted one week after the learning session. There were three problems in this paper-based test. Two problems were similar to the problems used in the first pair of the worked example-problem practice phase and the third one was analogous to the problems in the second pair. However, their cover stories, provided and unknown quantities were different from the corresponding problems in the example-problem pairs. Two steps based on the two physics principles could be used to solve each problem in this test. The participants could get a half mark if they used one of the two steps correctly to solve the problem. Thus, one mark was allocated for each problem, and there could be up to three marks totally in this test. The Cronbach's α value of this test was .88.

Mental effort ratings

A nine-point subjective rating scale was administered after each section of the learning materials (i.e., the first part of the learning materials, the introduction of principles, each worked example and each problem practice) and each problem in the delayed post-test. The participants were asked to rate how much mental effort they invested in learning the corresponding section or performing each test problem. The Likert-type scale ranged from 9 "very, very high" to 1 "very, very low". The Cronbach's α of the averaged overall mental effort indicator for the learning phase was .77 and for the delayed post-test was .89.

Experimental procedure

Introduction. The students had been given a ten-minute lecture by the researcher using PowerPoint to present the definitions of relevant physics terms appearing in the subsequent learning materials.

Learning stage. The students used paper-based learning materials. In the first learning phase, students in different experimental conditions had to complete the corresponding learning activities within 11 minutes. The participants in the problem-solving with principle guidance and reflection condition were requested to solve the problem within seven minutes and then write down their reflections on the difficulties during problem-solving within the remaining four minutes (the students could reflect earlier if they thought they had accomplished the problem-solving within seven minutes). The students in this condition were provided with a prompt which requested them to list the difficulties occurring in problem-solving after their attempt to solve the problem, for example, the difficulty in applying the problem quantities in the equations of physics principles or the differences between the existing knowledge and the two physics principles.

In the second learning phase, there were seven minutes for reading the introduction of the two physics principles, eight minutes for studying each worked example, and six minutes for practicing solving each problem. The students were requested to put aside the learning materials and not use them again as long as they thought they had completed the corresponding learning activity within the allocated time.

Test stage. One week later, students received a delayed transfer test. They had 18 minutes to do this test and rate their mental effort.

Results

The independent variable in this study was the instructional category in the first learning phase. The dependent variables included the average mental effort ratings for the learning phases and delayed post-test, as well as the total test score and the total test time. One-way ANCOVAs with the level of prior physics knowledge as a covariate were used to analyse the dependent variables.

Mental effort in the learning stage

A one-way ANCOVA found a significant difference between the four conditions in the first phase of learning, $F (3, 55) = 3.34$, $MSE = 1.67$, $p < .05$, $\eta_p^2 = .15$, the value of power $= .76$ (according to Gpower 3.1). Fisher's least significant difference (LSD) tests showed that the students in the problem solving only condition experienced significantly higher cognitive load than those in the other three instructional conditions. This result corresponds to a cognitive load theory view that pure problem solving can be very cognitively taxing for novice learners. There was no significant difference between the four instructional conditions for sub-jective ratings of mental effort in the second phase of learning, $F (3, 55) = 1.38$, $MSE = .99$, $p > .05$, $\eta_p^2 = .07$. Table 17.1 shows the descriptive statistics for the mental effort in the learning stage (in this and the following tables, the values of SDs are rounded to three rather than customary two decimal points, because with two decimal points, SDs would show identical values for several independent variables).

TABLE 17.1 Adjusted means and standard deviations of average mental effort in the first and second learning phases

Conditions	First learning phase		Second learning phase	
	M	SD	M	SD
PS only	7.58	.327	6.18	.251
PS+guidance	6.43	.323	5.69	.248
PS+guidance+reflection	6.24	.321	5.90	.246
WE+guidance	6.58	.383	6.40	.294

Note: PS = problem-solving; WE = worked example.

TABLE 17.2 Adjusted means and standard deviations for total scores, test time, and mental effort ratings in the delayed post-test

Conditions	Total scores		Total test time (sec)		Average mental effort	
	M	SD	M	SD	M	SD
PS only	.18	.198	567.93	65.024	6.44	.430
PS+guidance	.20	.196	594.39	65.067	6.77	.429
PS+guidance +reflection	.98	.197	692.25	64.978	6.80	.434
WE+guidance	.53	.240	624.99	78.433	6.94	.518

Note: PS = problem-solving; WE = worked example.

Delayed post-test

In the worked example group, a student was absent for this test. Table 17.2 shows the descriptive statistics for the dependent variables in this test. One-way ANCOVA demonstrated significant differences between the four conditions in total scores, $F (3, 54) = 3.57$, $MSE = .63$, $p < .05$, $\eta_p^2 = .17$, the value of power= .82. The Fisher's LSD test showed that the problem solving with principle guidance and reflection condition attained higher total scores compared to the problem solving only and problem solving with principle guidance conditions. On the other hand, there were no significant differences between the four conditions in the total test time, $F (3, 54) = .68$, $MSE = 6.75 \times 10^4$, $p > .05$, $\eta_p^2 = .04$, and the average mental effort, $F (3, 54) = .22$, $MSE = 2.95$, $p > .05$, $\eta_p^2 = .01$. Thus, the meta-cognitive reflection activity in addition to principle guidance enhanced the delayed transfer effect of initial problem-solving activity, although not sufficiently to outperform the comprehensive explicit guidance (worked example) group.

Discussion

For all the dependent measures in this experiment, there was no evidence found that any of the three instructional conditions in which the problem solving was presented prior to explicit instruction outperformed the condition in which a worked example was followed by the identical explicit instruction. This result aligns with the meta-analysis by Alfieri, Brooks, Aldrich, and Tenenbaum (2011) according to which students did not significantly benefit from the enhanced-discovery instruction that consisted of generation activity and guided discovery compared to worked example instruction. Considering that for the post-test the adjusted means are similar across most groups and the effect sizes are relatively low, it is reasonable to state that there are similar effects of the compared conditions across these groups. Therefore, the answer to the first research question is that both strategies are likely to work similarly in the acquisition of durable transferable knowledge.

The present experiment did not find any benefits of principle guidance in problem solving followed by explicit instruction over the equivalent condition without such guidance. This result is in line with the findings of Loibl and Rummel (2014a, 2014b) in which participants who received problem practice with guidance followed by explicit instruction performed equally in the post-tests to those who received the same problem practice without guidance. However, in the present experiment, the problem-solving with principle guidance and reflection condition attained significantly higher total scores in comparison to the problem solving only and problem solving with principle guidance conditions. Therefore, the answer to the second research question is that supplementing the learners' problem-solving attempts with guidance in relevant physics principles and learner reflection activities on their problem-solving attempts could potentially result in better outcomes.

In relation to cognitive load, the results demonstrated potential benefits of using principle guidance during problem solving (relative to problem solving without guidance) as well as benefits of using worked examples (relative to problem solving only) in reducing the mental effort invested in the first learning phase. This result accords with the findings of Schwartz et al. (2011) and DeCaro and Rittle-Johnson (2012) for procedure-related post-tests.

Finding a common ground for cognitive load and problem-first approaches

One of the possible means to resolve the apparently contradictory predictions of cognitive load theory and the problem-first approaches is to consider specific goals of various learner activities within complex learning tasks (Kalyuga & Singh, 2016). From this perspective, the above results are not unexpected if it is assumed that the same overall instructional goal could be potentially achieved by different pathways that involve different sets and sequences of specific goals of constituting activities.

When dealing with complex learning tasks, a variety of goals and corresponding learner activities need to be considered at different phases of instruction when deciding on the level of instructional guidance. The goals of creating cognitive or motivational prerequisites – such as intentionally activating learner relevant prior knowledge or engaging the learner with the task for motivational purposes – prior to the acquisition of domain-specific solution schemas may represent some of such goals (they could be generally labelled pre-instruction goals). These are kinds of goals that are usually associated with the problem-solving phase of productive failure or invention learning approaches, and they are different from the acquisition of domain-specific solution schemas as the focus of cognitive load theory and the instructional techniques consistent with it.

In different studies, the goals of the initial problem-solving phase within the productive failure approach were described as activating and differentiating any potentially relevant learner prior knowledge and ideas (Kapur, 2010; Kapur & Bielaczyc, 2012; Kapur & Rummel, 2012) or enhancing learner global awareness of their knowledge gaps (Loibl & Rummel, 2014a, 2014b; see Glogger-Frey et al.,

2015 for a review). Since none of these goals assume the immediate acquisition of domain-specific schemas (which is the goal of the following explicit instruction phase), the methods typically supported by cognitive load theory may not be best for achieving these goals. Instead, the suggested reduced-guidance activities could be suitable for the goals. From this perspective, the reported experiment demonstrated a potential instructional equivalence of the two different pathways to achieving the overall goal of learning durable and transferable knowledge that effectively applied different sets of specific goals: *schema acquisition* in both phases of instruction vs. *pre-instruction goal* followed by *schema acquisition*.

Limitations of the study and future research

A question concerning the exact conditions under which problem-solving first approaches such as productive failure are effective still remains to be answered. In relation to this, the role of specific goals of learner activities require further research. The optimal sets and sequences of goals in different instructional approaches need to be established empirically. For this, the pre-instruction goals should be specified more precisely than in the current explanatory framework.

Loibl and Rummel (2014b) demonstrated that explicit instruction combined with subsequent problem solving was superior to problem solving with subsequent explicit instruction in tests demanding procedural skills, however the latter outperformed the former in conceptual tests. DeCaro and Rittle-Johnson (2012) also obtained similar results. The present study did not use concept-related post-tests. It is therefore unclear if conditions with a pure or partially guided initial problem-solving phase could outperform fully guided/explicit instruction in such tests. Future studies may also need to use additional measures of problem-solving skills other than traditional post-test scores, such as the levels of creativity of the proposed solutions. Also, some form of activity that represents an equivalent of the reflection activity needs to be incorporated into the worked example condition (e.g., self-explanation prompts) to investigate its effect in comparison with problem solving with reflection condition.

In summary, the answer to the question posed in the title of this chapter is that both strategies may work well in achieving the goal of learning durable transferable knowledge. A clear practical educational implication of this study is that if the problem-solving first instructional strategy is chosen in a specific situation, problem solving during the first phase of instruction should be supplemented with guidance in relevant physics principles and learner reflection activities on their problem-solving attempts.

References

Arnold, J. C., Kremer, K., & Mayer, J. (2014). Understanding students' experiments—What kind of support do they need in inquiry tasks? *International Journal of Science Education*, 36 (16), 2719–2749.

Alfieri, L., Brooks, P. J., Aldrich, N. J., & Tenenbaum, H. R. (2011). Does discovery-based instruction enhance learning? *Journal of Educational Psychology*, 103, 1–18.

Atkinson, R. K., Derry, S. J., Renkl, A., & Wortham, D. (2000). Learning from examples: Instructional principles from the worked examples research. *Review of Educational Research*, 70, 181–214.

DeCaro, M. S., & Rittle-Johnson, B. (2012). Exploring mathematics problems prepares children to learn from instruction. *Journal of Experimental Child Psychology*, 113, 552–568.

Faul, F., Erdfelder, E., Buchner, A., & Lang, A.-G. (2009). Statistical power analyses using G*Power 3.1: Tests for correlation and regression analyses. *Behavior Research Methods*, 41 (4), 1149–1160.

Glogger-Frey, I., Fleischer, C., Grüny, L., Kappich, J., & Renkl, A. (2015). Inventing a solution and studying a worked solution prepare differently for learning from direct instruction. *Learning and Instruction*, 39, 72–87.

Holmes, N. G., Day, J., Park, A. K., Bonn, D. A., & Roll, I. (2014). Making the failure more productive: Scaffolding the invention process to improve inquiry behaviors and outcomes in invention activities. *Instructional Science*, 42(4), 523–538.

Hsu, C. Y., Kalyuga, S., & Sweller, J. (2015). When should guidance be presented in physics instruction? *Archives of Scientific Psychology*, 3(1), 37–53.

Huck, S. W. (2008). *Reading statistics and research*. Boston: Pearson/Allyn & Bacon.

Kalyuga, S., Chandler, P., Tuovinen, J., & Sweller, J. (2001). When problem solving is superior to studying worked examples. *Journal of Educational Psychology*, 93, 579–588.

Kalyuga, S., & Singh, A.-M. (2016). Rethinking the boundaries of cognitive load theory in complex learning. *Educational Psychology Review*, 28(4), 831–852.

Kapur, M. (2008). Productive failure. *Cognition and Instruction*, 26, 379–424.

Kapur, M. (2010). Productive failure in mathematical problem solving. *Instructional Science*, 38, 523–550.

Kapur, M. (2011). A further study of productive failure in mathematical problem solving: unpacking the design components. *Instructional Science*, 39, 561–579.

Kapur, M. (2012). Productive failure in learning the concept of variance. *Instructional Science*, 40, 651–672.

Kapur, M., & Bielaczyc, K. (2012). Designing for productive failure. *The Journal of the Learning Sciences*, 21(1), 45–83.

Kapur, M., & Rummel, N. (2012). Productive failure in learning from generation and invention activities. *Instructional Science*, 40, 645–650.

Loibl, K., & Rummel, N. (2014a). Knowing what you don't know makes failure productive. *Learning and Instruction*, 34, 74–85.

Loibl, K., & Rummel, N. (2014b). The impact of guidance during problem-solving prior to instruction on students' inventions and learning outcomes. *Instructional Science*, 42, 305–326.

Paas, F., & Van Merriënboer, J. (1994). Variability of worked examples and transfer of geometrical problem-solving skills: A cognitive-load approach. *Journal of Educational Psychology*, 86, 122–133.

Ross, B. H., & Kilbane, M. C. (1997). Effects of principle explanation and superficial similarity on analogical mapping in problem solving. *Journal of Experimental Psychology: Learning, Memory, & Cognition*, 23, 427–440.

Schraw, G., Crippen, K., & Hartley, K. (2006). Promoting self-regulation in science education: Metacognition as part of a broader perspective on learning. *Research in Science Education*, 36, 111–139.

Schwartz, D. L., & Bransford, J. D. (1998). A time for telling. *Cognition and Instruction*, 16, 475–5223.

Schwartz, D. L., Chase, C. C., Oppezzo, M. A., & Chin, D. B. (2011). Practicing versus inventing with contrasting cases: The effects of telling first on learning and transfer. *Journal of Educational Psychology*, 103, 759–775.

Schwartz, D. L., & Martin, T. (2004). Inventing to prepare for future learning: The hidden efficiency of encouraging original student production in statistics instruction. *Cognition and Instruction*, 22, 129–184.

Sweller, J., Ayres, P., & Kalyuga, S. (2011). *Cognitive load theory*. New York: Springer.

Sweller, J., & Cooper, G. A. (1985). The use of worked examples as a substitute for problem solving in learning algebra. *Cognition and Instruction*, 2, 59–89.

Van Gog, T., Paas, F., & van Merriënboer, J. J. G. (2008). Effects of studying sequences of process-oriented and product-oriented worked examples on troubleshooting transfer efficiency. *Learning and Instruction*, 18, 211–222.

Westermann, K., & Rummel, N. (2012). Delaying instruction: Evidence from a study in a university relearning setting. *Instructional Science*, 40, 673–689.

Wittwer, J., & Renkl, A. (2008). Why instructional explanations often do not work: A framework for understanding the effectiveness of instructional explanations. *Educational Psychologist*, 43, 49–64.

Wittwer, J., & Renkl, A. (2010). How effective are instructional explanations in example-based learning? A meta-analytic review. *Educational Psychology Review*, 22, 393–409.

18

THE CENTRALITY OF ELEMENT INTERACTIVITY TO COGNITIVE LOAD THEORY

Wayne Leahy

SCHOOL OF EDUCATION, MACQUARIE UNIVERSITY

John Sweller

SCHOOL OF EDUCATION, UNIVERSITY OF NEW SOUTH WALES

Cognitive load theory provides guidelines for instructional design founded on what we know about our cognitive architecture. That architecture is used to design instructional procedures that accord with our cognitive processes. The instructional procedures are relevant primarily to complex (high element interactivity) information that learners have difficulty understanding and assimilating (Sweller, 2010). The concept of element interactivity differs from other measures of complexity in that it not only considers the characteristics of the information being processed but also considers the prior knowledge of the learner. As knowledge levels increase, the element interactivity of the same information decreases. Thus, the complexity of information can vary either by changing the nature of the information or the knowledge levels of learners.

This chapter will firstly discuss human cognitive architecture, followed by categories of cognitive load. The relation of element interactivity to information structures and levels of learner expertise follow, along with an explanation of how that relation can resolve the contradiction between the generation and worked example effects. Similarly, the concept of element interactivity can explain the conditions under which the testing effect is obtainable. The chapter concludes with implications for practice and suggestions for further research.

Human cognitive architecture

Instructionally relevant aspects of human cognitive architecture apply to a category of human cognition identified by David Geary (Geary, 2008; Geary & Berch, 2016). Knowledge can be divided into biologically primary and biologically secondary categories. Primary knowledge is knowledge we have specifically evolved to acquire such as learning to listen to and speak a native language, recognise faces or engage in social relations. It often consists of generic-cognitive skills such as general problem solving, generalising from one task to another or self-regulating our mental processes. We acquire biologically primary knowledge easily, automatically and unconsciously without instruction. Biologically secondary knowledge is knowledge we need to function in a particular culture. Almost everything that is taught in schools is biologically secondary. It ranges on a continuum from elements of information that have relatively little interaction, for example the learning of facts and concepts, to more complex information with many separate interacting elements of information. Examples are the understanding of various principles in algebra or, a grammar of a language. Biological secondary knowledge as well, tends to be domain-specific. Learning to solve problems in general is biologically primary but learning how to multiply out a denominator in algebra to solve problems is biologically secondary. Acquiring biologically secondary information tends to be difficult, effortful and requires conscious effort. It is assisted by explicit instruction. Cognitive load theory is mainly concerned with biologically secondary knowledge because it is that knowledge that is the subject of instruction.

When dealing with secondary knowledge, the major, relevant structural components of human cognitive architecture are working and long-term memory. How these two primary mechanisms of human cognitive architecture interact, form the basis of our understanding of learning. That interaction between working and long-term memory can be encapsulated by five principles (Sweller & Sweller, 2006) that are analogous to principles of biological evolution. While the principles are concerned with the acquisition of biologically secondary knowledge, each of the principles constitutes an example of a biologically primary process that does not need to be taught because it is automatically acquired.

The information store principle. Long-term memory has a large, essentially unlimited capacity to store information.

The borrowing and reorganising principle. Almost all biologically secondary knowledge is borrowed from other people via listening, reading, and observing others. The transferred information is reorganized and merged with previous information stored in long-term memory.

The randomness as genesis principle. Borrowed information firstly must be created. It is created by a random generation and test process during problem solving. If knowledge is incomplete and cannot be borrowed from others, the learner has no other recourse except to generate possible problem solutions and test them for effectiveness. The correct solution is then retained in long-term memory and incorrect ones discarded.

The narrow limits of change principle. To randomly generate solutions to complex problems incorporating many elements runs the risk of combinatorial explosions. For this reason, human cognitive architecture has the structure of working memory, which limits the amount of novel information that can be simultaneously processed. This *combinatory* overload is overcome by the limitations of working memory in the number of elements of novel information that can be simultaneously processed and the duration during which they can be retained. Working memory limitations also protect information stored in long-term memory by not allowing rapid, major changes that may disrupt the long-term memory's information functionality.

The environmental organising and linking principle. The information held in long-term memory does not become dynamic until it has been activated by cues from the environment that prompt working memory to choose which knowledge set to use. The specific knowledge set held in long-term memory can be expended to direct complex behaviour that is appropriate for that environment. An unlimited amount of information can be transmitted from long-term memory to working memory. The limitations of working memory only apply to novel information and do not apply to structured knowledge transferred from long-term memory.

Categories of cognitive load

All learning material imposes a degree of cognitive load. Cognitive load is determined by levels of element interactivity that can be associated with either intrinsic or extraneous cognitive load (Sweller, 2010). A discussion of each of the loads is provided next.

Intrinsic cognitive load. For a learner to achieve a learning goal involves firstly the learner overcoming the degree of difficulty within the learning material. Instructional material is composed of elements and elements have a degree of interconnectedness, called element interactivity. The load can be lower or higher depending on element interactivity.

The effects of processing large amounts of information concurrently due to high element interactivity may be understood from research by Halford, Maybery and Bain (1986) and Maybery, Bain and Halford (1986). They used transitive interference problems for example, "a is larger than b, b is larger than c. Which is the largest?". When people endeavour to merge the two assumptions, cognitive load is at its maximum due to element interactivity being at its highest at this point.

A more concrete learning example is from chemistry instruction. When studying chemical element representation, to recognise that K is the chemical symbol for *Potassium* involves low element interactivity. K means *Potassium* and *Potassium* means K. This task is simple and working memory load is low as there are only two interacting elements. Of course, learning a long list of chemical symbols may be a difficult task not because of element interactivity but just because the list may be extensive. In contrast, in mathematics, learning to comprehend an algebraic equation of $y \times 3 = 15$ constitutes a higher element interactivity task that imposes a higher working memory load. The innate feature of this and any equation is that each element only makes sense in relation to the other elements. Unless all elements are understood and processed together, the equation is meaningless. Levels of intrinsic cognitive load are determined by element interactivity and that element interactivity cannot be altered other than by either changing the nature of what needs to be learned or, as discussed below, changing the levels of expertise of learners.

Extraneous cognitive load. This load also is determined by element interactivity but is related to the instructional design of the material to be learned rather than its intrinsic properties. Consider a Grade 5 Science class learning how to set up a simple way to transmit an electrical current. The instruction may involve a hands-on task of students manipulating a battery, wires, clamps and a lightbulb. Or, the same procedure can be shown by a video display. Other strategies may be by a textbook illustration, an audio recording or the teacher demonstrating the content by drawing on the whiteboard. Element interactivity changes within each of these instructional designs; each imposing their own level of extraneous cognitive load. Learning how to appropriately manipulate materials requires more elements to be simultaneously processed than watching a video. If the aim is to teach students how to manipulate the relevant objects, then the working memory load associated with manipulating materials is intrinsic. If the aim is to teach students concepts associated with electrical wiring, the element interactivity associated with learning to manipulate the objects is extraneous. It is extraneous because it is under the control of the instructor and can be manipulated to be higher or lower dependent on the strategy chosen. Extraneous load is relatively independent of the difficulty of the subject focus (intrinsic cognitive load) that is in the example, a method to demonstrate the transmission of an electrical current. Unlike intrinsic cognitive load that only can be changed by changing the nature of the task or the expertise of the learner, extraneous cognitive load is under the control of instructional designers. One aim of instructional design should be to reduce extraneous cognitive load.

Germane cognitive load. This term also is sometimes used. It does not constitute an independent source of cognitive load. Germane cognitive load refers to working memory resources that are devoted to dealing with intrinsic load rather than extraneous cognitive load. The more learners can devote their working memory resources to element interactivity associated with intrinsic load and the less resources are devoted to extraneous load, the more effective will be the instruction (Sweller, 2010).

Cognitive load, element interactivity and learner expertise

Clearly, from the aforementioned examples, material to be learned varies substantially in complexity. We may consider some material to be quite difficult for us, such as solving certain maths equations. Conversely, a relatively simple task such as learning part of a vocabulary of a foreign language may be viewed as a "simple" task. Element interactivity provides an index of complexity that simultaneously considers both the nature of the information and the knowledge levels of learners. Element interactivity is heavily influenced by the contents of learners' long-term memory. The environmental organising and linking principle above explain how the contents of long-term memory can alter performance. That alteration is mediated by element interactivity. Knowledge held in long-term memory can dramatically reduce element interactivity. For example, the transfer of knowledge for a student to learn the procedure for two-digit multiplication should be easier if the procedure for one-digit multiplication is already held in long-term memory.

Element interactivity levels can be determined by estimating the number of interacting elements in learning materials (Sweller 1994, 2010; Sweller & Chandler 1994; Tindall-Ford, Chandler & Sweller, 1997). Why an estimation? A precise metric of a learner's prior knowledge in a domain is, as far as we know, not possible. What may be a single element for one individual may be composed of multiple, separate elements for another. Thus, estimation is the only option.

To illustrate, consider three readers at different stages of expertise decoding the word "flower". A fluent reader of English would recognise the word and have developed in her/his mind an image of a "flower". That word acts as a single element in working memory. In contrast, a child of five years learning to read, has to potentially deal with six separate pieces of information or elements; the letters F, L, O, W, E, and R.

For a child at an even earlier reading stage, processing involves commencing with the first letter "F", itself being composed of separate elements. To the child it may be, a long vertical line with another horizontal line at the top right, with an identical line halfway down the first line. Thus for the fluent reader there is only one element, for the five year old reader six elements, and for a reader at a more elementary stage, the processing of multiple elements for the composition of each individual letter is required as well. Levels of element interactivity cannot be determined solely by decomposing the nature of the information. The knowledge of the learner is equally important.

Estimation of element interactivity was used in early cognitive load theory research by Sweller and Chandler (1994). Counting the number of steps a learner with a particular knowledge level would need to process to fully comprehend a construct can give an approximation of the element interactivity metric. This technique has been used by Leahy and Sweller (Leahy, Chandler & Sweller, 2003; Leahy & Sweller, 2004, 2005, 2008, 2016) in their studies of young children learning various instructional content.

An example of an estimation technique is the following approximate six steps required for a novice to understand how to read a three-day temperature graph (See Figure 18.1) and answer the question "What is the temperature on a Monday at 11 am?"

1. *Check legend box to identify a Monday line by,*
2. *Checking line type (if broken, unbroken, dotted).*
3. *Look at Time of Day axis for 11 am.*
4. *Follow line straight up until unbroken line to identify Monday.*
5. *Follow left to Temperature axis.*
6. *Identify the temperature of 34 degrees.*

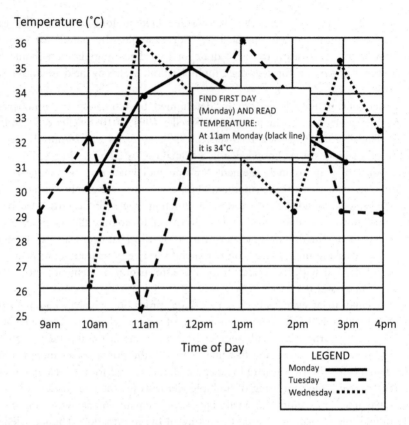

FIGURE 18.1 Three-day temperature graph

It was estimated that these steps were required for the novice students with little or no experience in reading a temperature graph. In contrast, for an expert who has had extensive experience using such a graph, the environmental organising and linking principle is likely to result in an element interactivity count of one.

From the above example, it can be seen that element interactivity associated with intrinsic cognitive load is usually only alterable by changing the nature of the material or changing the expertise of learners. For a given individual with a given level of expertise and a given task, element interactivity associated with intrinsic cognitive load is static. Element interactivity associated with extraneous cognitive load, however, can be changed. It is here that the design of instructional material, the extraneous cognitive load component, is critical.

With cognitive load theory's history of experimentation there has been development and evaluation of many instructional procedures that lower *extraneous* cognitive load. Nonetheless, at times the redesign has not resulted in any tangible benefit for the learner. The reason for this is the intrinsic degree of element interactivity within the learning content. All cognitive load effects are dependent on the degree of element interactivity and more specifically, require a high intrinsic cognitive load. Cognitive load theory rarely applies to low element interactivity information. Below, the worked example, generation and testing effects will now be examined to illustrate the differing consequences due to element interactivity.

Worked examples. Giving extensive scaffolding to instructions has a long history in education and one format is the worked example in which a step by step solution is provided. The worked example effect is manifested when students who are given a number of worked examples to study learn the concept or procedure more successfully than learners presented the same problems to solve themselves (e.g., Carroll 1994; Cooper and Sweller 1987; Kalyuga, Chandler, Tuovinen, and Sweller 2001; Sweller and Cooper 1985). Problem solving provides an example of generating a response rather than being shown the same response. Worked examples are a definitive form of guided instruction.

Generation and worked example effect contradiction. According to Slamecka and Graf (1978) the generation effect occurs when learners who have to generate answers while learning perform better than those who study presented answers to a problem. This result directly contradicts the worked example effect which immediately begs the question, how can the mode of being given a step by step solution (scaffolding) and the mode of generating answers (lack of scaffolding) be both effective? This contradiction is solved by examining the type of learning materials and their element interactivity.

The learning material used to test for the generation effect can be classified as low in element interactivity. Typical tasks are: recalling similar word pairs or opposite word pairs, finding missing words in sentences and simple arithmetic tasks. As previously indicated, cognitive load theory has established that effects generated by the theory are either weak or not evident if learning material is low in element interactivity. In contrast effects are clearly manifested if the material is high in element interactivity.

Chen, Kalyuga, and Sweller (2015, 2016a, 2016b) conducted several studies examining the contrasting findings of the worked example and generation effects. They found using mathematics problems that having students generate answers to problems is beneficial for low element interactivity material content such as memorising the names of geometric theorems. Those results demonstrated the generation effect. When learning to use the theorems to solve problems, studying worked examples proved superior to generating answers to the same problems. If those problems were presented to more knowledgeable learners for whom the solutions had a degree of familiarity, generating answers was superior to studying worked examples. As familiarity with solutions increases, element interactivity decreases and the worked example effect decreases or reverses. For novices for whom the material is high in element interactivity, a worked example format with explicit step by step instructions is a more efficient way to learn.

Testing effect. The testing effect has definitive similarities to the generation effect. The testing effect occurs when learners retain more information if they have a test after learning the information, rather than restudying the information

(Roediger & Karpicke, 2006a). In early research, both Gates (1917) and Spitzer (1939) discuss this phenomenon. Moreover, it has been later validated, albeit with material tapping low element interactivity knowledge, using a range of instructional content such as verbal learning (Hogan & Kintsch, 1971), word lists (e.g., Wheeler, Ewers & Buonanno, 2003), prose passages (Roediger & Karpicke, 2006b), videotaped lectures (Butler and Roediger, 2007), map reading (Carpenter & Pashler, 2007), factual information (Carpenter, Pashler, Wixted & Vul, 2008), animations (Johnson & Mayer, 2009), learning Swahili-English, symbol-word pairs (Coppens, Verkoeijen, & Rikers, 2011), remembering pictures and words (Lipowski, Pyc, Dunlosky & Rawson, 2014) and memorising word lists with a common immediate test from either of two languages (Verkoeijen, Bouwmeester, & Camp, 2012).

Although confirmed by the aforementioned research, other research is less consistent. Roediger and Karpicke (2006a) stated that the testing effect is only apparent using a delayed test. An immediate test may provide no difference or even a reverse testing effect with studying proving more effective than testing. In addition, Van Gog, Kester, and Paas (2011) using similar formats such as examples only and example-problem pairs found that both kinds were effective. Van Gog and Kester (2012) further explored the effect of examples only and example-problem pairs using both an immediate test and a delayed test a week later. No significant differences were found on either test. Moreover, a demonstration of a reverse testing effect was evident in another experiment also using an immediate test and a seven-day delay test. The examples only condition outperformed an example-problem pair condition on the later test. It was proposed by the authors that it may well be that the testing effect is not applicable for the acquisition of problem-solving skills from worked examples.

It is apparent that instructional format, content, age of participants, setting and the timing of testing have produced some conflicting results (e.g. Dunlosky, Rawson, Marsh, Nathan & Willingham, 2013; Roediger & Karpicke 2006a; Marsh, Roediger, Bjork & Bjork, 2007; Van Gog & Kester, 2012; Van Gog et al., 2011; Wiklund-Hörnqvist, Jonsson & Nyberg, 2014). Furthermore, although various explanations, e.g. forgetting, may be slower for tested items than restudied items have been hypothesised by Coppens et al. (2011) and Verkoeijen et al. (2012), consistent explanations of why the testing effect occurs and when it occurs has not been satisfactorily forthcoming.

More recently, Leahy, Hanham and Sweller (2015) and Hanham, Leahy and Sweller (2017) have completed research on the testing effect with primary school aged students as participants. In the work by Leahy et al. (2015), the content was structuring a written argument where rules were given and could be processed in any order. The material was low in element interactivity. In the testing condition, students studied a worked example and wrote their own argument as the test or studied two worked examples. The results of a common test showed a testing effect was evident despite immediate tests being used. Hanham et al. (2017) ran several experiments on the testing effect using both high and low element interactivity information. They were not able to obtain a testing effect on an immediate test with high element interactivity content such as composing a logic poem. This content involved simultaneous processing for comprehensive under-standing. However, they did demonstrate the effect using low element interactivity content with the text type of a debate. Here, the content required serially processing. In conclusion, there is evidence that the testing effect can most easily be obtained with low element interactivity information. Increases in element interactivity may be associated with decreases in the likelihood of obtaining the effect.

Implications for practice

This chapter has discussed the central importance of element interactivity for cog-nitive load theory. Element interactivity provides a strong indicator of why some material is difficult to learn. Instructional content may have only a few interacting elements such as learning the vocabulary of a foreign language or the notations of the periodic table in chemistry. For such low element interactivity information, cognitive load theory has little prescriptive advice. For an educator, it is less critical what type of presentation is utilised to teach these types of knowledge. Cognitive load theory was designed to provide instructional recommendations for high, not low element interactivity information. When intrinsic cognitive load is low, it may not be important to decrease element interactivity associated with extraneous cog-nitive load because the total load may not exceed working memory limits. In contrast, complex content imposes many elements which must be processed simultaneously before the content can be understood. Examples of this are the interpretation of diagrammatic material of a map, graph, spreadsheet and timetable or, the grammar of a second language. It is here that instructional design as recommended by cognitive load theory can be critical. A high intrinsic load from the content associated with a high extraneous load caused by poor instructional design, may overwhelm limited working memory resources.

The instructional importance of these theoretical points has been demonstrated using the worked example, the generation and the testing effects. The generation effect is more likely to occur when learning low element interacting information such as learning a vocabulary with the worked example effect requiring high ele-ment interactivity information such as a grammar. With respect to the testing effect, it is far more evident with instructional content imposing a low intrinsic cognitive load such as writing a prose passage of a persuasive argument. It can be obtained on either immediate or delayed tests but may be more easily obtained on delayed tests. If low element interactivity information is required for the testing effect, its characteristics may not be predictable using cognitive load theory.

Suggestions for further research

It has been suggested that the expertise reversal effect is a variant of the more general element interactivity effect (Chen et al., 2016a). The expertise reversal effect occurs when high element interactivity information is transformed into low element interactivity information due to increases in expertise. As indicated throughout this chapter, increases in expertise result in decreases in element interactivity and decreases in element interactivity can result in the disappearance or reversal of cognitive load theory effects. Some of those effects have been discussed in this chapter. Future research should investigate relations between element interactivity and all cognitive load effects. We can hypothesise that in general, reductions in element interactivity should result in reductions or the elimination of other cognitive load effects.

There may be some conditions under which cognitive load effects can be obtained using low element interactivity information. For example, there is recent research evidence (Smith & Ayres, 2014) that working memory can be compromised by pain, anxiety and emotion. The influence of affective variables on cognitive load effects requires additional work.

References

Butler, A. C., & Roediger, H. L.III (2007). Testing improves long-term retention in a simulated classroom setting. *European Journal of Cognitive Psychology*, 19(4–5), 514–527.

Carpenter, S. K., & Pashler, H. (2007). Testing beyond words: Using tests to enhance visuospatial map learning. *Psychonomic Bulletin and Review*, 14, 474–478.

Carpenter, S. K., Pashler, H., Wixted, J. T., & Vul, E. (2008). The effects of tests on learning and forgetting. *Memory and Cognition*, 36, 438–448.

Carroll, W. M. (1994). Using worked examples as an instructional support in the algebra classroom. *Journal of Educational Psychology*, 86, 360–397. doi:10.1037//0022-0663.86.3.360.

Chen, O., Kalyuga, S., & Sweller, J. (2015). The worked example effect, the generation effect, and element interactivity. *Journal of Educational Psychology*, 107, 689–704.

Chen, O., Kalyuga, S., & Sweller, J. (2016a). Relations between the worked example and generation effects on immediate and delayed tests. *Learning and Instruction*, 45, 20–30.

Chen, O., Kalyuga, S., & Sweller, J. (2016b). When instructional guidance is needed. *Educational and Developmental Psychologist*, 33, 149–162.

Cooper, G., & Sweller, J. (1987). The effects of schema acquisition and rule automation on mathematical problem-solving transfer. *Journal of Educational Psychology*, 79, 347–362. doi:10.1037//0022–000663.79.4.347.

Coppens, L. C., Verkoeijen, P. P. J. L., & Rikers, R. M. J. P. (2011). Learning Adinkra symbols: The effect of testing. *Journal of Cognitive Psychotherapy*, 23, 351–357.

Dunlosky, J., Rawson, K. A., Marsh, E. J., Nathan, M. J., & Willingham, D. T. (2013). Improving students' learning with effective learning techniques: Promising directions from cognitive and educational psychology. *Psychology Science in the Public Interest*, 14, 4–58.

Gates, A. I. (1917). Recitation as a factor in memorizing. *Archives of Psychology*, 6(40).

Geary, D. (2008). An evolutionarily informed education science. *Educational Psychologist*, 43, 179–195.

Geary, D., & Berch, D. (2016). Evolution and children's cognitive and academic development. In D. Geary, & D. Berch (Eds.), *Evolutionary perspectives on child development and education* (pp. 217–249). Switzerland: Springer.

Halford, G., Maybery, M., & Bain, J. (1986). Capacity limitations in children's reasoning: A dual task approach. *Child Development*, 57, 616–627.

Hanham, J., Leahy, W., & Sweller, J. (2017). Cognitive load theory, element interactivity, and the testing and reverse testing effects. *Applied Cognitive Psychology*, *31*, 265–280.

Hogan, R. M., & Kintsch, W. (1971). Differential effects of study and test trials on long-term recognition and recall. *Journal of Verbal Learning and Verbal Behavior*, *10*, 562–567. doi:10.1016/S0022-5371(71)80029-4.

Johnson, C. I., & Mayer, R. E. (2009). A testing effect with multimedia learning. *Journal of Educational Psychology*, 101(3), 621–629.

Kalyuga, S., Chandler, P., Tuovinen, J., & Sweller, J. (2001). When problem solving is superior to studying worked examples. *Journal of Educational Psychology*, 93, 579–588. doi:10.1037//0022-0663.93.3.579.

Leahy, W., Chandler, P., & Sweller, J. (2003). When auditory presentations should and should not to be a component of multimedia instruction. *Applied Cognitive Psychology*, *17* (4), 401–418. doi:10.1002/acp.877.

Leahy, W., & Sweller, J. (2004). Cognitive load and the imagination effect. *Applied Cognitive Psychology*, 18(7), 857–875. doi:10.1002/acp.106.

Leahy, W., & Sweller, J. (2005). Interactions among the imagination, expertise reversal, and element interactivity effects. *Journal of Experimental Psychology: Applied*, 11(4), 266–276.

Leahy, W., & Sweller, J. (2008). The imagination effect increases with an increased intrinsic cognitive load. *Applied Cognitive Psychology*, 22(2), 273–283. doi:10.1002/acp.1373.

Leahy, W., & Sweller, J. (2016). Cognitive load theory and the effects of transient information on the modality effect. *Instructional Science*, 44(1), 107–123. doi:10.1007/s11251-015-9362-9.

Leahy, W., Hanham, J., & Sweller, J. (2015). High element interactivity information during problem solving may lead to failure to obtain the testing effect. *Educational Psychology Review*, 27(2), 291–304. doi:10.1007/s10648-015-9296-4.

Lipowski, S. L., Pyc, M. A., Dunlosky, J., & Rawson, K. A. (2014). Establishing and explaining the testing effect in free recall for young children. *Developmental Psychology*, 50, 994–1000. doi:10.1037/a0035202.

Marsh, E. J., Roediger, H. L., Bjork, R. A., & Bjork, E. L. (2007). The memorial consequences of multiplechoice testing . *Psychonomic Bulletin & Review*, 14, 194–199. doi:10.3758/Bf03194051.

Maybery, M., Bain, J., & Halford, G. (1986). Information processing demands of transitive inference. *Journal of Experimental Psychology: Learning, Memory and Cognition*, 12, 600–613.

Roediger, H. L., & Karpicke, J. D. (2006a). The power of testing memory: Basic research and implications for educational practice. *Perspectives on Psychological Science*, 1, 181–210. doi:10.1111/j.1745–6916.2006.00012.x.

Roediger, H. L., & Karpicke, J. D. (2006b). Test-enhanced learning: Taking memory tests improves long-term retention. *Psychological Science*, 17, 249–255.

Slamecka, N. J., & Graf, P. (1978). The generation effect: Delineation of a phenomenon. *Journal of Experimental Psychology: Human Learning and Memory*, 4, 592–604.

Smith, A., & Ayres, P. (2014). The impact of persistent pain on working memory and learning. *Educational Psychology Review*, 26(2), 245–264.

Spitzer, H. F. (1939). Studies in retention. *Journal of Educational Psychology*, 30, 641–656. doi:10.1037/h0063404.

Sweller, J. (2010). Element interactivity and intrinsic, extraneous and germane cognitive load. *Educational Psychology Review*, *22*, 123–138.

Sweller, J. (1994). Cognitive load theory, learning difficulty and instructional design. *Learning and Instruction*, *4*, 295–312.

Sweller, J., & Chandler, P. (1994). Why some material is difficult to learn. *Cognition and Instruction*, 12, 185–233.

Sweller, J., & Cooper, G. A. (1985). The use of worked examples as a substitute for problem solving in learning algebra. *Cognition and Instruction*, 2(1), 59–89. doi:10.1207/s1532690xci0201_3.

Sweller, J., & Sweller, S. (2006). Natural information processing systems. *Evolutionary Psychology*, 4, 434–458.

Tindall-Ford, S., Chandler, P., & Sweller, J. (1997). When two sensory modes are better than one. *Journal of Experimental Psychology: Applied*, 3(4), 257–287.

Van Gog, T., Kester, L., & Paas, F. (2011). Effects of worked examples, example-problem, and problem-example pairs on novices' learning. *Contemporary Educational Psychology*, 36, 212–218.

Van Gog, T., & Kester, L. (2012). A test of the testing effect: Acquiring problem-solving skills from worked examples. *Cognitive Science*, 36(8), 1532–1541.

Verkoeijen, P. P. J. L., Bouwmeester, S., & Camp, G. (2012). A short-term testing effect in cross-language recognition. *Psychological Science*, 23(6), 567–571. doi:10.1177/0956797611435132.

Wheeler, M. A., Ewers, M., & Buonanno, J. F. (2003). Different rates of forgetting following study versus test trials. *Memory*, 11, 571–580.

Wiklund-Hörnqvist, C., Jonsson, B., & Nyberg, L. (2014). Strengthening concept learning by repeated testing. *Scandinavian Journal of Psychology*, 55, 10–16. doi:10.1111/sjop.12093.

19

CONCLUSIONS

John Sweller, Sharon Tindall-Ford and Shirley Agostinho

Cognitive load theory has been under continuous development for over a third of a century and can be expected to continue evolving as our insights into human cognitive architecture deepen and new cognitive load theory effects are found. The theory began with the simple assumption that humans' limited capacity and duration of working memory when dealing with novel information restricted our ability to learn during problem solving. Over the years, cognitive load theory has evolved with an emphasis on:

- the disappearance of working memory restrictions when dealing with familiar, previously learned information stored in long-term memory;
- the measurement of working memory;
- distinctions between categories of cognitive load;
- the role of element interactivity in determining cognitive load;
- evolutionary educational psychology and its consequences for cognitive load;
- distinctions between generic-cognitive and domain-specific skills;
- a connection between cognition and physical movement; and
- discovery of new cognitive load theory effects.

Those effects and the limits under which cognitive load theory effects could be demonstrated provided both a theoretical raison d'être and a major source of development. Of course, the cognitive load effects provided a large variety of instructional prescriptions and in turn, those prescriptions provided the ultimate justification for the theory. Without exception, all cognitive load effects have been based on multiple, randomised, controlled trials.

This volume documents some of the important work on cognitive load theory over the last decade. It is work that has been carried out around the globe that attests to the strength and dynamism of the theory. In these concluding comments, we will discuss several of the challenges facing the current version of the theory.

Independent measures of cognitive load

Initially, cognitive load was used to predict experimental results without independent measures of the construct. The Paas subjective rating scale (Paas, 1992) was the first attempt to independently measure the working memory load that was assumed to underlie experimental results. It still is the most commonly used measure of cognitive load. Other measures use secondary tasks (Brunken, Plass, & Leutner, 2003; Park & Brunken, 2014) and physiological procedures (Antonenko, Paas, Grabner, & van Gog, 2010; Paas & van Merriënboer, 1994).

These procedures all have involved global measures of cognitive load without attempting to differentiate between intrinsic and extraneous load. It is very unlikely that secondary tasks or physiological measures will be able to distinguish between categories of cognitive load but there have been recent attempts to use subjective rating scales for this purpose (Leppink, Paas, van Gog, van der Vleuten, & van Merriënboer, 2014). In order for these to succeed, learners themselves presumably need to be able to distinguish between the relevant categories. For example, if learners do not know that physically integrating information reduces cognitive load compared to split-attention conditions, they are likely to attribute difficulties in understanding and learning to intrinsic rather than extraneous load. In contrast, in contexts where learners have experience with the instructional methodology such as listening to lectures, they are likely to be able to determine whether the instructional material is intrinsically difficult to understand or whether the presentation procedures are poor, resulting in a high extraneous cognitive load.

Evolutionary educational psychology

Initial versions of the theory simply used the well-known distinctions between working and long-term memory. More recent versions have incorporated that distinction into an evolutionary educational psychology framework (Sweller & Sweller, 2006) in order to indicate the relations between various cognitive processes, relations that also occur in the natural world. In addition, Geary's distinction between biologically primary and secondary knowledge (Geary & Berch, 2016) has been used to indicate that cognitive load theory is predominantly concerned with biologically secondary knowledge.

These distinctions tend to be ignored but are critical for instructional design. Biologically primary skills are vastly more important than secondary skills. We can and frequently do survive without the secondary skills taught in educational institutions. In contrast, primary skills such as generalising learning or planning are essential to our existence as humans. If we are unaware that humans have evolved to acquire primary skills without tuition, the impetus to attempt to teach them is likely to be overwhelming. Successful teaching of a primary skill should transfer to a wide variety of secondary areas. As far as we are aware, there is a near blanket failure to empirically demonstrate far transfer due to explicit teaching of a primary skill (Sala & Gobet, 2017).

The other side of this coin is the suggestion that because skills are acquired so easily without explicit tuition outside of education establishments, explicit tuition is not required in the classroom. This advocacy flows directly from a failure to recognise a distinction between evolutionary primary and secondary knowledge. Primary knowledge does not need to be explicitly taught; the secondary knowledge for which schools were invented does need to be explicitly taught (Kirschner, Sweller, & Clark, 2006; Sweller, Kirschner, & Clark, 2007).

Generic-cognitive skills

In Chapter 1 the contention has been made that generic-cognitive skills such as general problem-solving skills or self-regulation skills are likely to be biologically primary (Tricot & Sweller, 2014). Can they be improved with tuition? There is a possibility, but there is little empirical evidence for far transfer after teaching these skills (Sala & Gobet, 2017; Sweller & Paas, 2017) despite over 100 years of such attempts. Of course, if an appropriate body of research is generated, both theory and practice will be obliged to follow the data.

Cognitive load theory and educational implications

Through randomised controlled experiments, the authors of this volume have investigated the efficacy of a range of instructional practices. Experimental findings provide evidence-based practices that can inform educators and instructional designers' work. Table 19.1 summarises the educational strategies presented in this book.

Discovering limits of cognitive load theory effects

Cognitive load theory has generated a large range of cognitive load effects, many of which are listed above and discussed in this volume. Each experimental effect refers to a novel instructional procedure that has proved to facilitate learning compared to more conventional instructional procedures. It is easy to fall into the trap of assuming that each effect is universal. In fact, it is probably the case that no instructional effect, whether generated by cognitive load theory or not, applies under all conditions. The educational adage of knowing the learner and teach accordingly (Ausubel, 1968), remains true for cognitive load effects. All CLT effects have limits and finding those limits is just as important as initially finding the effect. Indeed, many of the cognitive load effects derived directly from discovering the limits of other effects. The split-attention effect was found when the worked example effect could readily be obtained using algebra but not geometry problems formatted in the conventional fashion; the redundancy effect was found when the split-attention effect disappeared using redundant information; the transient information effect became obvious when the modality effect disappeared using lengthy, complex auditory information; intrinsic cognitive load had to be introduced when

TABLE 19.1 Summary of instructional guidelines

Enhancing student learning	Instructional strategies	Chapter
Instructional design and educational practices when: 　o Students are learning new information 　o Students are learning complex information (high element interactivity)	• Explicit instruction • Pre-train students on key concepts • Provide time for processing information • Segment or "chunk" information • Structured and systematic presentation of information	2, 17 2, 7, 17 4 2, 7, 18 2
Scaffold students' learning & provide opportunities for practice	• Deliberate practice • Mental rehearsal • Structured templates • Use of prompts • Worked examples	2, 17, 2, 17 2 2, 6 2, 17, 18
Support students to reflect on their work to inform next steps of learning: "*feedforward*"	• Assist student reflection • Improvement orientated feedback	2, 16, 17 2, 6
Support effective student collaboration	• Careful distribution of the number and type of activities amongst group members	3
	• Organise groups based on individual student's abilities and factor this into the composition of the group in relation to the task to be completed	3
	• Provide learners experiences so they develop and understand each other	3
	• Provide learners with support, structure and guidance to work together	3
Support students to manage their own learning	• Explicitly teach students the benefits of integrating relevant information the to-be-learnt information	13
	• Inform students on the structure and purpose of learning materials and encourage students to decide upon what information they need to process and how to process it to understand	14, 16
	• Provide students with a checklist that prompts them to self-assess their current performance and reflect on task selection	6
	• Teach students to integrate related sources of information by: 　o highlighting related information 　o linking related information with lines or arrows 　o where possible moving related information next to each other	13

Enhancing student learning	Instructional strategies	Chapter
Support student learning through the effective use of movement and gestures	• Encourage students to undertake movements that are meaningfully related to the learning task	9, 10–11, 12
	• ICT Tools that provide opportunities for observing and making gestures can support learning and problem solving	11
	• Incorporate pointing and/or tracing gestures into lessons, ensuring explicit guidance on the use of pointing or tracing	10, 11
	• Use apps that encourage gestures that are conceptually aligned with the to-be-learnt information	11
Principles for effective animations and multi-media materials	Design strategies	
	• Directly connect related information through arrows and highlights to reduce unnecessary visual search	5, 7, 8
	• Develop learners' visuospatial processing abilities	8
	• Integrate relevant information	8
	• Present animations in smaller segments	7, 8, 15
	• Pre-train students on key concepts presented in animation/ multi-media materials	7
	• Remove redundant information	8
	• Spatial ability, gender, and prior knowledge should be considered in the design of animations	7, 8, 15
	• Static images may be more effective than animations for some learners and for specific learning topics	7, 15
	• Support learner interactivity so they can stop and start animations to control the pacing of the animations	15
	• Use arrows and highlights to guide learners' attention to critical information	5, 7

no cognitive load effects could be obtained using low element interactivity information. All of these and other cognitive load theory-based findings depended on the use of randomised, properly controlled experiments. Accordingly, all cognitive load theory findings are falsifiable, constituting a major strength of the theory.

The chapters of this volume provide cognitive load theory informed educational strategies that can enhance educators' practices and in turn support student learning. The chapters also highlight possible future research areas for cognitive load theory. We expect there are new cognitive load theory effects to discover which will inform the continued evolution of the theory.

References

Ausubel, D. P. (1968). *Educational psychology. A cognitive view.* New York Holt, Rinehart and Winston, Inc.

Antonenko, P., Paas, F., Grabner, R., & van Gog, T. (2010). Using electroencephalography to measure cognitive load. *Educational Psychology Review*, 22, 425–438.

Brunken, R., Plass, J. L., & Leutner, D. (2003). Direct measurement of cognitive load in multimedia learning. *Educational Psychologist*, 38, 53–61.

Geary, D., & Berch, D. (2016). Evolution and children's cognitive and academic development. In D. Geary, & D. Berch (Eds.), *Evolutionary perspectives on child development and education* (pp. 217–249). Switzerland: Springer.

Kirschner, P., Sweller, J., & Clark, R. (2006). Why minimal guidance during instruction does not work: An analysis of the failure of constructivist, discovery, problem-based, experiential and inquiry-based teaching. *Educational Psychologist*, 41, 75–86.

Leppink, J., Paas, F., van Gog, T., van der Vleuten, C., & van Merrienboer, J. (2014). Effects of pairs of problems and examples on task performance and different types of cognitive load. *Learning and Instruction*, 30, 32–42.

Paas, F. (1992). Training strategies for attaining transfer of problem-solving skill in statistics: A cognitive-load approach. *Journal of Educational Psychology*, 84, 429–434.

Paas, F., & van Merrienboer, J. (1994). Variability of worked examples and transfer of geometrical problem-solving skills: A cognitive-load approach. *Journal of Educational Psychology*, 86, 122–133.

Park, B., & Brunken, R. (2014). The rhythm method: A new method for measuring cognitive load-an experimental dual-task study. *Applied Cognitive Psychology, 29*, 232–243. doi:10.1002/acp.3100.

Sala, G., & Gobet, F. (2017). Does far transfer exist? Negative evidence from chess, music and working memory training. *Current Directions in Psychological Science, 26*, 515–520. doi:10.1177/0963721417712760.

Sweller, J., Kirschner, P., & Clark, R. E. (2007). Why minimally guided teaching techniques do not work: A reply to commentaries. *Educational Psychologist*, 42, 115–121.

Sweller, J., & Paas, F. (2017). Should self-regulated learning be integrated with cognitive load theory? A commentary. *Learning and Instruction*, 51, 85–89.

Sweller, J., & Sweller, S. (2006). Natural information processing systems. *Evolutionary Psychology*, 4, 434–458.

Tricot, A., & Sweller, J. (2014). Domain-specific knowledge and why teaching generic skills does not work. *Educational Psychology Review, 26*, 265–283. doi:10.1007/s10648-013-9243-1.

INDEX